D0345751

Can war ever be justified? Why is it wrong to kill? In this book Richard Norman looks at these and other related questions, and thereby examines the possibility and nature of rational moral argument. Practical examples, such as the Gulf War and the Falklands War, are used to show that whilst moral philosophy can offer no easy answers it is a worthwhile enterprise which sheds light on many pressing contemporary problems.

A combination of lucid exposition and original argument makes this the ideal introduction to both the particular debate about the ethics of killing and war, and also to the fundamental issues of moral philosophy itself.

ETHICS, KILLING AND WAR

WA 1132445 7

ETHICS, KILLING AND WAR

UNIVERSITY OF GLAMORGAN
LEARNING RESOURCES CENTRE

Pontypridd, Mid Glamorgan, CF37 1DL
Telephone: Pontypridd (01443) 480480

Books are to be returned on or before the last date below

ONE WEEK LOAN

1 8 MAY 2000

- 5 MAR 1998

2 3 APR 1999

2 4 MAY 2000

- 4 APR 2000

1132445|7

Published by the Press Syndicate of the University of Cambridge
The Pitt Building, Trumpington Street, Cambridge CB2 1RP
40 West 20th Street, New York, NY 10011-4211, USA
10 Stamford Road, Oakleigh, Melbourne 3166, Australia

© Cambridge University Press 1995

First published 1995

Printed in Great Britain at the University Press, Cambridge

A catalogue record for this book is available from the British Library

Library of Congress cataloguing in publication data

Norman, Richard (Richard J.)
Ethics, killing and war: Richard Norman.
p.   cm.
Includes index.
ISBN 0 521 45539 1 (hardback)   ISBN 0 521 45553 7 (paperback)
1. War – Moral and ethical aspects.   I. Title.
U22.N67   1995
172′.42–dc20   94-6810   CIP

ISBN 0 521 45539 1 hardback
ISBN 0 521 45553 7 paperback

TAG

Learning Resources
Centre

Contents

Preface

I have never seen a war. Some people, I know, would say that this disqualifies me from writing a book in which I express views about the rights and wrongs of war. Only someone who has been there, they would say, can know how to assess the various facets of this unique experience, or can recognise that in the heat of battle there are things which have to be done, regardless of what any philosophical theory may presume to dictate.

One reply would be that, though the voice of experience has its own authority, the detached perspective also has something of its own to offer. In truth, however, we are none of us so very detached. The life of anyone in the twentieth century has been marked by the experience of war in some way or other. Though I say that I have never seen a war, I was born in the middle of one. The first years of my life were ones in which my mother waited anxiously for my father's return. My father had gone to war feeling instinctively that there could be no adequate moral justification for the waging of war, and he returned confirmed in that view. My parents' hatred of war decisively shaped my own attitudes, and led to my involvement in various campaigning activities in opposition to particular wars and particular military policies. That experience too is reflected in the arguments of this book. My philosophical concern with the ethics of war has been, in part, an attempt to think through the implications both of my parents' experience and of my own political involvements.

I should add, however, that the aim of the book is not primarily a partisan one. It is a philosophical work, not a political or moral tract. Though I proceed to certain practical conclusions, my intention in doing so is to exhibit philosophical thought at work, to introduce the reader to various ethical concepts, modes of argument and theoretical traditions with which people have tried to come to grips with the moral dilemmas of war, and to explore what can be done with those philosophical resources.

I am very grateful to those on whose help I have drawn: to Karen Jones, Anne Seller, Tony Skillen, Colin Radford and Peter Caws for reading sections and providing valuable comments; to audiences at the University of Kent, University of North London, University College London, and St David's University College Lampeter, where I read parts of the text; to Catherine Max, Judith Ayling, Christine Lyall Grant and Anne Rex at Cambridge University Press, who guided the book through the various stages of editing and production; to Jeff McMahan and Susan Mendus who read the book for the Press and provided extremely helpful advice; and to Carole Davies for her work on the preparation of the typescript. I could wish that I had done better justice to their efforts.

CHAPTER I

Moral thinking

War is, for most people, the big exception. It is generally accepted that the deliberate taking of human life is, more than any other action, utterly wrong. Insofar as there is a moral consensus within our culture, and beyond it, its most deep-rooted feature is the recognition of the wrongness of killing another human being. When it comes to the killing of thousands and even millions of people in war, however, this is widely accepted as a necessary and inevitable part of our way of life. There are perhaps not many people to be found who actually glory in slaughter; deaths in war, even enemy deaths, are normally acknowledged as a tragic loss. Nevertheless, for most people it is beyond question that nations have to pursue their interests or defend themselves by war if necessary, with the recognition that this will normally involve killing on a massive scale. Those who perpetrate the killing will be treated by their fellow countrymen not as moral outcasts but as heroes.

The majority of people accept this anomaly, but not everyone does. At the other extreme there are those who, because they see killing as the ultimate wrong, regard war as entirely unacceptable, as obviously and naturally so as the first group find it inevitable. Between these two positions are those who feel the force of the pacifists' rejection of war, but who also see no alternative to war in certain extreme situations, and who are therefore morally torn. War is therefore one of the most deeply divisive of moral problems. Of course there are other moral questions, and especially questions of life and death, over which people disagree deeply – issues such as abortion, euthanasia or capital punishment. In these cases, however, the consensus against the taking of life more or less dominates the argument, and the debate is about whether occasional exceptions are permissible in extreme cases, or indeed whether the possible exceptions are really cases of 'taking life' at all. The divisions on war and peace seem to go much deeper, and the opposed positions are much farther apart.

Philosophically, the extent of the dilemmas might seem to support those who say that there are no right or wrong answers to moral questions. In the end, so these philosophers maintain, moral argument breaks down, and reason then cannot resolve the disagreement. We reach the point where we can only say 'Well, that's your attitude, and this is mine.' There is no further reason which either of us could give to persuade the other. According to this philosophical view, we cannot say that either of us is right or wrong. We can only agree to differ.

In this book I want to explore the dilemmas of war and peace both in their own right, and as examples of philosophical questions about the scope of moral reasoning. In this first chapter, I shall sketch what I take to be a plausible general theory of moral reasoning. In subsequent chapters I shall look at the specific issues of war and peace in the light of this theory, and I shall then, in the final chapter, return to the general level and to the questions of how far moral reasoning can take us and whether it breaks down in the end.

There is one point of terminology which I want to clarify. I shall use the terms 'moral' and 'ethical' interchangeably to refer to fundamental practical questions about how we ought to live. I want to resist the over-narrow use to which the word 'moral' is often put. 'Moral issues' are often thought of as concerning only the conduct of individuals, as distinct from questions of collective action and political choice. I shall not use the word in this way. I shall treat the question 'Should this country go to war?' as no less a moral question than the question 'Should I, as an individual, participate in my country's war?' The word 'moral' also suggests a negative point of view. 'Morality' is thought of as a set of prohibitions, and when people and their actions are assessed from a moral point of view the primary term of appraisal is thought to be the negative term 'immoral'. These individualist and negative emphases lead to a focus on feelings of guilt as the way in which people reveal their possession of a moral conscience. Thirdly, insofar as 'morality' is thought to have a positive side, this is typically identified with behaviour which is altruistic, unselfish or even self-sacrificing. The 'morally good' person is thought of as one who performs acts of kindness and consideration. That of course is a possible view, but if we make it true by definition, we are again using the word 'moral' in a restrictively narrow way. Serious questions of right and wrong cannot be satisfactorily solved merely by a definition of the word 'moral'. It will be more useful to understand the word in such a way that it is an open question whether, and to what extent, it is morally desirable for us to act altruistically. The moral issues which I am concerned with, then, are moral issues in a broad sense, what are also less familiarly called ethical issues; they are fundamental questions about how we ought to live and what we ought to do.

SUBJECTIVISM AND OBJECTIVISM

Let us now look more closely at the idea that there are no correct or incorrect answers to moral dilemmas, and hence no rational basis for moral beliefs. Why might this be thought to be the case? What initially inclines people to this view is the existence of deep disagreements about questions of right and wrong. The depth of the disagreement about whether wars can ever be justified is one example. The opposing views seem so far apart, and seem to have so little in common; if the right answer could be arrived at by rational thought, how could different groups of people have arrived at such radically different conclusions? Perhaps, then, the difference between them is really a difference between two contrasting emotional stances, and in that case neither position can be said to be correct or incorrect.

It is not enough, however, just to point to the existence of moral disagreements, even recalcitrant disagreements. We have to ask *why* they are recalcitrant. The fact that people disagree quite fundamentally does not rule out the possibility that one side is right and the other is wrong. Compare the example of the disagreement between geocentric and heliocentric theories of the planetary system, or the disagreement between the flat-earth theory and the theory that the earth is spherical. At one time these were recalcitrant disagreements because of the absence of decisive evidence. This did not mean that there was no right answer, it merely meant that no one could say with confidence what the right answer was. Before anyone had circumnavigated the earth, or looked at it from space, the flat-earth theory and the spherical-earth theory might both have been plausible. With better evidence we now know that the earth is roughly spherical, and likewise we know that the sun is at the centre of the planetary system. To say that we 'know' this does not mean that disagreement is at an end. There may still be people – perhaps religious fundamentalists – who believe the opposite. If that is so, it does not show that there is no right answer, it simply shows that one group is mistaken.

If it is to be maintained that there is no rational way of establishing moral beliefs, then, it is not enough just to point to the existence of radical moral disagreements. What must also be claimed is that there is no way of resolving such disagreements. This is what some philosophers have indeed claimed. Bertrand Russell, for instance, was during the First World War a committed and active campaigner for peace and against the war policies of the British government, and he was imprisoned for his work for the No-Conscription Fellowship, but as a philosopher he maintained that his position, like that of his opponents, was in the end 'the outcome of feeling rather than of thought'. 'The fundamental facts in this as in all ethical questions', he believed, 'are feelings; all that thought can do is to clarify and harmonize the expression of those feelings.'[1] In support of this philosophical claim he argued that no rational way of resolving fundamental moral disagreements can be found.

If our views as to what ought to be done were to be truly rational, we ought to have a rational way of ascertaining what things are such as ought to exist on their own account, and by what means such things

---

[1] Bertrand Russell, 'The Ethics of War', p. 63, in *Prophecy and Dissent, 1914–16*, vol. XIII of *The Collected Papers of Bertrand Russell* (London, 1988).

are to be brought into existence. On the first point, no argument is possible. There can be nothing beyond an appeal to individual tastes. If, for example, one man thinks vindictive punishment desirable in itself, apart from any reformatory or deterrent effects, while another man thinks it undesirable in itself, it is impossible to bring any arguments in support of either side.[2]

If people agree about what things they regard as desirable for their own sake, says Russell, rational argument is then possible about how to bring those things into existence. Those who agreed that vindictive punishment is a good thing, for example, could then engage in rational argument about whether that end is effectively served by England's making war against Germany. But between those who disagree as to whether vindictive punishment is a good thing at all, no rational argument is possible.

The alleged absence of any rational way of resolving fundamental moral disagreements is, then, one reason for thinking that moral views ultimately rest on feeling rather than reason. A second argument which has been put forward by some philosophers for that conclusion is that moral views are thought to have a special connection with action. To regard something as right or wrong, good or bad, is to be disposed to act accordingly. Someone who professed to regard it as right to act in a certain way, but made no effort whatever to do so, would properly be described as hypocritical; we would say of him that 'He doesn't *really* think it's right.' But, so the philosophical argument goes, moral views can express themselves in action only if they engage with our feelings, and do so not just in an accidental way but because of their very nature. No mere rational recognition of the facts, it is said, can dispose us to action, only our feelings can do that.

These two arguments, then, have been put forward in support of what is often called the 'subjectivist' position: that our basic moral views derive from feeling rather than reason, and are therefore essentially subjective. What principally counts against that position, however, is that it seems to run counter to our

---

[2] Russell, 'The War and Non-resistance: Reply to Professor Perry', p. 186, in *Prophecy and Dissent*.

moral experience. Our sense of what is at stake in moral arguments seems to rest crucially on the assumption that there is a truth to be discovered, that we are concerned not just to uncover our feelings but to find out whether something really *is* right or wrong. To some extent the subjectivist position can account for this. It leaves room for the acknowledgement that in cases of moral disagreement and perplexity there will always be facts to be sorted out. Russell, we have seen, allows that there is room for rational argument as to whether a certain course of action will lead to a particular set of consequences; what he denies is that the view that the consequences are in themselves desirable can be true or false. However, experience suggests that even at the level of such fundamental moral beliefs we are doing more than recording our feelings. If I believe that killing is in itself wrong, or that we ought not to create unnecessary human suffering, it does indeed seem to be a *belief* I am expressing, not just an emotional dislike of killing or suffering. Beliefs are by definition things that are true or false. It is a deep-seated feature of our language that we talk about moral beliefs rather than moral feelings. Admittedly this may be an illusion. Language may mislead us, and perhaps we should change it and stop talking about moral beliefs. If it is an illusion, however, it is a very deep and pervasive one, and it needs explaining. If, on the other hand, talk of 'moral beliefs' is in order, then it follows that there is such a thing as a moral truth to be discovered, that that truth is in principle objectively ascertainable, and that it is the task of reason to ascertain what kinds of actions really are right or wrong. This is what is standardly called the 'objectivist' position. This philosophical dispute between subjectivism and objectivism is the theme of the present chapter, and it will be a continuing concern throughout the book, alongside my particular concern with the rights and wrongs of war.

HUME, GENERAL STANDARDS AND LANGUAGE

As a first step towards an answer to the general philosophical problem, I want to look at one of the classic formulations of the subjectivist position, by the eighteenth-century Scottish philosopher David Hume.[3] He maintains that reason cannot be 'the sole source of morals'.[4] He recognises that reason does have an important role to play in moral disputes. Like Russell, he allows that reason can instruct us in the tendencies of actions, can tell us what will happen if we do this or that, and this knowledge of consequences is of course essential in deciding what to do. But when all the facts are known, when we have discovered all that can be ascertained about the likely states of affairs to which our actions will lead, there still remains the question whether, in the light of all their consequences, such actions are to be the object of approval or disapproval. Here, says Hume,

the understanding has no further room to operate ... The approbation or blame which then ensues cannot be the work of the judgement but of the heart; and it is not a speculative proposition or affirmation, but an active feeling or sentiment.[5]

Hume thinks that one feeling in particular underlies our moral assessment of actions, and that is the feeling of 'sympathy' (which he also calls 'humanity' and 'fellow-feeling'). Through sympathy we identify with and are moved by the happiness and suffering, joy and sorrow, pleasures and pains of others. Under the force of this feeling we tend to express our approval of those actions which promote the happiness of the agent or of others, and our disapproval of actions which have the opposite effect.

So far, then, the picture is of moral assessments as the direct expression of the feeling of sympathy. Hume's position is, however, significantly modified in the following passage.

General language ... being formed for general use, must be molded on some more general views and must affix the epithets of praise or blame in conformity to sentiments which arise from the general interests of the community ... Sympathy, we shall allow, is much fainter than our concern for ourselves, and sympathy with persons remote from us much fainter than that with persons near and contiguous; but for this very reason it is necessary for us, in our calm judgements and discourse

---

[3] References are to David Hume, *An Inquiry Concerning the Principles of Morals* (Library of Liberal Arts edition, New York, 1957).

[4] *Inquiry*, Appendix I, 'Concerning Moral Sentiment', p. 105.   [5] Ibid. p. 108.

concerning the characters of men, to neglect all these differences and render our sentiments more public and social...The intercourse of sentiments, therefore, in society and conversation makes us form some general unalterable standard by which we may approve or disapprove of characters and manners.[6]

The important insight here is the role of *language*. Our shared language contains value-concepts which provide us with shared, impersonal standards for assessing human actions. Hume emphasises especially our vocabulary of words for virtues and vices, with which we praise or blame people for acting 'justly' or 'unjustly', for being 'generous', 'courageous', 'industrious' or 'honest', or for being 'cruel', 'cowardly', 'lazy' or 'dishonest'. I shall suggest in due course that these are only a limited range of our value-concepts, but for the moment the point is that insofar as these concepts are embedded in a public language they constitute a 'general unalterable standard by which we may approve or disapprove of characters and manners'. This however is a major shift in Hume's position. It appears that our moral judgements are not after all direct expressions of feeling. Our judgement can, Hume acknowledges, 'correct' our emotions, so that we can recognise a person or an action to be admirable or deplorable, whatever the feelings we may happen to have. The relation between our feelings and our evaluative language is therefore a complex one. It is because as human beings we share certain basic feelings that we are able to share also the same value-language. However, given that we do share such a language, our judgements can transcend our feelings and can have an impersonal character. We judge not on the basis of our feelings, but on the basis of the standards encapsulated in the language. Nevertheless our sharing certain natural human feelings is a precondition for our being able to employ those impersonal standards.

Hume, the archetypal subjectivist, is thus able to indicate, I suggest, how objective moral judgement is possible for us as language-users. I want to take this account further and, in doing so, to propose two substantial modifications to Hume's

---

[6] *Inquiry*, Section v, 'Why Utility Pleases', pp. 55–6.

version. First, Hume implies that the general standards in our language are deliberately and consciously adopted in order to make communication possible. We find it inconvenient to be limited to judgements which are as variable as our feelings, he seems to be saying, and therefore we decide to employ a common value-language instead. In fact, of course, language is not something which we deliberately invent. We inherit our language. Certainly we can change it; that is important, as we shall see hereafter, and it means that our evaluative vocabulary can develop over time. Nevertheless we do not invent language, and we do not invent the values it encapsulates.

PRIMITIVE RESPONSES

The second major addition which I want to make to Hume's account is that I take 'sympathy' to be just one example of an emotional response which is related to our evaluative language in the way that he indicates. There is a great range of such 'primitive responses', as I want to call them, which underlie our shared vocabulary of evaluation. There are, first, all those responses which give rise to our ways of assessing the quality of our lives and experiences. Some philosophers have tried to make 'the desire for happiness' do all the work here; they have put forward the concept of 'happiness' as the one basic concept with which to characterise a worthwhile life. This again is a massive over-simplification. Even if we did employ the term in this all-embracing way, it would be useless unless filled out with a host of more specific concepts. The fact is that we do not just assess situations and experiences as consisting in happiness or un-happiness. We assess them as 'interesting', 'exciting', 'ful-filling', 'demanding', 'amusing', 'comfortable', 'peaceful', or negatively as 'dangerous', 'boring', 'annoying', 'frustrating' and so on. We are able to use these evaluative concepts because we possess the natural human propensity to respond to situations with boredom or interest, frustration or excitement or whatever, though the use of a particular concept to appraise some aspect of one's own or another's experience is not necessarily a direct expression of the corresponding response. I can objectively recognise a situation as exciting without its being the case that either I or anyone else is actually experiencing feelings of excitement.

That then is one set of evaluative concepts, with which we characterise the components of a worthwhile human life. A second main set consists of the concepts with which we appraise our relations with one another. The response of sympathy plays its part here, underlying some of these concepts. If we did not have this capacity to be affected by, and to identify with, the experiences of others, we would not employ the evaluative vocabulary with which we praise actions as 'kind' or 'generous' or 'helpful', or criticise them as 'cruel' or 'thoughtless' or identify obligations to assist one another in situations of need. Again however I want to suggest that sympathy is not the only primitive response which underlies our evaluative understanding of our relations to one another. For a start I want to contrast it with the equally basic general response of *respect*. Whereas sympathy is primarily a response to others as passive experiencers, as beings who are affected by the world in various ways and who enjoy or suffer accordingly, respect is a response to others as active beings, as agents. So, whereas sympathy involves a spontaneous inclination to respond to other people's needs and interests as to one's own, respect may in contrast involve distancing oneself and recognising that others' projects are theirs, not mine. It is an inclination, not to live others' lives for them, but to stand aside and let them live their own life in their own way. If in the history of philosophy the idea of 'sympathy' is associated especially with Hume, that of 'respect' is linked with Kant.[7] Simplifying somewhat, I want to take from Kant the insight that whereas things, objects, have value because of their importance for persons, their place in people's lives and projects, persons themselves, as the source of this value, possess not value but dignity and, as such, the appropriate response to them is one of respect. A moral theory which was grounded

[7] The classic discussion is in Immanuel Kant, *Groundwork of the Metaphysics of Morals* (also translated as *Fundamental Principles of the Metaphysics of Morals* and as *Foundations of the Metaphysics of Morals*. There is also a conveniently available translation by H. J. Paton with the title *The Moral Law*).

solely in the attitude of sympathy would have what is called a 'utilitarian' character; human actions would be assessed solely on the basis of their tendency to promote happiness or prevent suffering. In due course I shall have a good deal to say about the inadequacies of a purely utilitarian morality, but for the moment I want to note one particular criticism that is made of it by many contemporary philosophers. If utilitarian morality is concerned simply with doing good, with promoting as much well-being and relieving as much suffering as possible, it may appear to justify using some people against their will in order to do as much good as possible. This may mean using them to promote the good of others, or it may mean trying to promote their own good in ways which they do not want. What utilitarian moral thinking seems to leave out, then, is values founded on respect, values such as 'freedom' and 'autonomy'. Most important of all, such values include a respect for life, whereas utilitarian thinking by itself justifies too easily the sacrificing of someone's life to promote the good of others. This will be a central theme of subsequent chapters, but for the moment I simply want to make the contrast between the two kinds of values, and to note finally that the two come together in the idea of *justice*, where we are concerned to promote the well-being of all the members of a community in a way which does not involve sacrificing some of them for others.

I have been contrasting the two basic responses of 'sympathy' and 'respect', and the moral concepts which arise out of them. The two are alike however in being quite general responses, attitudes which one might have towards any other human being. As such they contrast with a variety of more specific responses located in more specific relations between people – all the various kinds of love, affection, commitment and trust distinctive of friendships, sexual relations, family relations, relations between neighbours or colleagues or comrades. All of these give rise to their own specific kinds of loyalties, which all have their place within our moral understanding. We might try to formalise these as a list of 'obligations' or 'duties', specifying the distinctive moral obligations which we have to our friends, to our children, to our fellow citizens or fellow workers. How appropriate the language of 'obligations' and 'duties' is, I am not sure. In some cases the very use of such language might seem to indicate that the relationship is false or is dead; if I have to talk of my 'obligations' to my friend or lover or child, it cannot be much of a relationship. On the other hand I do not want to say that the behaviour appropriate to such a relationship is confined to the direct expression of the relevant emotions. As with sympathy and respect, so also these more specific responses and emotions give rise to a settled vocabulary in terms of which we understand and assess our behaviour. Thus I may decide that I ought to act in a certain way because of the particular responsibilities that I have to a friend, even though I may at this moment be feeling distinctly unfriendly towards her. Likewise any parent will recognise the remark that 'though I love my child dearly', at the moment 'I feel like murdering him'.

So far the various primitive responses which I have identified as underlying our moral vocabulary are, for all their diversity, all *positive* responses to others – sympathy, respect, love, affection and so on. But, it may be said, do we not also, and notoriously, respond negatively to others, with fear or hatred as well as with love or respect? Why then are these negative feelings not just as significant as the positive ones for our moral understanding? An easy answer would be that to see our relations to others in the light of these negative responses would not be to think in *moral* terms, since by definition to think and act morally is to be guided by a concern for the needs and interests of others. That however is *too* easy an answer. Nothing in all this should be made to hang on the possibly limited connotations of the word 'moral'. Thus Hume might have defended the central place allotted to 'sympathy' by saying that though of course we are motivated by a host of other passions, sympathy is the one which specifically explains our moral judgements. But what we want to know is not what kinds of practical judgement can be defined as 'moral'. We want to know how we ought to live and act, and if we are told that some of the reasons we might have for acting in certain ways are not distinctively moral reasons, that simply raises the further question 'Then why should I act morally?'

So what about negative feelings and responses to others? I want to say that they *do* help to shape the vocabulary with which we can rationally assess our actions. As beings who can be motivated by fear, for instance, we may quite appropriately see someone as a threat to us, and it may then be quite rational to defend oneself against that threat. Likewise it may be, in itself, rational to react adversely against those who have wronged us or wronged others, and if it is asked what exactly is rational about this, the answer must be that, insofar as responses such as 'anger' and 'hostility' are part of our make-up as human beings, this just *is* one of the ways in which we understand our relations to one another. It may be that we should sometimes seek to inhibit our anger, but to ask, say, of your response to someone who has just destroyed your treasured collection of ornaments 'Why be angry with him?' would be perverse. To recognise what anger is, just *is* to understand what makes that response a rational one in such a case.

One important part of our moral vocabulary which has its roots in these negative reactive responses is the vocabulary of 'guilt' and 'innocence'. We have the idea that if someone has done wrong they 'deserve' to suffer or be punished, and that inflicting suffering on such a person is morally different from inflicting it on someone who is 'innocent'. Clearly this is bound to create conflicts within our moral thinking. The idea that some people deserve to suffer is bound to come into conflict with the idea, grounded in responses such as sympathy, that it is in itself wrong to inflict suffering on anyone. Both these ideas are components of our moral thought. Which should give way to the other, and in what circumstances, is something that has to be worked out (and that will be one part of the argument to be pursued in the following pages). It may be that we should 'love our enemies', but even if we reach that conclusion, it remains the case that some people are indeed 'enemies' and that such a term remains an ineradicable part of our vocabulary for understanding our practical relations to one another.

I have been looking at the moral significance of our responses to other human beings. Our moral vocabulary also has to provide ways of understanding our relations to the non-human world, both animate and inanimate, and this too will be grounded in our primitive responses. Much of our behaviour towards the non-human world is instrumental; we make use of nature for our purposes. But some of our responses to other humans, such as sympathy or pity, are responses also aroused by other living things. Hence concepts such as 'cruelty' and our understanding of the wrongness of inflicting suffering will apply also to our treatment of animals which can suffer. How far our moral understanding of relations between human beings can be extended to our relations with the non-human world is a large question which I cannot pursue here, other than to say that it will depend in the end on the nature of our primitive responses to non-human beings. But I do want to note that there are also certain basic human responses which are *distinctively* responses to the *natural* world – responses such as 'reverence' and 'awe', for instance, which are specifically aroused by the foreignness and mystery of the non-human. Such responses might give rise to a whole way of seeing the natural world. I would suggest in particular that they underlie any religious view of the world. They also underpin more recent kinds of ecological thinking, which suggest that we should think more in terms of living in harmony with nature rather than on the basis of our present instrumental attitude. How far such ways of thinking can be sustained is another large question which I shall not go into. That they have an initial plausibility is because they draw on certain basic human responses to nature. The question is then how far they make sense of the overall pattern of our experience, and whether they put too much weight on particular features of that experience.

LANGUAGE, MEANING AND REASON

So far, then, I have sketched the beginnings of an account of how we can reason objectively about how we should act. I have suggested that we assess our actions by reference to the evaluative concepts embedded in our language. And I have suggested that we are able to share an impersonal language of evaluation because underlying it are the primitive responses which we share as human beings. Some of the reasons we give for how we have acted or how we ought to act refer directly to these feelings and responses. Thus I may give a reason for my behaviour by saying that I was angry, and show that anger was an appropriate response in the circumstances. I may say that people ought to act in a certain way because they ought to respect the freedoms or the lives of others, and this reason is rooted in the existence and nature of respect as a fundamental human response. Other terms in our moral vocabulary do not refer directly to these responses but presuppose them, for instance our vocabulary of virtues and vices such as 'generosity' and 'cruelty', our vocabulary of 'justice' or our talk of obligations and duties. I have suggested that we could usefully group our evaluative concepts in two broad classes, corresponding to two basic kinds of responses:

1. the concepts with which we characterise the components of a worthwhile life, and identify what human beings need if they are to live such a life;
2. the concepts with which we characterise our moral relations to one another, and our relations also with the non-human world.

These are not two watertight compartments. Our understanding of a worthwhile human life will of course include a recognition of our need for certain kinds of relations with others. Conversely it is because we stand in certain kinds of relation to others that we are concerned about their needs as well as our own. Nevertheless the classifications may serve to indicate the range of our evaluative concepts.

But now it may be asked: why give this privileged status to language? The account of moral thinking which I am trying to develop seems to imply that the reasons which we can give for or against particular courses of action depend on the evaluative concepts which happen to be enshrined in our language. Does this not look altogether too arbitrary? On the one hand, it might be asked, why should we be limited to the standards of rationality which are current amongst those with whom we share a language? On the other, why should we assume that the standards which are encapsulated in our language are genuinely rational? May not our language be as much a repository of error and illusion?

I want to claim that there is an important sense in which we cannot step outside our language. The fact is that it is only from within a shared language that we can see our actions as meaningful. A human action is not just a physical movement. What distinguishes even the most rudimentary actions from involuntary bodily movements such as breathing or the blinking of an eye is that the former have a meaning. Furthermore, 'meaning' can only be shared meaning, a meaning which is at least in principle communicable to others. Just as language itself can have a meaning only insofar as it involves publicly shared rules and criteria for its correct use, so likewise our actions can have a meaning only insofar as they can be characterised in meaningful ways within a shared language. Outside such a context, human behaviour cannot even be intelligible.[8]

What then is the connection between these considerations of 'meaning' and 'intelligibility' on the one hand and, on the other, the business of giving reasons in order to justify or criticise an action? Clearly they are not the same. To *understand* an action, to make it *intelligible*, is not necessarily to *justify* it as *right*. Nevertheless I think that they are closely connected, and my suggestion is that the concepts in terms of which an action could be made intelligible are the concepts which could count as reasons for or against an action. Consider an example: an act of killing. Suppose that an elderly couple are found killed by an intruder who broke into their house. 'Why were they killed?' we ask. Perhaps the intruder was a burglar, who was surprised by the couple whilst in the act of stealing. But suppose that we discover that nothing was taken. The killing now needs more explaining. Perhaps we discover that the killer was their son, who had been rejected by them many years ago and had long harboured a grudge against them. So now we can understand the killing as an act of vengeance. But suppose instead we find

---

[8] The claims which I make in this paragraph, and which derive from the philosophy of Wittgenstein, are defended at greater length in my book *Reasons for Actions* (Oxford, 1971), especially ch. 3.

that the killer had no previous connection with the couple. It now appears a 'senseless' act of killing. Then, from the questioning of the killer, it emerges that he is a lonely and embittered man, who feels that all his ambitions have been thwarted by a hostile world, who nurses a grudge against 'society'. This violent act which outrages everyone is his way of wreaking his revenge on a world which has rejected him. So now, at least, we can make sense of the action.

Quite clearly, understanding this action, making it intelligible, is not the same as justifying it or showing it to be right. Nevertheless, the considerations which make it intelligible – its being a means for the killer to acquire certain goods, or its being an act of vengeance, either personal or generalised – explain it because they are the sorts of considerations which could be used to justify an action. They explain it because they give us his reasons for doing what he did. Now what we are likely to say is: they may be *his* reasons, but they are not *good* reasons. What, then, is the difference between the two? Not, as might be supposed, that the former are purely private and personal whereas the latter are publicly acknowledged, for the fact is that 'his reasons' can be properly so called only if they really are *reasons*. If what he gave as 'his reasons' were in fact unintelligible (e.g. 'to get blood on my knife') they would explain nothing and therefore would not be recognised as genuinely his reasons, whatever he might say. To be reasons at all, they must make the action intelligible from a publicly shared standpoint. Since, then, we cannot drive a wedge between 'his reasons' and 'reasons', the important distinction must be between 'reasons' and 'good reasons'. Why might we say that the reasons in the example are not good reasons? There are two possibilities. One would be that the reasons, though they are in principle genuinely capable of being reasons, are not appropriate to this situation. If he kills the couple because he bears a grudge against the world, the obvious point to make is that they cannot be blamed for his misfortune. Such a case might be contrasted with the case where he bears a grudge against them because they rejected him as a child – though in that case too the reasons might not be good reasons if it turned out that he had been a very difficult child and the parents had done their best for him, eventually turning him out only because they thought he would be better off on his own. The other obvious point would be that though he has reasons for doing what he does, they are not strong enough to override the overwhelming objections to the act of killing. In other words, the reasons are indeed reasons, but they are being made to carry too much weight; they do not justify performing this particular action in these circumstances. 'Reasons' thus become 'good reasons' if they are sufficiently appropriate and sufficiently strong, bearing in mind the other reasons which are relevant to the case. There is no radical difference in kind between the two.

This may still seem too weak a distinction. Someone might say 'His desire for vengeance may make his action intelligible, but I don't think it is a good reason for doing anything at all. I don't think that people ought to be motivated by such considerations.' Recall Bertrand Russell's remarks about vindictive punishment; he implies that since some people just do regard it as a good thing for its own sake and others do not, the former would count it as a good reason for at least some actions whereas the latter would consider that it could never be a good reason for any action at all. What is correct here, I think, is that we can indeed reject particular moral concepts which are a feature of our language, and refuse to employ them as reasons. However, what I also want to emphasise is that our rejection is itself something for which we must give reasons, and those further reasons must themselves invoke concepts in our moral language. In other words, we can reject some of the evaluative concepts in our language by appealing to others, but we cannot stand outside our moral language altogether and invent reasons for ourselves. Thus one might reject concepts of revenge and retribution and the idea that people deserve to suffer if they have done wrong, and one's reason for rejecting them might be that their use has led to too much cruelty and additional suffering. Or one's reason might be that these ideas presuppose too strong a notion of individual responsibility, and that we can never plausibly attribute that degree of blame to individuals for the wrongs they have done. What one cannot do is simply deny the capacity for concepts such as 'desert' or 'revenge' or 'retribution' to furnish any reasons at all, without giving any reasons for rejecting them. Thus my account leaves room for radical conflicts between the proponents of different values, and for the radical rejection of conventional moral assumptions. It insists only that these conflicts and disagreements take place within a shared framework of evaluative language which furnishes the concepts invoked by contending parties, and that to step outside that framework altogether would be to abandon the possibility of seeing our lives and actions as meaningful.

HUMAN NATURE

So much, then, for my emphasis on the importance of language; but I also want to insist that language is not just a free-floating set of meanings. I have also maintained, with equal emphasis, that our evaluative language is rooted in our nature as human beings, in our basic human responses. This talk of 'human nature' may appear as problematic as my emphasis on language. Notoriously, claims about human nature often ascribe a false universality to forms of behaviour which are in fact culturally specific. Often these claims serve an ideological purpose, purporting to legitimise particular social institutions by making them appear inevitable. Thus advocates of a market economy may claim that human beings are naturally competitive, defenders of nationalism or militarism may claim that humans are naturally aggressive, and the striving for greater social justice may be countered with the claim that humans are naturally selfish. The falsity of these universal claims about human nature becomes apparent when we look at the great diversity of ways of life in different cultures, and when we consider how different modes of upbringing can foster different character-traits in individuals.

Talk of 'human nature' therefore has its dangers, but it does not follow that the very idea has to be abandoned just because of the spuriously universal claims that are made in its name. Notice, indeed, that the counter-claim that human beings are moulded by their environment and upbringing could not coherently be made unless there were something to be acted *on* by environment and upbringing. Some notion of human nature, then, is indispensable. My own employment of the idea involves not claims about the dominance of particular kinds of behaviour, but what I want to call a *repertoire* of basic responses which is drawn on in different ways by different cultures or groups or individuals. Thus aggression is a trait which may be fostered by some cultures and played down by others, but this could not be so unless a capacity to respond aggressively to some kinds of situations were a natural feature of human beings. Anger is a basic human response. In different cultures people may be taught to exhibit anger in different circumstances or in different ways, but anger itself, as a distinctive response, is a brute irreducible feature of human life.

Anger may be too easy an example. Can we always be so sure whether a particular feature of human life is natural or is entirely a cultural product? No, we cannot. Particular examples may be contestable. Take the case of jealousy, or in particular sexual jealousy. Is this a basic human response? Or is it a cultural product, a response fostered by a patriarchal culture in which women are seen as men's private and closely guarded possessions? In such cases there is no easy answer. We have no alternative but to examine the particular phenomena, to look at the facts of cultural variety or constancy and to look at the nature of the response itself and whether it presupposes specific social or moral beliefs. What we decided about sexual jealousy would in turn affect what we thought about moral concepts built on it, such as that of fidelity. Doubts about other examples which I have previously presented as uncontroversially basic responses could only be dealt with in the same way. None is immune from critical examination. But that some at least are authentically universal and basic can hardly be doubted.

The universality of basic human responses makes for at least a potential universality also of evaluative language. I have until now, with deliberate vagueness, referred to 'our' evaluative language. This should prompt the question 'Who are "we"?', for, like talk of human nature, such uses of the first-person plural lend themselves to a spurious universality. Philosophers, especially, are prone to pontificate about what 'we' would say on this or that, and thereby ascribe a general validity to what may be merely the assumptions of their own limited social group. It has to be recognised that different natural languages incorporate different evaluative concepts, and that a particular concept in one language may have no direct equivalent in another. When we read the ethical writings of the ancient Greek philosophers, for example, we find that some of their terms, such as the names for some of the virtues, cannot be easily translated into modern English, and that there are in ancient Greek no words for some modern ethical concepts (such as 'rights' and 'obligations'). This does not mean, however, that people are trapped within a particular ethical perspective represented by their own native language. Because human beings share the same basic human responses, they can come to understand the ethical concepts of another language and another culture, even if there are no obvious exact equivalents in their own language. They can do so just as a child can learn its own ethical language in the first place, in the context of its natural responses to shared human situations. A child learns concepts of 'justice' and 'fairness', for example, by encountering situations where conflicts have to be dealt with in what is basically a cooperative activity – the playing of games is an obvious context in which this may first be encountered. The child's ability to understand the force of remarks like 'It's not fair' depends on his or her experience of cooperation and of commitment to cooperative activities. But if this experience makes certain ethical concepts available to a child learning his or her own language, it makes them equally available to an adult human being from another culture. What counts as 'fair' or 'just' may vary from culture to culture, but we can come to see the point of alternative practices as ways of coping with the same basic experience. When I talk, therefore, of evaluative standards embedded in 'our' language I mean standards which are at least potentially employable by all human language-users. They may not coincide with the standards current within a particular natural language, but any such language is capable of being extended to incorporate concepts from other languages. The process of criticism and of acceptance or rejection of particular concepts in the light of others, to which I have previously referred, can take place not only within a particular language but between languages. It is in virtue of these possibilities of shared ethical reflection, grounded in shared experience and shared natural responses, that I think it appropriate to talk about the human community, the community of potential communicators, as a moral community.

To say that our moral thinking is grounded in a shared human nature is not to say that it is *about* human nature. Here I want to distinguish my position from a certain kind of ethical naturalism which maintains that our judgements of situations as good or bad or of actions as right or wrong are really reports of our responses to those situations or actions. On this view, 'This is good' means roughly 'I like this', and 'That action is wrong' means roughly 'I disapprove of it'. There is an obvious affinity between this version of naturalism and the subjectivism which I began by discussing. It is not a position which I want to defend. On my view, our ethical judgements are not about our responses, but are assessments of our lives and actions and relations to one another. They are judgements that particular human lives are fulfilled or unfulfilled, exciting or boring, rich or impoverished; that actions are cruel or kind, heroic or cowardly, honest or dishonest; that societies are just or unjust, free or unfree. I want to say that judgements of this kind can be objectively true or false. But what makes these concepts, and others, the appropriate concepts with which rationally and intelligibly to assess human lives and actions and societies is that they are features of our shared language, and they are so because we are the kinds of beings that we are, with the kinds of responses which we do have.

PROJECTION AND REIFICATION

To say that we view the world in the way that we do because we are the kinds of beings that we are, and because of the kinds of responses we share, may seem to invite the comment that what we are really doing is projecting our responses onto the world, or 'objectifying' those responses.[9] We might think, it may be said, that our ethical beliefs are objective assertions about an objectively existing reality, but in thinking this we are in error, and the error is a systematic error built into our moral language. When, for instance, we say of certain actions that they are right or wrong because they are honest or dishonest, just or unjust, we may suppose that we are saying something about the objective character of those actions. If, however, our use of concepts such as 'honesty' and 'justice' involves the projection onto the world of our own human responses, this may seem after all to warrant the subjectivist conclusion that what we are really doing in making such judgements is expressing our subjective feelings.

The terms 'projection' and 'objectification' may be a harmless enough way of describing the relation between our primitive responses and what they enable us to say about the world, but we should resist the inference that what is involved here is some kind of error.[10] To clarify the relation between our primitive responses, our language and objective features of the world, compare the example of humour. How is it possible for us to describe situations as 'funny' or 'comic'? There would not be such situations if there did not exist the irreducible human response of laughter. The existence of laughter is not something which can be explained further, it cannot be derived from any other features of human behaviour and attempts to explain it in that way have always been ludicrously inadequate. It is a basic feature of human nature. This is not to deny that some people lack a sense of humour, but the responses of humour and laughter are sufficiently widely shared to make possible also a shared language of humour, so that we can describe situations as 'funny', 'comic', 'hilarious', 'ridiculous' and so on. We could not talk in this way without a background of shared

---

[9] For such talk of 'projection' and 'objectification', see J. L. Mackie, *Ethics: Inventing Right and Wrong* (Harmondsworth, 1977), ch. 1. A 'projectivist' position, applied both to moral language and more widely, is developed by Simon Blackburn in *Spreading the Word* (Oxford, 1984), especially chs. 5 and 6.

[10] The 'error theory' is put forward by Mackie, *Ethics*, p. 35. Mackie therefore uses the ideas of 'projection' and 'objectification' in support of a subjectivist position. Blackburn claims that we do not need to talk of 'error' here, and argues for a position which he calls 'quasi-realism' (see especially *Spreading the Word*, p. 180).

responses, and what counts as 'funny' or 'comic', or whatever, is determined by the nature of those responses. In that sense it could be said that the application of those descriptive concepts is a 'projection' of our responses. No error is involved, however, in the use of such concepts in this way. There is nothing misleading in talking about features of the world rather than simply talking about our responses themselves.

There are limits to this analogy between ethics and humour. In the case of humour and laughter, the common ground of shared responses is not always universal. Though there need be no hesitation about describing laughter as a basic component of human nature, there is also no doubt that there is considerable diversity within this common ground. Different people laugh at different things, and though the diversity is not so great as to prevent us using the object-language of 'comic' situations, it is such that we sometimes just have to say, 'Well I find it funny even if you don't.' One of the questions which we shall in due course have to consider is whether we eventually reach a comparable point of breakdown in ethics too. However, notice one difference immediately; it does not matter that people differ in their sense of humour, but it does matter if people cannot reach agreement in ethics. If the common ground breaks down, that is itself a moral problem. There is therefore pressure to look for common ground and to try to reach agreement. We do not have to accept that pressure, and we might have moral reasons for resisting it, perhaps believing that at least in some cases conflict can be fruitful, but the pressure is there, and this constitutes a difference between the case of ethics and the example of humour.

Despite that difference, what the example of humour illustrates is that though our ways of characterising the world depend upon our shared basic responses, and though they could in a sense be described as 'projections' of those responses, there need be no illusion or error in such projections. I want to maintain that this is true also of our ethical language. Nevertheless, though at the general level the language of moral objectivity is not in itself erroneous, I do want to suggest that certain specific forms of ethical language do involve 'projection' in a stronger, derogatory sense, what I shall call 'reification'. There are certain kinds of ethical concepts, and ways of using them, which distort or conceal the relation of ethical judgements to our natural human responses. I want now to give some examples of such 'reified' or 'alienated' moralities.

A certain style of moral philosophy, influential in Britain in the 1920s and 1930s and epitomised in the work of W. D. Ross, placed at the heart of moral thinking the idea of certain fundamental and self-evident moral *duties*.[11] A comparable tendency in more recent years has been the revival of the idea of moral *rights*, and again these are often treated as though they were self-evidently valid, not standing in need of any further justification. The concepts of 'duties' and 'rights' are in themselves perfectly respectable concepts, and are indeed two sides of the same coin. The roles which people occupy, within social institutions of all kinds, carry with them various rights and duties, which serve to define the roles. For example, a person chairing a meeting has a duty to ensure that everyone gets a fair hearing, and with that goes the right to tell people to shut up if they are dominating the meeting and preventing anyone else from getting a word in. We could give innumerable other examples of institutional rights and duties of this kind, but the question then arises: what about the idea of rights and duties which are not attached to particular institutional roles? There are legitimate uses for this idea, but to use it intelligibly we should still have to ground rights and duties in the actual relations in which human beings stand to one another. We can meaningfully talk of rights and duties which we have in virtue of our informal pre-institutional social relations. Consider the duty to keep a promise, and the corresponding right to receive what has been promised to one. We can adequately explain why there is such a duty and such a right only by referring to the relation of trust and reliance which is created between promiser and promisee. What is wrong with the breaking of a promise is that it violates that relation of trust. In this way our moral duties are grounded in our concrete experience of our relations to one

---

[11] See for example W. D. Ross, *The Right and the Good* (London, 1930).

another. Contrast this with the idea of free-floating moral duties
which are supposed to be just self-evidently 'there', and whose
binding character we are supposed to recognise intuitively.
Where do such duties come from, and why should we be bound
by them? The idea remains wholly mysterious, because the
supposed duties are cut off from any grounding in human
experience.

The same goes for the idea of moral rights. We can make sense
of specific rights deriving from specific social relations, like the
right to what has been promised. But what about the idea of
basic 'human rights', which we are supposed to possess simply
in virtue of being human? This is a popular and extremely
influential idea, and we can, if we wish, give a sense to it. We
could say that though particular societies fail to grant certain
rights (such as a right to life, or to work, or to freedom of speech
and assembly), they *ought* to do so; these, we might say, are basic
human needs which every society must aim to satisfy if it is to
deserve the allegiance of its members, and in that sense they are
human rights even if they are not acknowledged social rights.
This concept of human rights would then be derivative from
ideas of human needs and ideas about what any society ought to
be like. What is misleading, however, is the suggestion that
there are 'self-evident' rights which are features of some pre-
existing moral universe, that there is a moral world constituted
by moral rights analogous to, but over and beyond, the social
world of social rights. This I regard as the projection of features
of the real human world into an imaginary world which has an
entirely illusory status.

The same, I suggest, is true of another influential concept,
that of 'the moral law'. This idea has a long history. It appears
in ancient Greek writers as the idea of 'the unwritten laws'. It
emerges again in the mediaeval tradition of 'natural law'
morality, and in Kant's notion of a moral law which takes the
form of a 'categorical imperative'.[12] As with the concept of

---

[12] For the Greek idea of unwritten laws see, for example, Sophocles' *Antigone*, lines
450–7. The most important mediaeval exponent of 'natural law' morality is Thomas
Aquinas; for a convenient introduction see D. J. O'Connor, *Aquinas and Natural Law*
(London, 1967). For Kant see fn. 7 above.

moral duties, the idea has an obvious social origin. The notion of the law of a society is unproblematic. What then happens is that the concept of 'law' is projected from the social realm into an imaginary moral universe whose status is quite mysterious. It becomes the idea of an external demand which we have to obey, a self-sufficient moral requirement which imposes itself on us. Why should we do what the moral law tells us? That question can be answered only if the content of the moral law is detached from its alien form, demystified and re-connected with its roots in our experience. The demands of this 'moral law' must be shown to be things which do in fact matter to us as human beings, for otherwise they can have no force for us.

This requirement should not be misunderstood. In particular, it should not be confused with the narrower and misconceived requirement that in order to explain why we should do anything, one has to show that it is in our own interests. That demand is misconceived because it is a fact of human nature that things do matter to us other than our own interests. We care about one another, for instance, in quite disinterested ways, and that care takes a variety of forms; our multifarious emotions, commitments, ties and loyalties are as much a part of us as are our desires for ourselves and for our own well-being. The attempt to reduce morality to self-interest is therefore a misguided enterprise, but the attempt to ground morality in concrete experience, in our natural human responses, is a quite proper one.

There is another, quite different way in which the idea of 'moral law' can be thought to acquire its force and its backing. The moral law can be thought of as one which is enacted by a divine legislator; it is the command of God. To mention this is to raise the whole question of the relation between morality and religion, and between religious and humanist perspectives in ethics. I have already said that 'religious' attitudes, understood in a broad sense, are a fundamental component of human experience. This however leaves room for great variety between people according to how large a role religious attitudes play in their lives and their thinking. In some people the principal focus is elsewhere, on human concerns and human relationships. In others, religious attitudes may come to occupy a dominant place. A further step is taken when the religious perspective is articulated in the terms of one of the orthodox systems of religious belief, ascribing to God or the gods a determinate personality and a determinate will which has manifested itself in history and which requires certain kinds of behaviour from human beings in the future. I cannot discuss here the question of the truth or falsity of religious belief. I shall simply state baldly my own position. I can understand the strength of religious attitudes, but the move beyond that to religious dogma, for example to claims about the existence and nature of a god, or to the confident assertion that the divine is fully revealed in the acts and sayings of a particular human being born in Bethlehem 2,000 years ago or in Mecca 1,400 years ago, seems to me to be without any rational justification. Having said that, however, the question then remains: how much room is there for fruitful moral argument and possible moral agreement between the religious believer and the non-believer?

My answer is that there is ample room so long as religious morality makes reference to human experience. Any religious morality which claims to appeal to reason will have to offer some account of the same range of experience which is the starting-point of a non-religious morality. It will have to address itself to the existence of human needs and desires and to the nature of human emotions and relations. So for instance a religious morality which posits a loving creator who desires the well-being of his creatures and who has endowed them with a nature which they need to fulfil will have a great deal of common ground with a humanistic morality. Indeed, the attempt by the religious believer to establish what God wills for his creatures will have to reason from the same facts of human need. Or take the experience of human solidarity. The idea of the brotherhood of man may gain an added resonance from the belief that human beings are all children of one God; but that notion of God as father is not just arbitrarily chosen, it is arrived at precisely as a result of the experience of fraternal relations between human beings and the sense that such relationships are rewarding and fulfilling.

So there is no limit in principle to the scope for agreement between a religious and a humanist morality so long as the former rests on the appeal to experience. On the other hand, the situation is quite different when a religious morality rests on an appeal to authority. Orthodox religious systems of moral belief typically claim to possess revealed moral truths, in the form of sacred texts or the reported utterances of past prophets or the current deliverances of divinely inspired religious leaders. In its most extreme form such a claim sets itself beyond rational argument, once the authority is accepted. It is then immune to the test of experience. However, the appeal to authority brings its own problems with it. The more religious morality tends in that direction, the more incapable it becomes of saying why anyone should accept that authority. What reason could be given? 'A voice spoke to me'? But many people hear voices – the Yorkshire Ripper heard voices telling him to kill prostitutes – so what makes this particular voice the voice of divine authority? 'It's written in a book (or on tablets of stone, or gold scrolls, or whatever).' But there are plenty of books around, including not a few which claim to be divinely inspired – why pick out this one? Tablets of stone are in shorter supply, but presumably it is not just the fact of being stone that is supposed to give them their authority. So what does confer that authority? If a certain body of moral teaching does impress itself strongly on people and appear to them to be authoritative, this can only be because it makes sense of people's moral experience, because it unifies that experience, illuminates it by pointing out and articulating insights previously only half glimpsed. We therefore come back to the fact that an appeal to authority can be convincing only insofar as it connects with people's experience. If it cuts itself off from that experience and becomes simply a set of commands, it is immune to rational argument but by the same token it loses its authority.

In the subsequent discussion of the ethics of war and peace I shall therefore feel no need to take account of moral claims which consist of no more than a bare appeal to authority. I do not, for instance, think that the argument for pacifism is advanced by pointing out that Jesus said 'Love your enemies' or that he told Peter to put up his sword. Knowing that he said these things may affect our estimate of him as a moral teacher, but in order to make that estimate we already need at least some moral understanding. We also need that prior understanding even in order to interpret these rather elusive sayings. Notoriously, they have been invoked by some as support for pacifism, whilst others have denied that they offer any such support. The argument between the two schools of interpretation is therefore likely to invoke all the same considerations as will occur in any argument for and against pacifism. Mixing the argument with an appeal to religious authority needlessly complicates the issue.

FORMS OF MORAL ARGUMENT

I have been distinguishing between reified moralities and moralities which are rooted in human experience. The former, insofar as they have a rational content, derive it from experience but project it into a 'beyond' which conceals its origins and presents it as a set of external demands to which human beings must conform – as transcendent duties or rights, moral laws or divine commands. To assess any of these ideas, I have argued, we have to bring them back to their roots in experience so as to identify the valid element in them.

I want now to look at two other styles of moral argument which also contrast with my own. The first of these consists in trying to deduce moral conclusions from some basic first principle. There are various examples of such an approach, but I shall concentrate on the one which has been most important and influential, the theory known as 'utilitarianism'.[13] I have already referred to it briefly, and I shall want to take issue with it at various points in this book. According to the utilitarian theory, the fundamental principle of morality is that actions are right insofar as they promote happiness or reduce suffering, and

---

[13] The most influential presentation and defence of utilitarianism is John Stuart Mill, *Utilitarianism* (first published 1861, various modern editions). For a recent defence of utilitarianism see J. J. C. Smart, 'An Outline of a System of Utilitarian Ethics', in J. J. C. Smart and Bernard Williams, *Utilitarianism: For and Against* (Cambridge, 1973).

wrong insofar as they reduce happiness or produce suffering. Concrete moral decisions are then to be made by ascertaining what would be the consequences of our actions, in order to assess how much happiness or suffering they are likely to produce for everyone who would be affected by them. The theory tells us to produce *as much happiness as possible* (where this is shorthand for 'the maximum net balance of happiness over suffering'). It is a *maximising* theory. When different people's interests conflict and we have to decide who is to benefit and who is to lose out, we are to settle the dilemma by asking what will produce the greatest amount of benefit overall, rather than by asking what would be 'fair' or 'just' or who 'deserves' to benefit or is 'entitled' to benefit. Considerations of the latter kind may enter into our deliberations in a subsidiary way, as rough guides to the best consequences. If, for example, we have to decide between alternative courses of action which will devote a limited amount of resources either to the needs of the homeless or to the needs of millionaires, we may reckon that more benefit will be produced if the resources go to the homeless. The rule of thumb here is that, other things being equal, the less well-off are likely to derive greater benefit from a given amount of resources, and to that extent our intuitive ideas of 'fairness' are likely to be a useful guide to the correct utilitarian conclusion. But these ideas play only a subsidiary role, derivative from the fundamental utilitarian principle. Moreover, the theory recognises no independent constraints on the means we may employ to produce happiness, in the form, for instance, of principles that it is wrong to kill or to lie or to deceive or to coerce. Such principles can again be no more than subsidiary rules, guides to the likely long-term consequences, serving to remind us that actions such as killing or lying are likely to create unhappiness and can therefore be justified only if they also produce enough happiness to outweigh the unhappiness.

In these respects utilitarianism may well appear morally contentious, and we shall in due course look more closely at various moral challenges to the theory. Its defenders argue, however, that in practice its implications will, on the whole, tend to coincide with our common-sense moral beliefs and assumptions, and the theory can claim to offer a plausible explanation of why those common-sense beliefs are the right ones. Its great advantage is that when common sense presents us with difficult dilemmas, the theory offers a single simple principle with which to resolve them, and by which to test all our moral intuitions.

The trouble is that it is too simple. It takes a single principle and elevates it to a special status amongst our practical concerns. If we ask where this principle comes from and why it should matter to us, the answer must be that it derives from some basic human attitude. Thus utilitarianism picks out the attitude of impartial concern for the happiness and suffering of everyone, and elevates it to a special status.[14] But *why* should it have this special status? One possible answer, we have seen, is that this attitude of impartial concern is built into the definition of what it is to act *morally*. This, however, is to beg the question. It is, I have previously suggested, a tendentious definition of morality, but in any case, even if violating the utilitarian principle amounts to a rejection of morality, this simply raises the question 'Why should I act morally?' If everyone's happiness and suffering are to matter to me, this can only be because I have, as a human being, the capacity to identify with others and be moved by their situation. This, as I have explained, is not to say that I should take account of other people's happiness or suffering only when I am actually being moved by them. It is, however, to say that the consideration of others' well-being would not give us reasons for performing this or that action unless we were, in general, beings who were capable of being moved in that way. But now the point is that the natural attitude to which the utilitarian principle appeals is just one human response among others. There can be no reason for giving it a unique status. If we are moved by a concern for other people's happiness and suffering, we are also, I have suggested,

---

[14] J. J. C. Smart says: 'In setting up a system of normative ethics the utilitarian must appeal to some ultimate attitudes which he holds in common with those people to whom he is addressing himself. The sentiment to which he appeals is generalized benevolence, that is, the disposition to seek happiness, or at any rate, in some sense or other, good consequences, for all mankind, or perhaps for all sentient beings' (Smart and Williams, *Utilitarianism: For and Against*, p. 7).

moved by a sense of *respect* for others – respect for them as *agents*, committed to their own actions and projects. Then, in addition to these two quite general responses, we are moved by all the various forms of love and affection for particular individuals, by loyalties of many different kinds, as well as by resentment and hostility and the like. Finally there is the special kind of concern which we each have for our own lives. This is not to say that egoistic attitudes must take predominance over altruistic ones, but simply to say that the problem of the relations between, and possible conflicts between, oneself and others cannot be resolved merely by mathematical and conceptual fiat, merely by incorporating one's own interests and one's own concerns into the total sum of 'the general happiness'.[15]

Our ethical vocabulary, then, reflects this diversity of human responses and concerns, and it is a mistake to try to reduce it to one basic self-evident principle or simple set of principles. Thus we should not approach practical moral issues by first adopting a schematic moral theory such as utilitarianism, applying it to the issues and reading off from it our practical conclusions.

Such an approach, however, what we might call 'foundationalism', does at least have the merit of adopting a critical stance towards common-sense moral assumptions. Whereas foundationalism is too restrictive, the method of moral argument which appeals to nothing deeper than common sense is excessively permissive. Many philosophical discussions of moral issues aspire to nothing more than extending to controversial cases those moral beliefs which are generally accepted as uncontroversial. Thus they will argue that 'of course we wouldn't think it right to do x' and therefore, to be consistent, we must also think it wrong to do y. To anticipate an example to which I shall return, writers on the morality of war often take it as obvious that there is a 'right of self-defence', meaning thereby that it is justifiable to kill in self-defence, and from this they conclude that it is equally obvious that pacifism is mistaken and that conventional justifications for war are acceptable. However, conventional moral beliefs, including many which

---

[15] This is an important theme of Bernard Williams' critique of utilitarianism in ibid.

would be commonly regarded as uncontroversial, are bound to include a fair share of prejudices and confusions. Utilitarians and other advocates of foundationalist theories then rightly respond that prevailing moral beliefs should not be accepted uncritically, but should be examined and questioned. With this I agree. The test of conventional beliefs should not, however, be whether they can be derived from some self-evident first principle. Rather, I suggest, we should ask whether the conventional beliefs make a proper use of the underlying evaluative concepts, and to gain a proper understanding of those concepts we must in turn identify the underlying natural human responses on which they build. In short, the test of our moral beliefs consists in asking how they are rooted in our pre-theoretical experience.

As an approach to moral reasoning this is of course extremely sketchy. What it might mean in practice is something I shall hope to demonstrate in the rest of the book. In the meantime I suggest that we can now see the possibility of a kind of objectivity in moral thinking. This objectivity consists in the fact that we can characterise our lives and our actions and our relations with one another by employing shared, impersonal evaluative concepts, and in the fact that these characterisations furnish objectively valid reasons for actions. At the same time, the account which I am offering can do justice to the arguments on both sides of the debate between objectivism and subjectivism. I initially noted three arguments.

1. I mentioned that moral disagreements typically give the appearance of being disagreements about *what is the case*. If two people disagree about what ought to be done, they cannot just agree to differ, as they could if it were simply a difference of tastes, for they will typically assume that one of them is *right* and the other is *wrong*. This is the assumption which supports objectivism. Of course it may be an illusion, but it still has to be accounted for, and I suggest that my view of moral reasoning can do so. Moral reasoning is indeed about 'what is the case', since it is a matter not of expressing feelings and attitudes but of characterising actions and situations as being of a certain kind. And our sense of what is at stake in moral disagreements is

accounted for by the fact that we are disagreeing about whether there really are impersonally valid reasons for or against performing this or that action.

2.   I also mentioned that, since our moral views must lead us to *act* in certain ways, it might seem that they must be intimately connected with our feelings, and this appears to support the subjectivist position. There is indeed such a connection, but it is more indirect than subjectivism maintains. Our moral views are not direct *expressions* of our feelings. But the concepts which we employ in making moral judgements are concepts which have a practical significance for us because we are the kinds of creatures that we are, with the kinds of feelings and responses which we do have.

3.   The other point which I mentioned as appearing to support subjectivism was that there might seem to be no way of resolving deep moral disagreements. On this point I must for the time being reserve judgement. I have tried to show that we can argue rationally about moral issues, and that this means not just establishing the relevant facts, but arguing rationally about their moral significance. It remains possible, nevertheless, that such arguments may sometimes leave a residue of irresolvable disagreement. We can find out how far rational argument can take us only by giving it a try. This I shall do by looking at the rights and wrongs of war. At the end of the discussion I shall consider whether, and if so in what sense, rational argument still leaves us with an irreconcilable clash of opinions.

CHAPTER 2

The wrongness of killing

VIOLENCE

Moral arguments about the acceptability of war are often conducted using the concept of 'violence'. Pacifists often assert that they oppose war because they reject violence as a way of settling disputes. Their opponents may then attempt to demonstrate that violence is sometimes necessary, and thence conclude that war can sometimes be justified. Unfortunately, however, 'violence' is one of the most confused terms in our moral vocabulary. The simple opposition between the two views I have just mentioned is only part of the picture. We find politicians who are unquestioningly committed to the maintenance of the country's armed forces and who unhesitatingly give orders for the use of those forces to control territory or put down a rebellion, but who also declare that 'violence is never acceptable' and resolutely condemn the 'violence' of, for instance, strikers who get into fights with the police. The assumption here seems to be that 'violence' is by definition illegal, so that actions against the established authorities can be called 'violence' but actions carried out by or ordered by the authorities cannot be so called. This narrowing of the concept is matched by a widening of it on the other side of the political argument. A connection is made between 'violence' and the 'violating' of a person's rights, and this may then be used to suggest that features of individual behaviour or social life not normally thought of as violent may nevertheless embody a kind of violence. Behaviour which is emotionally damaging or distressing may be described as 'psychological violence'.

Poverty and deprivation resulting from certain kinds of social institution may be described as 'institutionalised violence'. The suggestion would be that the normal day-to-day workings of a social system may violate the rights of members of particular social groups by restricting their options and denying them the opportunities which other groups enjoy. No overt violence may be needed to bring about this result, and yet the effect on people's lives may be just as devastating and crushing as the effect of what we normally call 'violence'. It is in order to draw attention to these hidden violations of people's rights that the phrase 'institutionalised violence' has been coined.

Further confusion is created by the everyday connotations of the term. Doing something 'violently' is equated with doing it energetically, with sudden or rapid movements. If I cannot get the tomato ketchup out of the bottle by holding it upside down or shaking it gently, I may then shake it 'violently'. These connotations tend to colour arguments about whether damage to property is violence. Protesters who proclaim their commitment to non-violence may nevertheless be accused of violence if they pull down a fence outside a missile base. If they paint slogans on a wall, the accusation of violence sounds less plausible, for of course their physical movements are likely to be slower and more careful, but that can hardly be of great moral significance.

I conclude that moral arguments are unlikely to be advanced one way or another if they are conducted primarily in terms of the concept of 'violence'. This is because people's use of the term is likely to be determined by prior moral positions which they have taken up, and therefore the concept of 'violence' cannot itself be used to defend those positions. We have first to sort out our moral beliefs, and only then can we determine how, if at all, the term 'violence' may be useful in enabling us to make some of the moral distinctions we want to make.

Now I would suggest that when people use the term 'violence' for a moral critique of war, what they see as the central moral consideration is the taking of human life. War is the deliberate killing or maiming of human beings in vast numbers. And though the physical acts of war, such as shooting and bombing,

do not normally involve any discrimination between the intent
to kill and the intent to maim, it is, I think, the fact of killing that
is morally fundamental. It is this that makes intelligible the
position of pacifism as an absolute moral rejection of war. If
pacifism is formulated as an absolute rejection of violence, it can
easily be ridiculed by drawing on the ambiguities of the term
'violence', so as to suggest, for instance, that the pacifist must
refuse even to parry a blow or pin down an assailant.[1] What the
pacifist really objects to is killing, and he or she typically
maintains that nothing which might be achieved by war can
justify the massive taking of human life. Of course there are
other evils of war: the wholesale disruption of civil life, the
laying waste of the land, the destruction of buildings and cities
and works of art. If these were the fundamental moral concerns,
however, the question of war would belong in the same category
as moral concern about such things as environmental destruction. Though there are indeed connections with such
issues, the moral problem of war belongs essentially with other
dilemmas concerning the taking of life.

I suggest that in thinking about the rights and wrongs of war
we take pacifism as our starting-point, for the pacifist position
draws attention to the radical disparity within conventional
moral thinking which I mentioned at the beginning of the
previous chapter. There is normally taken to be a very strong
moral presumption against the taking of human life. Controversial cases, such as abortion or euthanasia or the death
penalty, are controversial because there is disagreement about
whether there are special reasons in these cases for making an
exception or for thinking that the presumption against killing
does not apply here. But whereas the uncompromising rejection
of abortion or of euthanasia or of the death penalty are widely
held views, pacifism, the uncompromising rejection of killing in
war, is the position of a small minority. Many people who are
bitterly opposed to abortion, or to embryo experimentation, or
the termination of the lives of severely deformed babies, exhibit

---

[1] See for example Jan Narveson, 'Pacifism: A Philosophical Analysis', in *Ethics* vol. 75
    (1965), reprinted in Richard Wasserstrom (ed.), *Today's Moral Problems* (New York,
    1975).

no such opposition to war, although it claims many more lives. Even those who oppose particular wars, or particular military policies such as nuclear deterrence, are rarely pacifists. Most people in our society accept war and the preparation for war as an inevitable, if regrettable, feature of social life. Often even the regret is muted; wars have been heralded as glorious, and the successful completion of a war has often been the occasion for celebration. No one, I think, whatever their views on abortion, would propose putting out flags to celebrate the successful completion of abortions. So war seems to be an anomaly. There is moral disagreement about it, but the centre of gravity in such disagreements appears to be located at quite a different point from its location in other comparable disagreements about the taking of life.

Why is this? Can it be justified? In this and the following chapters I shall try to answer those questions. I shall first try to clarify the nature of the normal presumption against killing, and I shall then consider what special factors might affect the application of that presumption to the case of war.

What exactly is the nature of the moral objection to the taking of human life? What are its roots in our experience? Two phrases are often used to describe the objection: the idea of a 'right to life', and the idea of 'the sanctity of life'. I want first to look at each of these.

THE RIGHT TO LIFE

I have already mentioned that the idea of basic moral rights is problematic. The concept of rights is essentially a social one. We enjoy rights through our occupancy of particular social positions, whether institutionalised or informal, and we can identify what rights people have by consulting the rules and conventions which define the relevant social positions. As a member of an Athletics Club I have rights to use certain facilities, to stand for office in the club and so on. As a citizen who is included on the electoral roll of a particular political community, I have a right to vote, and that is a right with which I am endowed by the law of my country. The idea of a 'right to life' is not like that. It is supposed to be a universal human right, a *moral* right, not dependent on the laws or rules of particular social institutions. Indeed, particular laws may be criticised precisely on the grounds that they fail to respect the moral right to life. How are such moral rights to be identified, then? How do we know whether we have them or not? Others besides the right to life are often claimed. Do we have a moral right to unlimited free speech? A moral right to enjoy pornography if we want to? Do we have a moral right to carry firearms, or a moral right to the fruits of our own labour? The examples are all contentious, and the questions cannot be answered simply by appealing to the concept of a right.

There are no self-evident moral rights. The concept of a moral right may have a use, but it is not morally basic, and whether or not we have particular moral rights such as a right to life can be determined only by appealing to prior moral considerations. Further argument is needed; we have to go deeper, and cannot simply appeal to any supposedly self-evident truth that people have a right to life.

THE SANCTITY OF LIFE

What about the idea of 'the sanctity of life'? Does this fare any better? What is immediately striking about the phrase is that it has religious connotations. The precise nature of those connotations is, however, unclear. The intended meaning may be that life is sacred because it is created by God and is therefore not ours to destroy. The trouble with all such appeals to the purposes of an omnipotent creator, however, is that since they apply to everything in creation, morally speaking they leave everything as it is. They endorse everything and therefore tell us nothing. If indeed life is created by God, then presumably also diseases, earthquakes, droughts, old age and even our human propensities to murder are likewise the product of divine creation. So, from the fact that life is created by God, it does not follow that the destruction of life is wrong.

The deeper interpretation of 'the sanctity of life' would see it not as a principle to be derived from religious beliefs about divine purposes or divine commands, but as itself the direct expression of some fundamental religious impulse, such as the response of 'reverence' or 'awe' which I mentioned in the previous chapter. Religious feelings of this kind are the source of, rather than the product of, more formal religious beliefs. Talk of 'the sanctity of life' could thus be seen as a way of articulating our natural human response to the wonder and mystery of life, and as an indication that such a response properly involves a moral refusal to take life.

It is doubtful, however, whether such a moral principle accurately reflects our underlying responses. If the sanctity of life really does mean a principled refusal to take life, because life as such is sacred, then consider what this would entail in practice. We should have to regard it as wrong to kill any living thing, not just any human being, but any animal or plant. It would be wrong not only to kill animals for food, which vegetarians would of course accept, but also to harvest crops if this involves killing the plants. It would be wrong to kill weeds in the garden, or to destroy germs to prevent diseases. It is possible to live in such a way, and some people have tried to do so. It can, moreover, be made more plausible as a way of life if interpreted to allow that the wrongness of killing can sometimes be overridden by other considerations. This would mean that the killing of a weed or a germ could sometimes on balance be justified, perhaps to preserve another living thing, but would still be a moral loss. Such a conception still remains extremely remote from most people's moral thinking; most people would think it no loss at all to destroy a germ. That does not automatically invalidate such a moral position. I have warned against appealing uncritically to conventional moral beliefs. Nevertheless this literal interpretation of 'the sanctity of life' is so distant from most moral thinking that we should at least wonder whether it properly reflects our underlying moral experience.

Those who are committed to the idea of 'the sanctity of life' might well, at this point, reply that what they really maintain is 'the sanctity of *human* life'. Such a position would indeed be much more in keeping with prevailing moral attitudes, but again that does not automatically make it right, and the position raises its own problems. It should prompt us to ask, what is so special about human life? If we maintain the sanctity of human life simply because it is human, this looks like an arbitrary bias in favour of our own species. Such a stance has been labelled 'speciesism', implying a comparison with racism and sexism.[2] Just as the extreme form of racism or sexism would consist in believing that whites should be favoured just because they are whites, or that the interests of men should take precedence over those of women for no other reason than that they are the interests of men, so, it is suggested, giving a special status to human life not because it is life but because it is human constitutes an equally arbitrary piece of discrimination. The reply might be that as human beings we just do respond to fellow humans in a way different from how we respond to other living things, and that this brute fact is the basis for our giving a special status to human life. In the end I shall, indeed, maintain a position not so very different from that. Still, something more needs to be said. What exactly is it that we are responding to when we respond in a special way to other human beings? What *is* so special about human life?

An initially plausible answer would be that human beings possess distinctive qualities which mark them off from other species. What might these be? The favoured candidates are likely to be certain mental qualities: perhaps that human beings alone possess rationality, or that they alone possess self-consciousness in the strong sense that, unlike other animals, they are capable of forming some overall conception of their lives, seeing themselves as beings with a past and a future, assessing the past and making plans for the future.

Whether human beings are the only living things to possess these qualities is a matter for debate. It may be that the intellectual capacities of some animal species, such as chimpanzees or gorillas or dolphins, are greater than has been generally recognised. Still, there is no doubt that qualities of this kind distinguish human beings from most other animals, and if

[2] Peter Singer, *Practical Ethics* (Cambridge, 1979), p. 51.

species such as chimpanzees come on the human side of the divide, the 'sanctity of life' principle could apply to them while still avoiding the paradoxical implication of embracing every form of life. What is more problematic is that the qualities in question are not possessed by all human beings. A new-born baby is certainly not yet rational or self-conscious. Its level of awareness and its capacity for intelligent behaviour are a good deal lower than that of the average bird or rodent. There are also human beings who are so severely handicapped mentally that they can be said to possess little or no rationality or self-consciousness.

One might simply accept this implication and conclude that the principle of the sanctity of human life does not apply to babies or mentally defective humans. Such a conclusion is not as grotesque and callous as it may sound. It does not mean that we can simply slaughter babies and the mentally handicapped with no compunction. There remain very strong reasons of an indirect kind for not killing these human beings. Most obviously, to do so would normally cause unbearable grief for the parents and others who are emotionally close to the human being in question, and these considerations remain relevant even though 'the sanctity of human life' does not apply. Even so, we may feel uneasy about an interpretation of the sanctity of human life which excludes large classes of human lives in this way.

Another move which might be made, at least to explain the wrongness of killing human infants, is to bring in the idea of 'potentiality'. Babies are not yet rational or self-conscious, it may be said, but they are potentially so, and that is why it is as wrong to kill them as to kill an adult human being.

This idea of 'potentiality' is a popular one but it is by no means straightforward. In due course I shall suggest that it does indeed have a role to play in our moral thinking, but for the moment I want to indicate the difficulties. The concept has been invoked not only to explain the wrongness of killing human infants, but also, by moral critics of abortion, to argue that a human foetus is likewise a potential rational and self-conscious person and should therefore not be destroyed. Others have countered this move with the argument that if the status of a foetus is sacrosanct because of its potentiality, then by the same token a human ovum has the potentiality to develop into a human being if it is fertilised by a sperm and would therefore have to be treated with the same respect as a human foetus and a human infant – a conclusion which appears manifestly absurd. 'That's not the same', the anti-abortionist might reply – but what this shows is that those who want to invoke the idea of 'potentiality' owe us an account of what is meant by it. If we are to say that a baby is a potential rational and self-conscious being, must we then say the same of a foetus? And if we do, are we then also committed to saying that an unfertilised ovum is a potential rational and self-conscious being? In all these cases there is clearly some kind of causal continuity, but what more, if anything, is needed for an x to be a potential y?

A further reason why the idea of 'potentiality' needs careful handling is that, even if we can agree that x is a potential y, it is not clear what moral implications, if any, this should have for our treatment of x. Why should we base our moral treatment of any being on what it *could become* rather than on what it *is*? To take an example used by Peter Singer,

Prince Charles is a potential King of England, but he does not now have the rights of a King. Why should a potential person have the rights of a person?[3]

Surely the moral status of anyone or anything should depend on what it is now, not on the fact that it will be or could be a different kind of being in the future. I shall come back to the idea of 'potentiality' later, but for the moment it is enough to note that it offers no easy solution to the problems with which we are at present concerned.

UTILITARIAN OBJECTIONS TO KILLING

We have seen that if the idea of the sanctity of life is understood literally, it seems to put all life on a par and make it wrong to kill any living thing. If we modify our position to that of the sanctity of human life, we have to explain what is morally special about human life, and this must consist in something more than its

---

[3] Ibid., p. 120.

simply being human. Qualities such as rationality and self-consciousness may seem suitable candidates, but the problem is that these qualities are not possessed by two large groups of human beings, infants and those who are severely mentally defective. The concept of 'potentiality' might help to explain why 'the sanctity of human life' still applies to human infants, but we have now seen that it involves problems of its own.

At this point we might try a new approach. If qualities such as rationality and self-consciousness are too restrictive, perhaps we should focus on qualities which really are possessed by *all* human beings. A baby does not possess a sophisticated intelligence or self-awareness, but it can experience pleasure and pain, it can be happy and can suffer. Is that not sufficient reason why we should be concerned for it? Of course, these capacities for pleasure or happiness or suffering, capacities which have been summed up in the term 'sentience', are not unique to humans. Being broad enough to be possessed by all humans, they are also possessed by many other animal species (though not by plants). Perhaps, however, we should simply acknowledge that implication and accept that our moral concern should extend to all living things which experience pleasure or suffering.

This is indeed a new approach, and it could be suggested that we are now looking at something quite different from the idea of the sanctity of life. If these are the qualities which set the limits of moral concern, then perhaps what we should really be aiming at is not the protection of life as such, but the promotion of pleasure or happiness and the prevention of pain or suffering. This is in effect the moral perspective which I have previously labelled 'utilitarian'. It and the idea of 'the sanctity of life' represent two distinct approaches to questions about the taking of life. This is apparent from the way in which arguments about controversial cases typically go. Take the case of abortion. In part, of course, disagreement here is about whether a human embryo really is a human 'life'. That however is not the only point at issue. Many people who argue for the acceptability of abortion would feel that the important questions are about the likely effects on the future well-being of the woman if she is forced to go through with the pregnancy, and about the future happiness or unhappiness of the child who will be brought into the world if the foetus is not aborted. They consider that whether an abortion would be justified in a particular case depends on the concrete benefits or harms which would follow, and they are, I think, likely to be impatient with the question whether the embryo is a human life not so much because they consider that the answer is obvious but because they think that it is not the important question. Consider again the question of infant euthanasia and the view that we should not prolong the lives of babies born with defects such as severe spina bifida or severe Down's syndrome. Those who take this view are likely to do so from a consideration of the suffering which would otherwise ensue for the child and the parents. They will be opposed by those who insist that the sanctity of human life does not permit it to be destroyed for such reasons. Here then we have a contrast between two broad approaches to such issues, approaches which are naturally and spontaneously adopted by many people and are not just the product of philosophical theorising.

It can hardly be denied that considerations of a broadly utilitarian kind should play *some* role in our moral thinking. The harms and benefits which consist in the experiencing of suffering or happiness can hardly be denied moral relevance. It can hardly be denied also that some dilemmas are properly dealt with by weighing one set of harms or benefits against another. Consider a family dispute, where one child is revising for a very important examination the next day and the other child wants to play her stereo at full volume. Over an extended period some fair apportionment of time to the two preferences could no doubt be fixed, but on this particular occasion the lesser interests just have to be outweighed by the greater, even though the child denied her decibels will be miserable as a result.

Utilitarian thinking, then, is sometimes appropriate. It does not follow, however, that it is always the only appropriate form of moral thinking. In particular, those who are committed to the idea of the sanctity of life will deny that it is the only or even the principal way of thinking about the rightness or wrongness of killing. Utilitarianism in the strict sense, then, is the view that *all* moral considerations ultimately come down to utilitarian ones. The rightness or wrongness of any action, whether an act of killing or anything else, is to be determined by assessing the amount of happiness or suffering which the action will lead to or will prevent. And in any situation the right action to perform will be the one which will produce more happiness overall than any alternative, or, if no available action will produce a net gain in happiness, then that which will lead to the least amount of suffering. Here is a distinctive approach to moral questions. It purports to provide a key to unlock our moral difficulties. In the light of our problems with the idea of the sanctity of life, let us see whether utilitarianism can provide a more satisfactory account of when and why it is wrong to kill.

There are obvious utilitarian reasons why it will usually be wrong to kill someone. In most cases it will create terrible grief and suffering for the family and/or friends who suffer the bereavement. That will usually be an overwhelming reason against taking the life. The death will often also be a loss to the wider society, depriving others of the benefits and services which the dead person could have conferred. These considerations do not always apply. Some people live isolated lives and their death is no great loss to anyone. More to the point, these considerations do not yet account for the idea that killing someone is a wrong done *to the person who is killed*, not just to those who are bereaved. This too, however, admits of a utilitarian explanation. For a start, killing someone usually involves inflicting considerable pain on the victim. It may not do so – some deaths are painless and/or quick – but more important is the fact that to kill someone is to deprive them of all the future happiness which they could have experienced. Most people's lives presumably contain on balance more happiness than suffering, for otherwise they would not be worth living. This loss of happiness is therefore, for the utilitarian, the principal reason why it is normally wrong to kill someone. Normally, but not always. The utilitarian is bound to recognise exceptions. These will include various kinds of mercy-killing, perhaps of severely handicapped infants in the cases I have already mentioned, or of the old or the sick when it is a kindness to them to put them out of their misery. There will also be cases where killing people would indeed deprive them of that happiness and create grief for others, but where the utilitarian would justify it on the grounds that it will overall do more to prevent suffering or promote happiness for people in general. A utilitarian case for killing in war would have to take some such form. Thus utilitarians cannot be absolutists about the taking of life, that is to say, they cannot maintain that killing is always, without exception, automatically ruled out. Whether killing is wrong depends on the circumstances. Advocates of the sanctity of life, on the other hand, could be absolutists, but they do not have to be. They could accept that there are exceptional cases where the sanctity of life is outweighed by other considerations which are very strong indeed. Nevertheless they are more likely to take an absolutist position, and are at any rate bound to recognise a strong moral presumption against killing which it is very difficult to overrule, whereas for the utilitarian the presumption against killing is merely a general rule stating that killing is likely to have bad consequences in most cases.

What are we to make of the utilitarian account? Consider the following example from Dostoevsky's novel *Crime and Punishment*. Raskolnikov is an impoverished law student. He has noble aspirations. He wants to complete his studies so that he can serve his fellows, and so that he can better the lives of his mother and his sister, who are devoted to him. Raskolnikov has previously borrowed money from a money-lender, an old woman whose life is a misery. The only person who could be said to be in any sense close to her is her feeble-minded sister, who lives with her and whom she torments. Raskolnikov decides to kill her and take her money so that he can complete his studies.

His decision is, in part, formulated in utilitarian terms, and from a utilitarian point of view it is difficult to see what is wrong with it.[4] The old money-lender would have got no pleasure from

---

[4] Raskolnikov's thoughts take shape when he overhears a conversation in a restaurant between a student and an army officer. The student says that he is only joking but, playing with the argument simply for the fun of it, he puts the case for killing the old

her life, no one will miss her or mourn her passing and Raskolnikov will put her money to much better use than she would have done. As it turns out, he blunders, kills the simple-minded sister as well, is racked by feelings of guilt, is arrested and punished. The consequences do not, therefore, in retrospect provide a utilitarian justification for the murder. The proper conclusion for the utilitarian to draw, however, need not be that Raskolnikov should not have committed the murder but only that he should have been more careful and not given way to irrational guilt-feelings. Admittedly the utilitarian picture may be more complicated than that. There are long-term consequences to consider. If, in order to reap the benefits of the murder, Raskolnikov would have to resist any inclination to feel remorse, he might thereby turn himself into a ruthless and callous criminal, one who is prepared to kill on other occasions where the utilitarian justification is absent. On the other hand, he might not; he might be able to remain a clear-headed utilitarian who can distinguish between cases like this one and other cases where killing will have no such benefits for others. In any case, to reason in this way is to concede the essential point, that the utilitarian can have no objection to killing *in this particular situation*; utilitarian arguments against killing the old woman will have to refer to the consequences for *other* situations.

What does the example show, then? Certainly it shows that

woman: 'on the one hand, we have a stupid, senseless, worthless, wicked and decrepit old hag, who is of no use to anybody and who actually does harm to everybody, a creature who does not know herself what she is living for and who will be dead soon, anyway... On the other hand, we have a large number of young and promising people who are going to rack and ruin without anyone lifting a finger to help them, and there are thousands of them all over the place. Now, a hundred or even a thousand of them could be set on the road to success and helped at the very start of their careers on that old woman's money, which is to go to a monastery. Hundreds, perhaps thousands of lives could be saved, dozens of families could be rescued from a life of poverty, from decay and ruin, from vice and hospitals for venereal diseases, and all with her money. Kill her, take her money, and with its help devote yourself to the service of humanity and the good of all. Well, don't you think that one little crime could be expiated and wiped out by thousands of good deeds? For one life you will save thousands of lives from corruption and decay. One death in exchange for a hundred lives, why, it's a simple sum in arithmetic! And, when you come to think of it, what does the life of a sickly, wicked old hag amount to when weighed in the scales of the general good of mankind?' (Fyodor Dostoyevsky, *Crime and Punishment*, trans. David Magarshack (Harmondsworth, 1951), p. 84).

utilitarianism may conflict with conventional moral views, but we should again remember that that is not by itself a sufficient criticism. Convention may be wrong and utilitarianism may be right. The deeper criticism is the one which I made in the previous chapter. Utilitarianism is too simple. Its plausibility rests on certain features of our moral experience and our basic human responses, but if these are elevated into a complete moral theory which claims to be all-embracing, then whole areas of our moral experience will simply have been left out. What then is missing from the utilitarian perception of the Raskolnikov example? One answer would of course be: the sanctity of life. There are other things to be said, however, and one important way of looking at it would be this: whatever Raskolnikov may think about the advantages of killing the old woman, it is not his decision to make. *It is her life, not his*, and therefore he cannot take it upon himself to dispose of her life for however worthy an end.

RESPECT FOR AUTONOMY

This dimension of the situation has been referred to by some writers as the requirement of *respect for autonomy*.[5] By 'autonomy' is here meant 'the capacity to choose, to make and act on one's own decisions'.[6] Most people want to go on living. To kill them, against their will, represents a failure to respect their autonomy. This is therefore a fundamental reason why it is normally wrong to take human life. It will not always apply. Sometimes people may decide that they wish to end their lives. Their autonomy will then be respected by accepting their wish to die, not by frustrating it, and in this way one could in principle justify acts of suicide or voluntary euthanasia. Here the contrast with the idea of the sanctity of life is apparent. From the latter point of view any act of terminating a life is, as such, wrong, even if the life is one's own, and hence suicide or voluntary euthanasia could not be justified.

It is equally important to recognise the contrast with

---

[5] Jonathan Glover, *Causing Death and Saving Lives* (Harmondsworth, 1977), pp. 74ff. Cf. Singer, *Practical Ethics*, pp. 83–4.   [6] Singer, *Practical Ethics*, p. 83.

utilitarian attitudes to the taking of life. From a utilitarian point of view one could, in principle, justify not only voluntary but also involuntary euthanasia, that is, taking someone's life *against* their own wishes, on the grounds that it will ease their death and be kinder to them to do so. In practice it would be very difficult to come up with such a justification; a utilitarian would have to take full account of the danger of misjudging another person's interests, as well as the fears and insecurities which would be created if involuntary euthanasia were to become a general practice. Nevertheless, *if* one could be certain that euthanasia against someone's own wishes was in their own best interests, and that there would be no further harmful consequences, this would be a reason for performing such an action, whereas respect for autonomy would be a reason against it. The contrast is even clearer in cases such as the Raskolnikov example, where utilitarianism could in principle justify taking someone's life against their wishes in order to promote other people's interests.

We should beware of assimilating 'respect for autonomy' to a utilitarian way of thinking. The utilitarian might accept that autonomy is an important component of a good human life, and that therefore we should seek to promote people's autonomy along with other aspects of their happiness and well-being. 'Respect for autonomy', however, is not primarily a matter of producing as much autonomy as possible. Here I want to recall my remarks in the previous chapter about 'respect' as a basic response to another person. I contrasted it there with an attitude such as 'sympathy', which involves identifying with another's interests and seeking to promote them as though they were one's own. Such an attitude gives rise to acts of benevolence and charity which, if generalised, add up to a utilitarian perspective. Respect, by contrast, involves a kind of distancing of oneself from the other person, not the distancing of indifference but a recognition that others have their own choices and decisions to make, their own life to live, and that one should not try to live it for them. This use of the word 'respect' is not its use to indicate a sort of admiration, a looking up to someone in virtue of certain particular qualities which they possess, as when one respects someone for their athletic prowess or their intellectual distinction or their moral integrity. Rather, the kind of respect that we are talking about is that which is due to any person in virtue of their capacity to make their own choices and live their own life.

In considering the idea of 'respect for autonomy', then, we have taken an important step forward in understanding the wrongness of killing, a step which takes us beyond the opposition between 'the sanctity of life' and utilitarian considerations. We can see why it is wrong to sacrifice someone's life for the sake of their own or others' greater good, without being committed to according the same moral treatment to every living thing. At this point, however, I want to introduce a doubt about the use of the word 'autonomy'. At least as some writers have employed it, it carries strongly intellectualist connotations. To respect people's autonomy in this strong sense is to respect their consciously formulated desires and decisions. As Jonathan Glover puts it, 'I override your autonomy only where I take a decision on your behalf which goes against what you actually do want, not where the decision goes against what you would want if you were more knowledgeable or more intelligent.'[7] Quite consistently with this, Glover recognises that taking someone's life does not involve overriding their autonomy if they are not capable of formulating the desire to go on living. This means, in particular, that there can be no objection of this kind to the killing of foetuses or new-born babies.

> The claim that killing is directly wrong because it overrules someone's autonomy does not apply to ... abortion or to the killing of a new-born baby. However much one may regard a new-born baby as a person, it would be absurd to suppose that it has any desire not to die, or even the concepts of being alive or dead on which such a desire depends.[8]

The same would be true of the killing of animals or of severely mentally defective adult humans. (Bear in mind, once more, that in many of these cases there may well be other kinds of reasons for not killing, such as the utilitarian consideration that killing babies will usually create devastating grief for the parents.) It is not enough to say that *if* a young baby could

[7] Glover, *Causing Death and Saving Lives*, p. 77.   [8] Ibid., pp. 138–9.

understand the choice between living and dying, it would want to go on living. It does not in fact understand that choice, therefore it does not have the desire to live, and killing it would not constitute a failure to respect the baby's autonomy. Granted, babies and animals may engage in behaviour which as a matter of fact keeps them alive. The baby will suck the breast or the bottle, the animal will defend itself against attack. They do not, however, perform these actions with the conscious aim of preserving their lives. To formulate that aim requires quite a sophisticated understanding. One must be able to envisage one's own non-existence. This means being aware of oneself 'from outside', so to speak, as one living thing among others in a world which is independent of oneself. It requires a developed understanding of time, beyond the immediate past and the immediate future, so that one can envisage the time before one's birth and the time after one's death. It is quite striking that children take a long time before they can even begin to make sense of the idea of 'what it was like before I was born'.

If 'respect for autonomy' is understood as respect for people's consciously formulated desires, then, it will have similar practical implications to the position which we looked at earlier, that the lives of human beings are valuable insofar as they possess rationality and/or self-consciousness. In both cases the particular objection to killing applies only to mature human beings with developed intellectual capacities. As before, we could simply accept this implication. We could say that utilitarian considerations are usually (but not always) reasons against taking the lives of human beings and of animals which are capable of experiencing pleasure or suffering, and that, in addition, respect for people's autonomy is normally a stronger reason against taking the lives of mature human beings with a developed awareness of life and death. This is a position which some contemporary writers have taken.[9] It would require a revision of conventional moral assumptions, but it is a coherent position and it has a certain plausibility. Nevertheless I think it

[9] I think it could fairly be taken to summarise the positions of Jonathan Glover and Peter Singer. The arguments which I have considered in reaching this point in the discussion owe much to their work.

unsatisfactory, not because it conflicts with conventional beliefs, but because this narrow interpretation of 'respect for autonomy' unduly restricts the proper range of the attitude of 'respect'. Recall the phrases which, I suggested, naturally come to mind in cases like the Raskolnikov example: 'she has her own life to live; it is her life, not his'. Our use of such phrases seems to me to point to the idea that the primary object of respect is individuals and the lives that they lead, rather than autonomy in the narrow sense. I have mentioned in chapter 1 the Kantian origin of ideas of 'respect' and 'autonomy'. In Kant's moral philosophy the relevant core concept is that of 'respect for persons' – but what is a 'person'? Modern philosophers have taken up this term and, as with the term 'autonomy', have given it a rather narrow specialised sense: not all human beings are 'persons' in this narrow sense, and to be a 'person' one must again possess the required level of rationality and self-consciousness. I would suggest that the broader concept which we need is that of 'respect for life', meaning the recognition that everyone has their own life to lead. This is also the point at which we could, with justification, introduce the vocabulary of 'rights', and talk of respect for everyone's right to live their own life. I warned earlier against over-hasty appeals to the concept of rights. There are no self-evident rights, and if we want to ascribe rights to people, the justification for this must derive from more fundamental moral considerations. I now want to suggest that the concept of 'respect' may provide such a justification. The idea of 'respect' involves this recognition that each person has his or her own life, which others may not appropriate or destroy, and it is such a recognition which we might want to formulate by saying that each person has a 'right to life'.

It is this idea of 'respect for life' which I now want to explore, the idea of a moral attitude towards human lives as such, which avoids the pitfalls of our earlier discussion of 'the sanctity of life' but, like it, provides a strong non-utilitarian reason against the taking of life, and is suitably linked to a broader version of the idea of 'respect for autonomy'. Can we develop a coherent account of such a concept?

RESPECT FOR LIFE

I want to begin by looking at an attempt by the American philosopher James Rachels to formulate a concept of this kind.[10] Rachels distinguishes between 'being alive' and 'having a life'. The concept of 'life' is, he says, ambiguous between these two uses. The sense in which we can ascribe 'life' to all living things is what he calls the *biological* sense of 'life'. He contrasts this with the *biographical* sense in which some living things may 'have *a* life'. Not everything which is alive can be said to have a life.

Insects, while they are doubtlessly alive, do not have lives. They are too simple. They do not have the mental wherewithal to have plans, hopes, or aspirations. They cannot regret their pasts, or look forward to their futures.[11]

Rachels also suggests that some human beings, such as someone in a permanent coma, do not have lives. He then argues that the primary moral concern should be to protect lives rather than to preserve as many living things as possible. The rule against killing is, he says, 'a *derived* rule'; the point of not killing living things is to enable them to have lives. Consequently the rule against killing does not apply to living things which are not capable of having lives, including many animals and some humans.

I find Rachels' distinctions useful in helping to clarify a notion of 'respect for life' which does not extend to the inviolability of all living things. Nevertheless his account throws up some problems which we have to negotiate. He appears to imply that it is just a contingent fact that one has to be alive in order to have a life. It is surely not just coincidence that we apply the same word 'life' to the two concepts. Is there not a closer link than that? Do not all living things, in some sense, have a biography? Here is Rachels' example, a potted biography of the chess champion Bobby Fischer:

Bobby Fischer was born in 1943 and grew up in New York City; he learned to play chess at age six and devoted himself single-mindedly to the game thereafter. He became the United States Champion at 14 and dropped out of high school; he won the world championship in

[10] James Rachels, *The End of Life* (Oxford, 1986).   [11] Ibid., p. 26.

1972 and has been a recluse ever since. He has always suspected Russian players of trying to cheat him, and more generally, trusts almost no one. He was involved with an off-beat religious cult in California, but that ended in a public dispute. At last report, he was devoting his days to researching the theory that the world is run by an international conspiracy of Jews.[12]

What makes this a biography? Every living thing grows and develops over a period of time, from birth to death; that is what makes it a living thing. In that sense, every living thing has a history. Compare the following chronological story.

This oak tree began life as an acorn planted 300 years ago. Within ten years it was a strong young sapling, and after 100 years it had become a mighty oak spreading its branches across a diameter of 20 metres. Since then it has suffered various kinds of damage, most recently in the 1987 hurricane, but each time it has recovered, though often with the loss of a bough here and there, so that it now looks gnarled and lop-sided.

Why is this not a biography?

So, on the one hand, there are difficulties in establishing a distinction between 'being alive' and 'having a life'. In some sense, everything that is alive has a life. On the other hand, some of Rachels' ways of attempting to establish the distinction are in danger of making it too sharp. We have seen that he links 'having a life' with various mental capacities. He refers to the having of 'plans, hopes, or aspirations', the ability to be aware of one's past and one's future. He talks of 'a conscious life', and by this he presumably means not just the life of a being which is conscious of its surroundings, but the life of a being which is conscious of itself as having a life, in other words, a *self*-conscious life. Here we seem to be back with the strong requirements of rationality and self-consciousness and the narrow sense of autonomy. The dangers of this line of thought become apparent if we note that the principal concern of Rachels' book is the ethics of euthanasia. I have already mentioned that one kind of case where Rachels says that a person no longer has a life, and where the objection to killing therefore lapses, is the case of someone in an irreversible coma. Here are two other cases. He

¹² Ibid., p. 25.

says of a woman suffering from Alzheimer's disease and killed by her husband that 'when her husband shot her, her life was already over. He was not destroying her life; it had already been destroyed by Alzheimer's disease.'[13] Rachels also discusses the case of a man who killed his thirteen-year-old son who 'had suffered a brain injury at birth that left him virtually mindless, blind, mute, deformed in all four limbs, and with no control over his bladder or bowels'.[14] Rachels says of him that 'the tragic brain injury prevented him from ever having a life' (though, significantly, he also says at one point that 'his whole life was spent in a small crib'). Rachels may be right about all these cases, but they also illustrate the dangers. If 'having a life' is going to depend on the possession of relatively sophisticated mental capacities, and if, moreover, the possession of these is a matter of degree, the way may be open to saying of anyone who has limited intelligence, or who has little in the way of 'plans, hopes, or aspirations', that really he or she has no life and there is no objection to killing him/her.

The dilemma is, then, that if 'having a life' means having a history it seems to collapse back into being alive, and if it depends on possessing specific mental capacities it may become too sharply demarcated from being alive. However, we may perhaps be able to clarify the concept which we need if we try to synthesise these two lines of thought. We want a notion of 'respect for life' which is respect for a life as a whole, as a continuing process of development extended over time, not just the isolated exercise of mental capacities. But what is distinctive of a human life is the ability of the individual human being to shape his or her own life in his or her own individual way, and in part this does involve certain kinds of mental ability. It involves, as Rachels says, a certain degree of self-consciousness, some ability to think about the direction of one's life, to look back on one's past and to have hopes and aims for the future. But we are not talking here about a particularly sophisticated set of intellectual abilities. Some people think deeply about their lives. They may go in for rigorous self-examination. They may

---

[13] Ibid., p. 6.   [14] Ibid., p. 29.

have a carefully formulated life-plan which they consistently follow. Others lurch from crisis to crisis, constantly changing their minds. Others again may drift through life, in a fairly uneventful and unexciting way, choosing a particular kind of work and life-style and family life for no other reason than that it is what is expected of them. But all of them are, in the required sense, shaping their lives, living their own lives in their own way. They all act in the way that they do by reacting to and building on past experiences, whether thoughtfully or uncritically. They are all, in that sense, engaged in a process of development, and it is a process which begins not with the acquisition of particular mental skills but, literally, at birth. With birth, *experience* begins, not just a series of stimuli and responses, but the building up of a picture of the world, and the ability to act in the light of that awareness and thus to exercise control over one's environment. It is the beginning, therefore, of a process of *learning*, and thus of development and growth in that strong sense. The particular activities in which a new-born baby engages are not in themselves impressive or distinctive. Even after a few months the baby's repertoire of sucking, crying, grasping and crawling leaves it well below the level of ability of a new-born lamb or calf. The human baby's activities have their particular significance, however, in the light of the later stages of growth and development. They are the beginning of the process which, with the gradual acquisition of self-awareness and awareness of past and future, becomes the conscious shaping of a human life. In this sense the living of one's own life begins at birth.

I am, in a way, reintroducing here the concept of 'potentiality'. I am saying that respect is owed to the human infant in virtue of its potential. I have previously noted the difficulties raised by the employment of this concept. In talking now about the potentiality of a human infant, I am using a strong notion of 'potentiality' which does not imply that we could make any comparable claims about, say, the potentiality of a human embryo. Nor am I committed to any general implication that, if an *x* could become a *y*, we owe an *x* the same moral treatment as a *y*. We owe respect to the life of the new-born baby in virtue of what it already is, and what it is already doing. What it is doing has to be understood in the light of the later stages of the process, and in that sense we are talking about its potential. But it is already acting, learning, living its own life. In respecting it for its potential, therefore, we are respecting it for what it now is, not merely for what it will be.

The common-sense notion that life begins at birth is, then, well founded, and properly informs our moral ideas of respect for life. It is no accident that we celebrate *birth*days as marking the stages of a life, and that the question 'How old are you?' is answered by counting the time since one's birth. There is indeed an element of convention in this (I am told that the Chinese do it differently), and we *could* date our lives from the moment of conception. Nevertheless it is not pure convention. I have argued that there are good reasons why we typically think of a life as beginning with the emergence from the womb. This is, moreover, the moment of entry into the communal world, the world of shared meanings, in which the baby's movements take on a significance as meaningful activity. It is the beginning of meaningful interaction with other human beings. We have a culturally shared notion of a normal human life-span, as extending from birth through childhood and maturity to old age and death. And so we think of killing as the interruption of this process, preventing someone from living out the normal span of their life. This is reflected in our characteristic reactions of grief and mourning. A human death at any age is a loss, the removal of a unique individual life, but what is tragic is an early death. We mourn especially the death of a child, whose evident potentialities will now never be realised. We mourn especially the death of an adult cut off in his or her prime, whose life is unfinished. Behind these reactions lies the idea of the characteristic and natural shape of a human life. The details will vary from culture to culture, but the basic pattern remains the same. What is tragic about an early death is, therefore, not just that it deprives the person of a certain quantity of worthwhile experiences, but that it interrupts and frustrates their living of their own life. And killing always, to some degree or other, does that.

The concept of a human life is thus a blending of the

biographical and the biological, of activity and of process. It involves the notion of a natural biological process, from birth to death, but also the notion of the activity whereby each individual gives a particular character to this natural process. The biological life is, as it were, an outline which is filled in differently by each person. Moreover, the process is more than just a biological process. Things happen to us. We experience a succession of events which are not of our making, and which affect the course of our lives, but they do so only insofar as we respond to them, giving them a significance as obstacles or opportunities and building them into an intelligible history. The life is the interaction of the active and the passive. I have talked of people 'shaping' their lives. The metaphor is an attempt to avoid an over-intellectualist way of putting it. Leading a life is not necessarily a matter of following out a carefully formulated 'life-plan'. 'Shaping' suggests an analogy with artistic activity: creatively working on a naturally-given material in such a way as to give a sense and a significance to it. The analogy is useful up to a point, but again has its dangers. I want to avoid suggesting that 'living a life' is a matter of meeting certain criteria of *success*, as though only those who measure up to a certain intellectual or artistic standard can qualify. I am almost inclined to say that 'living one's life', in the sense which I am concerned to define, is something which everyone does – but there *are* exceptions. Like Rachels, I think that there are some human beings, such as those suffering from massive brain damage, who are incapable of even that minimal level of mental activity which counts as the leading of a life, and I shall say a little more about such cases in a moment. Beyond that minimal threshold, however, 'living one's life' is something which every human being does.

I conclude that we can indeed formulate an adequate notion of 'respect for life' which is distinct from that of 'the sanctity of life' and does not lapse into the idea of a prohibition on the destruction of any living thing. 'Respect for life' means respect for people's right to live their own lives. 'Living one's own life' means shaping one's life through one's activities, from birth, over time, accumulating experiences and learning from them, making decisions for oneself in the light of these experiences and of one's sense of one's past, and making an intelligible pattern out of them. As applied to the developed human being, the practical implications of 'respect for life' will be largely similar to the implications of 'respect for autonomy'. Emphasising that 'this is *my* life' means recognising that it is also primarily for me to decide what risks to take with my life, and whether and when to end my life. Just as 'respect for autonomy' was taken to imply that when someone wants to terminate his or her own life, suicide or euthanasia may become acceptable, so 'respect for life' will have the same implication. (A play dealing with these issues was appropriately titled *Whose Life Is It Anyway?*)[15] Of course this does not mean that the person's own wishes are the only consideration. Someone's desire to end his or her own life may well affect other people, and this may well generate powerful reasons for not acting on that desire. It is not *just* one's own life that is at stake. What we can say, however, is that respect for life does not rule out the taking of life if someone genuinely wishes to end their own life.

'Respect for life' and 'respect for autonomy' may, then, come to much the same thing in some contexts. Nevertheless I want to maintain that the concept of 'respect for life' provides the more satisfactory account of the wrongness of killing. In practical terms we have seen that it does justice to our sense of the wrongness of killing infants: they may not be able to formulate the desire to go on living, but they have begun to live their own lives. More fundamentally, if the wrongness of killing is derived from respect for autonomy, this makes it sound as though the desire to live is just one desire among others. The suggestion seems to be that, other things being equal, respect for autonomy requires us not to frustrate people's desires, and that therefore if people desire to go on living we should not frustrate that particular desire. Killing someone would, to that extent, be on a par with frustrating their desire for a cigarette or a cream bun, and the seriousness of the violation of autonomy would depend simply on the strength of the desire. Deriving respect for

---

[15] Brian Clark, *Whose Life Is It Anyway?* (Ashover, 1978).

life from respect for autonomy in this way seems to me to get
things precisely the wrong way round. If we take individual
desires in isolation, it becomes quite unclear why they are a
proper object of respect. Why should I respect someone's desire
for a cream bun? If we are to respect people's desires, it must be
because of the nature of the desires. Particular desires get their
importance from their place within the life as a whole. A desire
for a cream bun is, as it stands, a trivial desire. A desire to pursue
a certain career, or to practise a certain religion, is likely to be
much more central to a person's life, and the respect which it
calls for is correspondingly greater. This suggests that we respect
particular desires not simply because they are desires, but
because of their importance for the person who has them, and
that the primary object of respect is the life itself. Of course a
desire to go on living would be as fundamental a desire as any,
but even if a person does not formulate this as a conscious and
explicit desire, his or her life is still owed respect. I should add
that to focus on isolated individual desires is in any case an
unsatisfactory narrowing of the concept of 'autonomy'. 'Autonomy' itself is better understood as the ability to control one's
own life, and in that case 'respect for autonomy' comes closer to
the idea of 'respect for life' as I have presented it.

MARGINAL CASES

A recurrent problem with the various moral concepts which we
have been considering in this chapter is the problem of
boundaries. Where do we draw the line around those beings
whose lives it is wrong to destroy? We saw that 'the sanctity of
life', if taken literally, implies too wide a boundary to be
plausible, embracing all living things. If the concept is narrowed
to 'the sanctity of human life', this is, as it stands, arbitrarily
narrow, since it offers no reason other than mere assertion for
distinguishing between one species and others. 'Respect for
autonomy', in the form in which we initially encountered it,
draws the boundaries even more narrowly. It constitutes a
reason against killing only those beings who are sufficiently self-
conscious to understand what it would be for them to die or to

continue living, and who are therefore able to formulate the relevant desires. Utilitarian considerations apply in principle to any being which is capable of experiencing pleasure or suffering, but whether they provide a reason for not killing such a being will depend on the particular case and the likely prospects of pleasure or suffering. What then are the boundaries implied by the concept of 'respect for life' as I have interpreted it? What are we to say of the various marginal cases which have emerged as problematic – new-born babies, foetuses, severely defective human beings, those who no longer want to go on living, non-human animals and so on?

The first thing to be said is that these are indeed marginal cases. The paradigm case where respect for life is appropriate is as a response to beings who are capable of shaping their own lives in the light of their past experience and their awareness of future possibilities. I have said that almost all human beings fall into this category. Nevertheless the description does not establish firm boundaries. There is no sharp line between beings which do and beings which do not possess such a capability. As we move away from the paradigm case, the task becomes one of assessing the extent to which the marginal cases match the paradigm, looking for similarities and differences. Perhaps the only firm conclusion we can reach may be that a particular case really is borderline, and then we have to find the moral response appropriate to that conclusion. So, for instance, the one moral view about the problem of abortion which seems to me to be undeniably mistaken is the one which says that there is no problem. This view may come from those who say that a foetus at any stage of its development is just obviously a human life eliciting precisely the same moral response as any other human being. It may equally come from those who say that at no stage of its development does the foetus elicit anything like the same moral response as a human life, and that therefore there are no moral grounds for any hesitation at all about destroying it. To both versions I want to say that abortion *is* a borderline case.

I have argued previously that the proper focus of respect for life is a life as a whole. The truism that life begins at birth does mark a morally significant boundary. Respect is due as much to

the life of the new-born baby as to that of the adult human
being. I referred here to a strong notion of potentiality: we
respond to the baby in the light of our knowledge of what it will
become, but that knowledge also entitles us to say that the baby
has already started living its own life, acting in the world and
learning from experience in ways which will increasingly enable
it consciously to direct its life. The foetus is different, and
abortion is different from infanticide. That, however, is not the
end of the matter. It cannot be irrelevant that, as the foetus
grows, it comes to look more and more like the new-born baby,
and that our knowledge of this makes it increasingly easier for us
to respond to it accordingly. Of course, it is not just a matter of
how it looks. An extremely life-like plastic doll, which looked
just like a baby, would not elicit the same response from us as a
baby once we realised that it was just a doll. What is relevant in
the case of the developed foetus is not just that it looks
increasingly like a baby but that it is on the way to becoming
one. This is what I have called the weaker notion of potentiality,
and I have acknowledged that, from the fact that x will become
y, it does not follow that x should be treated in the same way as
y. Nevertheless, when the knowledge that a developed foetus is
on the way to becoming a baby is combined with the fact that
it looks increasingly like one, this is bound to affect our response
to it. It may be said that this is just an emotional reaction and
should not be allowed to determine our moral beliefs. However,
as I argued in the previous chapter, our moral beliefs, though
not identical with, are in the end grounded in the emotional
responses which are natural to us as human beings. An
emotional response may be inappropriate or misguided in a
particular case, if for instance it involves false beliefs about the
object of the response. If our reaction to the developed foetus
stems from our attributing to it thoughts such as 'I'm really
looking forward to being born and getting on with my life', then
of course our response is misguided. But insofar as the foetus
really does to some extent share some of the features of a living
human being, and insofar as this leads us to respond to it in
something like the way in which we respond to a living human
being, this must have a moral significance.

To an extent, then, I agree with those who see the abortion issue as a matter of dates and time-limits. A 28-week foetus *is* more like a living human being than is a 14-week foetus, and the latter *is* more like a living human being than is a 14-day embryo. So a late abortion is harder to justify than an early abortion, and an early abortion is harder to justify than is experimentation involving the destruction of embryos up to 14 days. One complicating factor must also be mentioned. I have defended the moral relevance of the fact that life begins at birth, with the implication that abortion is morally different from infanticide. But of course a very late abortion is also, in effect, an early birth, if the aborted foetus is capable of surviving. Thus birth itself is not a straightforward cut-off point, and this is why a concern with 'viability' properly enters into the debate. And since the point at which a foetus becomes viable (capable of surviving outside the womb) will vary from case to case and will depend on the current state of medical technology, we are back with the moral indeterminacy of blurred boundaries.[16]

The debate about abortion is one moral controversy having to do with marginal cases. The issue of euthanasia is another. I have said that 'respect for life' as I have interpreted it has the same practical implications as 'respect for autonomy' in many cases. In particular, it implies a morally relevant distinction between voluntary and involuntary euthanasia. The right to live one's own life carries with it a right to end one's own life. Voluntary euthanasia may therefore be justified, for instance in cases where people are terminally ill, in great pain and wish to end the agony. 'Respect for life' will mean respecting their wishes. That does not settle the argument as to whether voluntary euthanasia should be made legally permissible. Some would argue that the dangers are too great. If voluntary euthanasia becomes legal, might people be pressured into asking for it against their own better judgement? Are there reliable ways of ensuring that people's request for euthanasia is

---

[16] It is *because of* this moral indeterminacy that the idea of 'a woman's right to choose' is also important. If abortion were, uncontroversially, murder, 'women's rights' arguments would be out of place; and if there were no moral objection whatever to abortion, 'women's rights' arguments would be unnecessary.

genuine and is a considered decision? These are difficult
empirical questions, but my claim here is simply that 'respect
for life' does not furnish a moral objection to voluntary
euthanasia. Conversely, it does of course furnish a very strong
objection indeed to euthanasia which is involuntary, that is,
against the person's own expressed wishes.

The most difficult cases to consider are those which raise the
possibility of *non-voluntary* euthanasia. This would be euthanasia
to end the life of someone who was not capable either of
requesting it or of refusing it. Examples where the question
might arise would be severely deformed babies, or people in an
irreversible coma. These are the sorts of case of which Rachels
says that though the person may be alive, he or she may not
have a life. I mentioned in the last section the dangers of making
such a distinction, but I agreed that it can sometimes be made.
The clearest case would be that of someone in an irreversible
coma, where there would be no possibility of further activity at
all and therefore no possibility of the person continuing to live
his or her own life. 'Respect for life' would not be an objection
to killing in such a case. Something similar might be said of
babies born with severe brain damage such as microcephaly or
anencephaly, capable of only the most rudimentary conscious-
ness and of performing actions only in the most limited sense.
Perhaps the crucial test is, as Rachels suggests at one point, to
ask whether the possibility of living or dying can matter to the
person concerned.[17] This is not to ask, from the perspective of
'respect for autonomy', whether the person wants to go on
living, but to ask whether the possibility of living or dying
matters from the point of view of the person's life as a whole. I
think we should then have to say of the severely brain-damaged
infant that it does not matter to him or her, since nothing
matters or ever will matter to such a human being, and
therefore that killing is not a wrong done to him or her. More
problematic are cases such as Rachels' example of a woman in

[17] Rachels puts it as follows: 'We may ask of Repouille's son whether his "life" did *him*
any good. Did it have any value from *his* point of view? And immediately we
encounter the crucial problem that he did not *have* a point of view, in any but the
most primitive sense' (*The End of Life*, p. 30).

the advanced stages of Alzheimer's disease.[18] She is certainly capable of performing some identifiable and meaningful actions. These actions, however, never add up to anything meaningful overall, since what she lacks is any sense of past or future and therefore any continuity in her activity. Whether she can be said to be leading a life is debatable. I shall not try to answer the question, but merely suggest that this is where the indeterminate border area is located.

Abortion and euthanasia raise questions about marginal cases among human beings. What about non-human animals? I do not want to make dogmatic assertions about the abilities of animals, a subject which arouses strong passions and tends to provoke indignant claims on behalf of people's favourite cat or dog, but I doubt whether most animal species could be described as capable of 'shaping their lives' in any very strong sense. Most animal behaviour is a response to an immediate situation, whereas 'living one's own life' in the sense which I have discussed involves having some awareness of one's own past and one's own future and hence having a sense of one's life as a whole. I have warned against too intellectualist an interpretation of such capacities, which would confine them to the far-sighted and the single-minded. I have also stressed that respect for someone's life is not dependent on their *success* in exercising such capacities. In referring to people's capacity to give a shape and a sense to their lives, I am not implying that some people's lives are too meaningless to be worthy of respect. Of course people do sometimes find their lives meaningless, lacking any shape or pattern, but that is still a statement about how they see their lives. The very fact that they experience this as a problem is itself significant. At the other extreme there are people who do not even need to raise the question whether their lives are meaningful, since the course of their lives is already mapped out for them by their society and their cultural tradition. The fact that their lives have a clear pattern is no achievement on their part; they proceed along the stages of life's way without even having to ask which direction to take. But any of these things

---

[18] Ibid., p. 2.

can be said only of beings whose lives can have a sense for them, and I suspect that no, or almost no, non-human animal species fall into that category.

Even if 'respect for life' in the full sense does not extend to non-human animals, however, it does not follow that our attitude to the lives of animals should be one of moral indifference. Two further points in particular should be noted. First, I suspect that my remarks about abortion, the development of the foetus and its progressive approximation to the paradigm case, apply also to animals. The more that animals are, objectively, like us, the more we identify with them and extend the idea of 'respect for life' to include them. We see it as marginally more objectionable to kill a fly than a germ, and considerably more objectionable to kill a dog or a horse. Again the response may be that this is just a psychological fact about our feelings, and again my reply is that our moral beliefs must ultimately be grounded in such feelings.[19] The second additional point to make is that even if 'respect for life' in the full sense is not applicable to non-human animals, there may be other reasons for not destroying animal lives. I mentioned in the previous chapter the attitude of 'reverence' as a response to the natural world. This seems to me to be significantly different from the attitude of 'respect'. In particular, whereas 'respect' is primarily an attitude to individuals and a recognition of the uniqueness of individual lives, 'reverence' is, I suspect, more characteristically an attitude towards the natural world as a whole. It may underpin our recognition of the moral importance of preserving natural environments and habitats, protecting threatened species and so on, but within that context we may be more inclined to see individual animal lives as replaceable. Utilitarian considerations also may be applicable to our

---

[19] Peter Singer, the philosopher who has most effectively emphasised our moral obligations to animals, criticises the view that because we have closer relationships with other humans than with animals, our moral obligations are correspondingly stronger. 'This argument,' he says, 'ties morality too closely to our affections ... The question is whether our moral obligations to a being should be made to depend on our feelings in this manner' (*Practical Ethics*, p. 66). Agreed, our moral beliefs should be more than just direct expressions of our feelings, but ultimately that is what they do depend on.

treatment of animals, even when 'respect for life' is not. Other things being equal, it is wrong to inflict suffering on animals, and this itself is enough to rule out many of the ways in which animals are currently killed.

My discussion of marginal cases may seem disappointingly inconclusive. Confronted with indeterminate boundaries, I have done very little to make them any more determinate. That however has not been my purpose. I have been concerned to locate the areas of indeterminacy, not to eliminate them. I want to emphasise that the existence of borderline cases does not give any support to moral subjectivism. The fact is that certain cases just are, objectively, borderline, and from the fact that in such cases we cannot give a clear answer to the question 'What ought we to do?' it does not follow that we can never do so. On the contrary, it is precisely because there are paradigm cases where an action would be a violation of respect for life that we can say of other cases, such as the killing of an animal or a severely brain-damaged human infant, that to some extent they do and to some extent they do not approximate to the paradigm case. This does not make moral reasoning as a whole subjective, any more than the existence of the duck-billed platypus makes it a subjective matter what we count as a mammal. The trouble is that in the practical sphere, as contrasted with the theoretical, there is pressure to make the indeterminate cases more determinate. In theoretical matters we can rest content with the answer 'Well, it is and it isn't (a mammal, or whatever).' In practical matters, however, when we ask the question 'Is it wrong?' the answer cannot be left as 'It is and it isn't', since we have to make a decision one way or the other. The parents of a severely brain-damaged baby have to decide whether or not the child should live. A pregnant woman has to decide whether or not to have an abortion. There is normally no 'third way' which is the practical equivalent of recognising that the case is borderline. The problem is even more acute when it comes to deciding what the law should be. In law there have to be hard and fast lines, and if they cannot be discovered they have to be created. We have to decide whether abortion or euthanasia should or should not be illegal in this or that kind of case. I shall

return in a later chapter to the problem of how we resolve moral
dilemmas. Here my concern has been to identify which cases are
borderline when it comes to respect for life.

CONCLUSION

I have tried to work out a satisfactory interpretation of the
principle of respect for life. I have argued that this is the most
important reason why it is normally wrong to kill. I have tried
to show how the principle is grounded in our natural responses
to other human lives. Note that this is a case where I want to use
the same term, 'respect', to refer both to the moral principle
and to the basic human response in which it is grounded. The
principle here is one which requires us to apply the natural
response objectively and rationally. Having clarified what
'respect for life' is as a component in our range of natural
human responses, we are in a position to say that these are the
cases in which it is appropriate, and these are the practical
implications which it has.

This still leaves open the question of how much weight it
carries. For all that I have said in this chapter, it remains
possible that killing is wrong for the reasons I have identified,
but that this is of limited importance. The wrongness of taking
life might even be of a minor kind, always relevant but often
outweighed by other considerations. To me this seems intuitively implausible. I am inclined to say that it is a moral
consideration of very great weight indeed, playing a quite
fundamental role in our moral thinking. I cannot prove this. I
do not even know what argument I could offer to someone who
doubted it. Perhaps I can only point to the fact that most people
just *do* regard it in that way. The philosophical argument of this
chapter could, however, be seen as giving support to that
assumption in the following way. The assumption that killing is
a very great wrong tends to go with the idea that killing is wrong
in itself – that its wrongness is not derivative from, and
dependent on, other considerations. Now that idea has, as we
have seen, been questioned philosophically, and it might have
turned out to be vulnerable to such questioning. I might, in this

chapter, have agreed with the philosophical arguments for the view that the wrongness of killing is derivative from utilitarian considerations, or from 'respect for autonomy'. I have not done so. I have defended the idea that killing is independently wrong, and I have argued that this idea can be coherently formulated and defended against objections. It does not follow logically that the idea has the degree of moral importance which it is commonly thought to have. The two conclusions are separable from one another. Nevertheless my philosophical discussion, if successful, could be seen as establishing that our fundamental intuitions about the wrongness of killing are 'in good order' as it were (whatever our disagreements about the application of them). They are not the product of confusion or muddled thinking. They are authentically grounded in the 'primitive responses' which, I suggested in the previous chapter, are the underpinning of all our moral understanding. To that extent we may feel confirmed in the importance which we attach to them.

I want to suggest one other way in which we might attempt to illuminate the importance of 'respect for life' as a moral idea, and that is by looking at its relation to our other, non-moral attitudes to death. Consider again the phenomenon of grief as a reaction to someone's death, independent of any moral response. The death may occur from natural causes or by accident and may raise no questions about anyone's moral responsibility for it; I am for the moment concerned simply with our response to it as a death. I think it is fair to say that grief at a death has a quite unique and special place among our emotions. It may be grief at the loss of a loved one, or at the death of a colleague or an acquaintance, or of a person well known in public life, or it may be a response to a news report of a particularly tragic death of someone quite unknown to us – perhaps a child killed in a road accident. Each of these cases has its own special features, but common to them all is the response to that unique kind of loss which is the loss of an irreplaceable life. It is not the same as our sense of the loss of the happiness which the person could have experienced, or of the benefits which he or she could have conferred on others; again those features may well be present, but they are different. Even in those cases where the life had little more to offer, and where we might see it as a merciful release, we still grieve at the death itself. The loss of the life leaves an emptiness which cannot be equated with any other kind of loss. Think too of the rituals of mourning which exist in every human society, and of the evident need which we have for these. Now none of this proves that we are right to attach a correspondingly great importance to the moral wrongness of killing. What I am offering here cannot be called an argument. What it suggests, however, is that the special place of such grief among our emotions, and the special importance we attach to the wrongness of killing, are all of a piece. Our moral understanding of killing and our non-moral understanding of death make up a coherent whole, and thereby reinforce one another.

I should add that although for much of this chapter I have been contrasting the moral attitude of 'respect for life' with a utilitarian perspective, in practice the two will in the vast majority of cases coincide. There will normally, as I have said, be a very strong utilitarian case against the taking of a life. In most cases the killing of a person will mean the loss of the happiness which that person could have experienced, and will mean terrible suffering for others, and this will outweigh any benefits which someone else might think to derive from the killing. Normally utilitarian considerations point the same way as the attitude of 'respect for life'. Normally – but not always. There are problem cases, and killing in war may be one such case, where the two kinds of consideration sometimes pull in different directions. We therefore have to consider what to say of such conflicts. Even if the wrongness of killing carries the weight which I have ascribed to it, it does not follow that killing is *always* wrong. Although the taking of human life cannot be justified *simply* on utilitarian grounds, it remains arguable that sufficiently weighty considerations of harm and benefit might sometimes override the principle of respect for life. I shall consider these problems in the next chapter.

CHAPTER 3

Killing and letting die

ABSOLUTISM AND CONSEQUENTIALISM

The simplest and probably the commonest way of trying to justify waging war is in terms of its consequences. Particular wars are held to be justified by what they achieve. Their achievements are almost always bought at enormous cost, but sometimes, it may be said, the alternative to war is even more dire. The following judgement by the historian A. J. P. Taylor is an example of that consequentialist way of thinking.

> The Second World War was fought to liberate peoples from Nazi, and to a lesser extent Japanese, tyranny. In this it succeeded, at however high a price. No one can contemplate the present state of things without acknowledging that people everywhere are happier, freer and more prosperous than they would have been if Nazi Germany and Japan had won ... It was a war justified in its aims and successful in accomplishing them. Despite all the killing and destruction that accompanied it, the Second World War was a good war.[1]

If we were to take the view that the only relevant considerations, in assessing war or anything else, are consequentialist ones, and if we were to equate good and bad consequences with happiness and suffering, our position would be a utilitarian one. I have argued in the previous chapters that utilitarianism is an oversimple moral theory, and in particular it fails to recognise that the wrongness of killing carries

---

[1] A. J. P. Taylor, *The Second World War* (Harmondsworth, 1976), p. 234.

an independent moral weight. Nevertheless it is clear that the consideration of consequences must at least play an important part in our moral thinking, and we therefore have to ask what the relationship is between these two kinds of moral consideration.

One answer which has traditionally been given takes the following form: granted that consequences must play a substantial role in our moral thinking, there are nevertheless also certain *absolute* moral principles which we ought to accept, principles which specify that certain kinds of actions are always right or wrong, whatever the consequences. The term 'absolutism' is used to refer to the view that there are absolute moral principles. What the content of these absolute principles might be is a further question, and different versions of absolutism would give different answers. 'The taking of human life is always wrong' would be one candidate for an absolute principle, and the acceptance of it would commit one to absolute pacifism. It is not however the only candidate. In moral debates about war and other life-or-death dilemmas, the traditional absolutist position has taken the form of a different principle: 'It is always wrong to kill innocent human beings.' The precise interpretation of 'innocent' is very much a matter for discussion, and I shall discuss it in chapter 5. Traditionally it has been taken to allow the possibility that killing in war is permissible, since enemy combatants are not in the relevant sense innocent. It might also allow the killing of individuals in self-defence, and the killing of criminals as a punishment. This version of absolutism has been prominent within the Christian tradition, and especially in the moral doctrine of the Roman Catholic Church. Philosophical discussion of absolutism has also tended to focus on this particular example of a possible absolute principle. The general question, however, is whether *any* absolute moral principles can be maintained.

We must be clear just how strong a claim is being made by an absolute principle. We should distinguish it from claims which might be made on consequentialist grounds that specific kinds of actions ought never to be performed, because performing them is always likely to have worse consequences on balance

than refraining from performing them. Consider for example
the difference between absolutist pacifism and consequentialist
pacifism. One could be a pacifist on consequentialist grounds,
taking the view that the disastrous consequences of war are
always likely to outweigh anything positive which might be
achieved. Such a position however must always be provisional,
always open to revision in the light of new cases or new evidence
about consequences. Someone who had hitherto been a consequentialist pacifist might, for example, have said in 1939:
'Confronted with the historical record, I have until now held
the view that wars never achieve sufficient good to justify the
enormous moral price that has to be paid, but we now face, in
Nazism, a quite unprecedentedly evil regime, and even the
terrors of war are likely to be outweighed by the horrors of
allowing this regime to continue.' That person's provisional
commitment to pacifism would then have to be revised in the
light of the new circumstances. I am not saying that the
consequentialist pacifist would have to abandon his or her
pacifism in this particular case. The judgement might go the
other way. The point is, however, that consequentialist pacifism, and any general moral principle based on beliefs about
likely consequences, must always be open to possible revision of
this kind.

An absolutist position, then, is stronger than a consequentialist position which says that certain kinds of actions are
always likely to be ruled out by their bad consequences.
Absolutism is also stronger than the position which I reached at
the end of the previous chapter. I suggested there that the
wrongness of killing is not just a matter of its bad consequences;
the idea of 'respect for life' carries an independent moral
weight, and it seems plausible to say that that weight is very
great indeed. This however falls short of an absolutist formulation. It leaves open the possibility that though killing is in
itself wrong, its wrongness could in extreme cases be overridden
by sufficiently weighty consequences. In contrast, someone who
is an absolutist about killing would say that taking a life is *always*
wrong, *whatever the consequences*, and its wrongness can *never* be
overridden by other considerations.

We therefore have three general positions:

(a) the consequentialist position that the rightness or wrong-
    ness of actions is solely a matter of the overall goodness
    or badness of their consequences. (Utilitarianism is one
    version of consequentialism, adding that good and bad
    consequences are to be identified with happiness and
    suffering.)
(b) The view that certain kinds of action are *intrinsically* right
    or wrong, that is, right or wrong because of the nature of
    the action itself and not just because of its consequences.
(c) The view that certain kinds of action are not just
    intrinsically wrong but *absolutely* wrong, always wrong
    whatever the consequences.

It may seem that position (b) is an unstable one. In distinguishing it from absolutism, we allow the possibility that the
independent wrongness of actions can sometimes be overridden
by consequences. Does this not mean that in any particular case
we shall always have to take account of the consequences of the
action, and does this not then collapse into consequentialism? I
hope to show that this intermediate position, precarious though
it appears, is nevertheless defensible. It is the position which I
reached at the end of the previous chapter, and the conclusion
of this chapter will be to endorse it. My arguments towards that
conclusion will, however, proceed by looking at the debate
between the more extreme positions of consequentialism and
absolutism. I shall consider how consequentialists would criticise the absolutist position, and then discuss some of the
traditional defences of absolutism against such criticisms.

A general consequentialist argument against absolutism is
likely to take the following form. In assessing actions, what we
are concerned with is surely what difference they make in the
world. What is wrong with killing, for instance, is surely the fact
that people end up dead. In that case, however, we have to
recognise that in some situations killing a person may be the
only way of preventing even more deaths. Suppose, for instance,
that someone is carrying a highly contagious and fatal disease
for which there is no treatment or cure, and that killing him

immediately is the only way to prevent thousands of other people from contracting the disease and dying. If our concern is to prevent deaths, then we ought surely to kill the one person on the grounds that one death (especially if it is the killing of someone who will in any case die soon) is a lesser evil than thousands of deaths. Once we have made that concession, however, and allowed that killing may be necessary in order to prevent even more deaths, it would seem that to be consistent we should also allow for the possibility that killing might be necessary in order to prevent other kinds of bad consequences. Suppose that, to modify our previous example, the disease in question is not fatal, but that those who contract it will go blind, be permanently crippled and suffer excruciating pain for the rest of their lives. Might it not then be legitimate to kill the one person in order to prevent such appalling suffering for thousands of others? I have put the argument in terms of killing (and will continue with that case), but a similar consequentialist criticism could be made of any candidate for an absolute principle. If the significance of our actions is that they make a difference in the world, that they bring about certain effects, then it is surely by their effects that we should judge them.

ACTS AND OMISSIONS

That, then, is a general argument against absolutism. Are there any ways to rebut it? One way would be to appeal to what has come to be called, in recent philosophical writing, the 'acts and omissions doctrine'. This is the view that there is a morally important difference between *doing* something and *allowing* something to happen. The doctrine states that even though a certain kind of action is wrong, allowing an identical set of consequences to occur is not necessarily wrong. Killing, for example, and allowing someone to die are not morally equivalent, although each has the consequence that the person dies. Letting someone die is not necessarily as bad as killing someone. If we were to make use of the distinction between acts and omissions in this way, we could consistently maintain that killing people is always wrong. To the objection that a refusal to kill may result in even more deaths, we could reply that the refusal to kill would then be a case of letting people die, and this is not absolutely prohibited, whereas killing is.

Note that the claim is not merely that there is a difference between acts and omissions – this would be a trivial claim – but that the difference is morally important. On the other hand, it is not the implausible claim that there is nothing wrong with failing to prevent a death. Clearly there are occasions when we ought to act to prevent someone from dying, and a failure to do so would be wrong. The question is whether the wrongness of letting someone die is on a par with the wrongness of killing.

There does seem to be a certain plausibility in making a moral distinction here. Compare two examples. I mentioned in the previous chapter the example of Raskolnikov in Dostoevsky's *Crime and Punishment*, who kills an old woman to take her money. Let us now imagine a partly parallel example. Vokinloksar is also a young law student. He is struggling to complete his studies on a meagre grant, but is worried that he will have to give up his course in order to get a job and support his mother and sister. Suddenly he receives a completely unexpected legacy of £100,000 from a distant relative. However, his good luck brings publicity, and a few days later he receives a letter from an old woman saying that £100,000 is exactly the sum she needs to pay for heart surgery, without which she will die. Will he pay for her? He refuses, and she dies.

Let us suppose that all the relevant circumstances and consequences in the two cases are the same, except that Raskolnikov kills an old woman and Vokinloksar lets an old woman die. Is the failure to save a life, in the one case, morally on a par with the act of killing in the other? It may be objected that the consequences never can be the same. An act of murder will always have further undesirable consequences. It will contribute to a general atmosphere of insecurity. It will either produce agonising feelings of guilt in the murderer, or will so corrupt his character that he will be more inclined to commit other murders in the future. The same consequences will not follow from the failure to save a life. Now this may be true (though I suspect that the differences are sometimes exaggerated, and may also be question-begging – perhaps someone who fails to save a life *ought* to be wracked with guilt). There may well be good consequentialist reasons for regarding murder as normally worse than a failure to save a life. However, we still want to know whether there is a moral difference between killing and letting die *as such*. So, for the sake of the argument, and although it may put a severe strain on our imaginations, let us suppose that the consequences in the two cases really are the same. Vokinloksar's refusal to give the money to the old woman, which would have saved her life, is not literally an act of murder, but is it morally equivalent to murder? Is it just as wrong as Raskolnikov's act? This seems highly implausible. Even if you think he should have given the old woman the money (and you may well not even think that), his refusal to do so can hardly be equated with Raskolnikov's act of murder. Why not? A plausible difference would seem to be that whilst Raskolnikov has actively killed someone, Vokinloksar has not.

We can also, at least initially, provide some backing for this distinction. I have allowed that consequences are morally relevant, and what the argument above (p. 76) does establish is that consequences can never be simply discounted. However, I have also indicated in the previous chapters that they are not the only thing which is morally relevant. In particular, the relations in which we stand to one another have their own independent significance; indeed, I have argued that it is impossible to understand why we should have any concern for one another at all unless we recognise the moral relevance of our particular relations to one another. I have also argued that these moral relations are diverse. Other people may be the potential beneficiaries or victims of our actions, and then the focus is on the consequences of our actions for others, but this is not the only morally significant relation in which we stand to others. I have suggested that the attitude of respect grounds a different kind of moral relation. It involves seeing others as agents in their own right rather than as the recipients of our own actions. I distinguished in chapter 1 between moral obligations which derive from the fundamental attitude of respect and those which derive from the distinct fundamental attitude of sympathy. 'Respect' is linked with a suitably broad notion of 'autonomy'; it involves standing back from the lives of others, letting them live their own lives but not necessarily requiring us to act on their behalf. Obligations deriving from 'sympathy' may require us to intervene in the lives of others, to help or protect them. Respect, I have argued, underlies our recognition of the wrongness of killing, but it is at least possible that the case of saving lives is different. 'Killing' and 'not saving someone's life' involve different relations between one person and another, and it is therefore conceivable that they have a different moral significance.

Reflection on further examples, however, suggests that a simple contrast between acts and omissions is unsatisfactory. Consider two other examples. Thomas Hardy's short story 'A Tragedy of Two Ambitions' concerns two brothers, Joshua and Cornelius Halborough, sons of a village millwright, ambitious to rise in the world through a career in the church and anxious not to be frustrated by the social embarrassments created for them by their father, a habitual drunkard. They pack him off to Canada, have taken the first successful steps along their ecclesiastical careers, and are hopeful of seeing their younger sister Rosa betrothed to Mr Felmer, the local landowner and a widower. They then come upon their father, returned from Canada, again the worse for drink, and walking along the riverbank towards Felmer's house intent on introducing himself, an action which will blight all their hopes. After an altercation with the brothers he continues on his way to the house. They hear a splash.

'He has fallen in!' said Cornelius, starting forward to run for the place at which his father had vanished. Joshua, awaking from the stupefied reverie into which he had sunk, rushed to the other's side before he had taken ten steps. 'Stop, stop, what are you thinking of?' he whispered hoarsely, grasping Cornelius's arm. 'Pulling him out!' 'Yes, yes – so am I. But – wait a moment –' 'But, Joshua!' 'Her life and happiness, you know – Cornelius – and your reputation and mine – and our chance of rising together, all three –' He clutched his brother's arm to the bone; and as they stood breathless the splashing and floundering in the weir continued; over it they saw the hopeful lights from the manor-house conservatory winking through the trees as their bare branches waved to and fro. In their pause there had been time to save him twice over.[2]

By the time they reach the spot there is no trace of their father, and nothing they can do.

My second example is not fictional, and so has the disadvantage that the facts are contested. It returns us to the subject of war. In 1944 the Russian army was pushing the Germans back through Poland. It halted on the outskirts of Warsaw. The Polish government in exile, in London, anxious that the Poles should liberate their capital city for themselves before the Russians arrived, called on the people of Warsaw to rise against the Germans. The uprising was crushed. The Russians made no attempt to come to its aid. It was convenient for them that the non-communist Polish Resistance should be destroyed by the Germans, so that it would present no challenge to Russian authority in liberated Poland.

It is a matter for dispute whether the Russians could have given effective aid to the uprising. Perhaps they could not have advanced further without over-extending their supply lines. For the sake of the example, however, let us suppose that they deliberately allowed the uprising to be crushed.

The pertinent feature of the two examples is, I hope, obvious. The point is not just that the brothers should have saved their father, or that the Russians should have tried to prevent the Warsaw uprising from being crushed. As I have mentioned, advocates of the acts and omissions distinction can perfectly well accept that we have *some* obligation to save lives and to render other kinds of aid. What the examples suggest is that omissions can sometimes be morally equivalent to acts. Morally speaking, the brothers killed their father. The Warsaw example is less clear-cut, but some would certainly say that the Russians betrayed the uprising and, in effect, destroyed the Polish Resistance. What inclines us to say this is the element of *intention*. In my earlier example, Vokinloksar fails to save the life of the old woman but he does not intend her to die. Here, by contrast,

---

[2] Thomas Hardy, *The Distracted Preacher and Other Tales* (Harmondsworth, 1979), p. 185.

the brothers want their father dead, and though they are reluctant to admit it even to themselves, that is their intention in delaying; the Russians want the Resistance wiped out, and that is their intention in delaying. It is no excuse to say, in either case, that they did nothing. Their omission, their failure to act, was the means which they deliberately adopted in order to secure the deaths which they wanted.

This may seem to suggest that the morally important distinction is not between acts and omissions, but between intended and unintended consequences. The distinctions will often coincide, for if I intend to bring about a certain consequence, I am more likely to have to do it by means of an act rather than an omission. If I intend to bring about someone's death, I would normally have to do it by killing them. The opportunity to do it by letting them die will not often occur. However, it will sometimes do so, as the examples show. The morally relevant factor is then the intention to bring about the death, rather than whether this is done by actively killing or by letting someone die.

The acts-and-omissions distinction was introduced as a way of supporting absolutism. It seemed initially plausible that certain kinds of actions might be absolutely ruled out, though not the corresponding omissions. The possibility which we should now consider is that some kind of absolutism could be sustained by saying that what is always and absolutely wrong is the *intentional* bringing about of certain states of affairs. A possible absolute principle would be that it is always wrong to intend the deaths of other human beings. This need not commit one to the principle that it is always wrong to fail to prevent deaths which one does not intend. Even if intentionally bringing about someone's death is sometimes the only way of preventing even worse consequences (such as even more deaths), the absolutist can still maintain that it is wrong, since the consequences one then failed to prevent would be unintended consequences.

THE DOCTRINE OF DOUBLE EFFECT

The distinction between intended and unintended consequences has historically taken the form of a principle known as 'double effect'. The phrase refers to the fact that actions may sometimes have two sets of consequences, one set being the intended consequences for whose sake the action is performed, and the other set being unintended side-effects. Suppose that an action is itself of a kind which is morally permissible, and is performed for the sake of a good result. Suppose that the action also has foreseeable but unintended bad consequences, and that it is absolutely wrong ever intentionally to bring about such consequences. The doctrine of double effect states that it may be permissible to perform such an action, since the bad consequences are unintended side-effects and are not intentionally procured.

The doctrine of double effect has traditionally been a component of Catholic moral teaching, where it is typically applied in conjunction with absolute principles, such as the prohibition against killing the innocent. I have previously mentioned (and will examine in a later chapter) the idea that in war civilians are 'innocent' but combatants are not. This implies that an intentional attack on civilians in war is the intentional killing of the innocent, and is therefore ruled out. The deliberate bombing of cities in the Second World War, for instance, both by the Germans and by the British and American forces, has been condemned on these grounds. The following is the kind of case in which the doctrine of double effect then comes into play. Suppose that the intention is to bomb a military target. Let us assume that the war is itself a just war, and that this military action will help to defeat the enemy. Attacking a military target involves killing combatants, but that is in itself permissible. Suppose, however, that a foreseeable but unintended side-effect of the action is that a certain number of civilians living nearby are likely to be killed. It would be wrong intentionally to bring about their deaths. The doctrine of double effect says that bombing the military target, with these side-effects, may nevertheless be permissible, since it is not the intentional killing of the innocent.

As with the acts and omissions doctrine, an initial caveat is needed. I said that the acts and omissions doctrine does not mean that omissions do not matter. Similarly, the doctrine of double effect does not mean that unintended consequences do not matter. It does not mean that an action can be justified no matter how many unintended deaths of innocent persons it may bring about. Unintended side-effects are still subject to other moral limitations, such as the requirement of proportionality. The harm which they constitute must not be out of proportion to the good which could be achieved by allowing them. One could not, for example, bomb a target of only slight military importance, killing nearby civilians in huge numbers, and claim that their deaths did not matter because they were unintended. What the doctrine of double effect does is make it possible to apply an absolutist standard to the intended action and its intended consequences, while applying a consequentialist standard to the unintended consequences. Absolutist principles such as the prohibition against killing the innocent can then be kept intact, for, even though a refusal to perform the prohibited action may lead to even worse consequences, these are unintended consequences and therefore, though they should of course be prevented if possible, they cannot outweigh the absolute principle.

A particular controversial topic to which the principle of not killing the innocent and the principle of double effect have been applied is the issue of nuclear deterrence. The idea of deterrence is that by threatening to use nuclear weapons in retaliation, one can prevent other countries from launching a nuclear attack. It is claimed by many people that if Britain (or the United States or any other favoured country) did not employ nuclear weapons as a deterrent, the use of nuclear weapons by 'the other side' would be even more likely. However, employing nuclear weapons as a deterrent means being willing to use them, for if the possessors of the weapons were not willing to use them, they would not deter. And being willing to use them means being willing to kill millions of people, perhaps destroying whole societies, and possibly producing climatic and environmental effects which will entirely eliminate the human species.

There are two possible moral criticisms of nuclear deterrence. It can be argued that a policy of nuclear deterrence is unacceptable because it involves the build-up of nuclear arsenals and therefore increases the risk of the ultimate catastrophe of an all-out nuclear war. Abandoning nuclear deterrence has its dangers but it can be argued that, taking into account both their relative magnitude and their relative probability, the dangers of nuclear disarmament are out-weighed by the dangers of deterrence. Such consequentialist arguments seem to me to be persuasive, but I cannot make them here.[3] The moral criticism of nuclear deterrence which concerns me here is the absolutist argument. One cannot threaten to use nuclear weapons, even in retaliation, unless one is willing to carry out the threat. If one could be entirely certain that deterrence would succeed, it would be possible for a government to follow a deterrent policy in the confidence that it would never have to carry out the threat. In fact, however, no such certainty is available, and governments which follow such a policy therefore have to recognise that the policy may fail and that they must be willing to carry out the threat. (Making deterrent threats which are really a bluff is theoretically possible, but unlikely to be feasible in practice, given the nature of the political and military command structures, and in any case the deterrent policies of the nuclear-armed states are not based on bluff.) But, the absolutist argument maintains, one should not be willing to use nuclear weapons in any circumstances, since to use them would be to engage in the deliberate killing of the innocent. Nuclear deterrence is therefore not a morally accept-able way of preventing other states from using nuclear weapons. *Whether or not* it is an effective means of preventing them, it is not a permissible means, since it requires one to be willing to violate

---

[3] The consequentialist case against nuclear deterrence has been made most effectively by Douglas Lackey. See his 'Ethics and Nuclear Deterrence' in James Rachels, ed., *Moral Problems* (3rd edition, New York, 1979), and 'Missiles and Morals: A Utilitarian Look at Nuclear Deterrence' in *Philosophy and Public Affairs* vol. 11 (1982), reprinted in *International Ethics*, ed. C. R. Beitz, M.Cohen, T. Scanlon and A. J. Simmons (Princeton, 1985).

the absolute prohibition against the intentional killing of the innocent. If, as a result of our country's refusal to maintain a nuclear deterrent, another state were actually to launch a nuclear attack and kill millions of innocent people, this would be an *unintended* consequence of our refusal. The prevention of this unintended consequence could not justify a willingness intentionally to violate the absolute principle.[4]

The absolutist criticism of nuclear deterrence, then, is one example of how absolutism can be reinforced by the distinction between intended and unintended consequences which is contained in the doctrine of double effect. What are we to make of the doctrine? One problem is the inherent slipperiness of descriptions of intentions. The doctrine seems to lend itself to evading one's moral responsibility by redescribing one's intention, by saying 'I didn't intend that, what I really intended was ... ' Thus advocates of the bombing of German cities in the Second World War might have said 'We don't *intend* to kill civilians, what we intend is to destroy German morale. And whilst the intentional killing of civilians is indeed morally unacceptable, destroying German morale is a permissible act.' The doctrine then seems to become empty, for given sufficient verbal agility one can justify anything whatsoever.

To some extent the doctrine can be defended against this criticism. Any doctrine or principle can be misused, and though the doctrine of double effect perhaps lends itself to misuse more easily than most, misuse is still misuse. Intentions are not

[4] Examples of the absolutist rejection of nuclear deterrence are G. E. M. Anscombe, 'War and Murder' and 'Mr. Truman's Degree', in *Ethics, Religion and Politics*, vol. III of her *Collected Philosophical Papers* (Oxford, 1981), and Anthony Kenny, *The Logic of Deterrence* (London, 1985). See also essays by Kenny, Dummett and Ruston in *Objections to Nuclear Defence*, ed. Nigel Blake and Kay Pole (London, 1984).

    An attempted moral defence of nuclear deterrence might be that, although one cannot be *certain* that deterrence will succeed, it may *in fact* succeed (and has done so); therefore, though the practitioners of the policy must be *willing* to do what is wrong, it may turn out to be the case that they do not *in fact* do wrong. This defence depends on the premise that it may be morally permissible to be willing to do something which it would be wrong actually to do. Whether that premise is acceptable is a question I shall not pursue further, other than to note that it is unlikely to cut much ice against the kind of absolutism we are considering here, which is allied to the 'double effect' principle and accordingly stresses the moral importance of intentions.

infinitely redescribable. For a start, an intention incorporates not just an ultimate aim but the intended means of achieving that end. So, in the example, destroying German morale may be the aim, but bombing cities is the chosen means of achieving it. It is not a side-effect, it is the intended means, and is therefore an inseparable element in the full description of the intention.

One can of course *say* what one likes about one's intentions; that is how the 'intentional/unintentional' contrast can be misused. The important question, however, is not how a person describes his or her intentions, but whether the description is a true description, and this is a matter of objective fact, even though it may be difficult for others to ascertain. It has sometimes been suggested, for instance, that a doctor who is opposed to euthanasia but whose patient is dying slowly in great agony can resolve his/her dilemma by administering a pain-killing injection which will also, 'as a side-effect', hasten the patient's death. The 'double effect' principle is invoked to suggest that the doctor is not intentionally terminating the patient's life, since the intention is to ease the pain. If this is advocated as a resolution of the doctor's dilemma, it is simply dishonest. The doctor's dilemma consists of her thinking it wrong intentionally to end a life, but recognising that it may be better for her patient that she should do so. If, in response to this dilemma, she deliberately administers a particular kind of pain-killing injection *because* it will also hasten death, then she *is* intentionally terminating a life. The fact that her intention is also to relieve pain makes no difference; if she says that she is not intentionally ending the patient's life, she is deceiving either herself or others.

Moreover, correctly describing the agent's intentions is not just a matter of ascertaining the psychological facts, but also in part concerns the nature of the action itself. The action may itself be such as to exclude certain possible intentions. Consider again the case of nuclear deterrence. Defenders of the deterrent policy have sometimes tried to reconcile it with the prohibition on killing the innocent by advocating what is called a 'counter-force' rather than 'counter-city' policy. 'If,' it is said, 'the deterrent takes the form of nuclear weapons targeted on military installations we would admittedly, if we used them, kill millions of innocent civilians, but our intention would be to destroy the military installations.' This defence fails because nuclear weapons, with their massive destructive power, do not permit that discrimination of intentions. By their very nature they destroy everything and everyone within a large area, and in using them you cannot intend to destroy some of the things or people and not others. Intending to use them against, say, a missile silo *is* just intending to use them against the whole area in which the missile silo is located. The intended goals to be achieved may be different, but the intended actions are indistinguishable. (Compare hitting a nail with a hammer: you can intend to hit the head of the nail, but you cannot intend to hit this particular spot on the nail-head rather than that.)

It may be objected that I seem to be incorporating too much into the description of intentions. I may seem to be moving towards the claim that all aspects of an intended action which are known to the agent must be part of the agent's intention. That, however, would run together precisely the two things between which the doctrine of double effect is supposed to discriminate – the action and its side-effects. In my earlier example of the conventional (i.e. non-nuclear) bombing of a military installation, are we to say that the concomitant deaths of civilian passers-by, or of civilians hit by bombs which fall off target, are an intrinsic part of the intended action? The doctrine of double effect as traditionally applied does not carry that implication. It says that these would be side-effects. If, by contrast, we are to say that in the case of nuclear bombing the destruction of the civilian population is an essential part of the intended action and therefore cannot be described as un-intended, then the distinction between 'action' and 'side-effects' is going to have to carry a good deal of moral weight, and it is not clear that the distinction is sufficiently sharp to do so. Thomas Nagel, in a discussion of 'double effect', considers the example of American actions in the Vietnam War, bombing villages in which guerrillas are suspected to be hiding. Inevitably the victims were mostly unarmed women and children, but 'the government', he says, 'regards these civilian casualties as a regrettable side-effect of what is a legitimate attack against an armed enemy'.[5] One might counter that the action is an indiscriminate attack on the village and therefore on guerrillas and civilians alike, discrimination between them being impossible, but the reply, Nagel envisages, might be that the action is obliteration bombing of the *area* in which the guerrillas are located, with civilian deaths as side-effects. Because of the inconclusiveness of arguments about the appropriate description of the action, Nagel says that the principle of double effect 'introduces uncertainty where there need not be uncertainty'.[6]

I think it has to be agreed that the boundary between 'intended actions' and 'unintended side-effects', though perhaps not as indeterminate as Nagel implies, is not a sharp one. This might not matter. As I suggested in the previous chapter, in our moral thinking we may have to live with vague boundaries and grey areas. Perhaps the grey areas in the doctrine of double effect are greyer than most, but this is not the heart of the problem. Suppose that we can in fact draw a relatively workable distinction between 'intended actions', with their 'intended consequences', and 'unintended side-effects'. Suppose we were to satisfy ourselves that, in the Vietnam example, bombing the whole village is the intended means of killing the guerrillas, whereas in the other case bombing the airfield near a heavily populated area would lead to civilian deaths only as unintended side-effects. Even if the distinction holds, I think that the underlying worry is likely to be: how can such a fine distinction make so much moral difference? I mentioned previously the impression often created by the 'double effect' principle, that it is an evasion, that it lets people off the hook. I have noted one crude way in which it furnishes an evasion: either through dishonesty or self-deception, someone might attempt to evade responsibility for an action by claiming that it was unintended and that their real intentions were morally acceptable. This would be a misuse of the doctrine.

[5] Thomas Nagel, 'War and Massacre', in *International Ethics*, ed. Beitz *et al.* (see fn. 3 above), p. 61. The article originally appeared in *Philosophy and Public Affairs* vol. 1 (1972), and is also reprinted in Nagel, *Mortal Questions* (Cambridge, 1979).
[6] Ibid., p. 60.

Even if it is employed honestly, however, we may still feel that
this focus on the distinction between the 'intended' and
'unintended' effects of actions puts the emphasis in the wrong
place. The distinction seemed appropriate when we looked at
examples of the intended and unintended consequences of
omissions. The Halborough brothers' responsibility for their
father's death seems akin to murder because they intentionally
let him die, whereas if Vokinloksar fails to save the old woman
by giving her his legacy, he does not intend her death. In the
airfield example, however, the civilian deaths, even if not
intended, are the foreseen consequences of the attackers' *actions*.
Killing the civilians is *what they do*. I have acknowledged that the
'double effect' principle is not supposed to absolve the attackers
of all responsibility for the unintended side-effects; civilian
deaths are still supposed to be avoided if possible. I can
acknowledge also that the difference between intentionally
killing civilians as the means to some end, and killing them as an
unintended side-effect, may have *some* moral importance. It
may seem, then, that the issue is simply that of *how much*
importance the distinction should have. In the context of the
present discussion, however, that is indeed a crucial question,
for the distinction is supposed to make all the difference between
thinking in absolutist terms and thinking in consequentialist
terms. And we may doubt whether it can plausibly do this. If
killing civilians as an intended means to some military goal is
thought to be so morally appalling as to be absolutely ruled out,
can it then be morally acceptable on consequentialist grounds
to bomb a military target knowing that what one is also doing,
though unintentionally, is killing civilians? There *is* a distinction, but many people's intuitive response will be that it
cannot carry that much weight.

What re-emerges from such examples, I suggest, is the
importance of *agency*. The acts and omissions distinction and the
double effect principle have both been introduced as common
ways of defending absolutism, and in that guise they both seem
to point in the same general direction. The weakness of each,
however, turns out to be its neglect of the plausibility of the
other. The acts and omissions distinction fails to take account of

the importance of intentions; it neglects the fact that intentional omissions may be on a par with actions. The double effect principle emphasises the importance of intentions but neglects the importance of agency; it fails to recognise the important difference between the unintended consequences of omissions and the unintended, but foreseeable, side-effects of intentional actions.

The importance of agency is a deep-seated feature of the way in which we view our lives. Consider the following case. Suppose that a child runs out into the road in front of a car without any warning; it is quite impossible for the driver to stop or to swerve in time, and he knocks down the child and kills her. It might be quite correct to say that there was nothing the driver could have done to avoid killing the child, and that he is therefore not to be blamed in any way. I do not want to resist that moral conclusion, but I do want to point to the fact that the driver is nevertheless likely to feel distraught at *what he has done*.[7] This is quite distinct from the grief which any observer may feel at the tragedy of the child's death. What is likely to preoccupy the driver is the thought that, however blamelessly and unintentionally, *he killed her*, and his feelings about this will be very different from his feelings about the fact that there are many other children in the world who have died and whose lives he could have saved if he had lived his own life differently. If the driver feels terrible about what he has done, I do not think that such a feeling is irrational. What it points to is, I think, a deep connection between one's *agency* and one's *identity*. The things that I have done go to make up my life, they are distinctive features of my sense of who I am. This is not normally true of my omissions. It might be in particular cases; the experience that someone's life has depended on me and I have failed to save them may be a distinctive event in my own life-history. But this is not true of the myriad other harms in the world which I, along with innumerable other people, could have prevented.

Now I am not saying that, when my failure to prevent harms is a failure I share with others rather than a failure that is special

[7] Cf. Bernard Williams, 'Moral Luck', p. 28, in *Moral Luck* (Cambridge, 1981).

to me, this makes it morally acceptable. Indeed I want to emphasise again that in the example of the driver I am not drawing any moral conclusions at all. What I am trying to do is to explain why, in cases where questions of moral responsibility do arise, it may be plausible to make a distinction between actions and omissions. I am suggesting that it gets its plausibility from the link we make between our agency and our identity, and that the significance of this link is confirmed by the way in which we think about non-moral cases such as the driver example. It may be said in response that we should change this feature of our thinking – that we should regard our omissions as being just as definitive of our lives as our actions are. I doubt whether this is possible. For reasons which I shall come back to later in this chapter, I suspect that any such proposed conceptual revision would turn out to be incoherent. For the moment, however, I simply want to draw attention to the pervasiveness of the idea that killing someone, even if the death is unintended, has a different significance from failing to prevent someone's death.

At this point in the discussion we might conclude that, having come full circle, what we need is a combination of the 'acts and omissions' principle and the 'double effect' principle. The 'acts and omissions' distinction fails to take due account of the fact that intentionally letting someone die may be morally on a par with killing them. The 'double effect' doctrine fails to take due account of the fact that knowingly killing someone, even if the death is unintended, is importantly different from unintentionally failing to save lives. Perhaps what we need, then, is a theory which takes account *both* of the difference between acts and omissions *and* of the difference between intended and unintended deaths. Such a theory might state that we are as responsible for the intended consequences of our omissions, and for the unintended but foreseeable consequences of our actions, as we are for our intended actions and their intended consequences, but that we are not in the same way, or to the same degree, responsible for the unintended consequences of our omissions. This hybrid theory could provide the necessary support for an absolutist prohibition of killing (or of killing the innocent). The absolute principle would be that it is always wrong knowingly and avoidably to kill (innocent) people, or intentionally to let (innocent) people die. It would be wrong even if that were the only way of preventing other, unintended, deaths. Faced with a situation where, whatever we did, people would die, it would still be wrong to violate that absolute principle. Since the resulting deaths would be unintended, the principle would not be shown to be inconsistent in the way suggested by our original consequentialist criticism of absolutism.

I do indeed think that a satisfactory theory needs to take account of the plausible elements in both the 'acts and omissions' principle and the 'double effect' principle. As yet, however, such a conclusion has something of an *ad hoc* air about it. The argument so far has consisted in assessing the intuitive plausibility of those two principles when tested against various examples. By proceeding in this way we can patch up an anti-consequentialist position which looks reasonably coherent, but it does not take us to the heart of the matter. I want now to attempt a more thorough-going analysis of what is wrong with consequentialism, and to do so by looking more closely at the central concept of 'responsibility'. I shall suggest that the consequentialist account of responsibility is inadequate in three fundamental respects: (i) it is implausibly individualistic; (ii) it is indeterminate; (iii) it is morally question-begging. I shall elaborate each of these three claims in turn.

CONSEQUENTIALISM AS INDIVIDUALISTIC

Bernard Williams usefully characterises the consequentialist notion of responsibility as that of 'negative responsibility': 'If I am ever responsible for anything, then I must be just as much responsible for things that I allow or fail to prevent, as I am for things that I myself, in the more everyday restricted sense, bring about.'[8] This of course is just another way of saying that consequentialism rejects anything like the 'acts and omissions'

---

[8] Bernard Williams, 'A Critique of Utilitarianism', in J. J. C. Smart and Bernard Williams, *Utilitarianism: For and Against* (Cambridge, 1973), p. 95.

distinction. What it also brings out is the fact that consequentialism offers a purely *causal* picture of moral responsibility.
What I am responsible for is simply a function of the
consequences which are causally affected one way or another by
my actions and inactions. To decide what I ought to do in any
situation, I have to consider all the various states of affairs
which are likely to come about if I act in various ways, which
will turn out differently if I act differently, and for which I am
to that extent responsible; and I have to decide which of all
these states of affairs is on balance the best.

As Williams also points out, this picture takes no account of
the fact that, in some cases, what will come about as a result of
my acting in a certain way will come about because of *other
people's* actions:

> from some, at least, non-consequentialist points of view, there is a vital
> difference between some such situations and others: namely, that in
> some a vital link in the production of the eventual outcome is provided
> by *someone else's* doing something. But for consequentialism, all causal
> connections are on the same level, and it makes no difference, so far as
> that goes, whether the causation of a given state of affairs lies through
> another agent, or not.[9]

In other words, consequentialism leaves no room for the idea
that in the case of some of the consequences of my actions, I am
not responsible for them because someone else is responsible for
them.

We must be careful what use we make of this idea. Consider
an example proposed by Alan Gewirth.[10] A group of terrorists
possesses an arsenal of nuclear weapons, and they threaten that
they will use them to destroy a large city unless one of their
political opponents named Abrams tortures his mother to
death. (Their aim is perhaps to demonstrate their power and
humiliate their opponents.) Should Abrams accede to their
demand? Surely, it might be said, a mother's right not to be
tortured to death by her own son is absolute. But if Abrams

---

[9] Ibid., p. 94.
[10] Alan Gewirth, 'Are There Any Absolute Rights?', in *Theories of Rights*, ed. Jeremy
Waldron (Oxford, 1984). The article originally appeared in *Philosophical Quarterly*
vol. 31 (1981).

refuses, won't he then be responsible for the deaths of all the innocent inhabitants of the city?

Gewirth's example may appear far-fetched, but the recent annals of terrorism make it not too difficult to construct a modified and plausible example. In 1989, for instance, Iranian Muslims issued a death sentence against the novelist Salman Rushdie and demanded that the British government hand him over for execution. We can all too easily imagine a group of terrorists hi-jacking an airliner and threatening to blow it up, thereby killing the hundreds of passengers on board, unless Rushdie is delivered up for execution. The absolutist would presumably say that it is wrong to send an innocent man to execution in order to appease terroristic demands. The consequentialist could then ask: if the British government refused to do so, would they not then be responsible for the deaths of the passengers? (There are also consequentialist reasons for not giving in to the hi-jackers. Accepting their demands would set a precedent and encourage similar terrorist actions in the future. Moreover, in any actual case one could not be certain that the terrorists were not bluffing, and one might therefore decide that it was worth taking the risk of refusing their demands in the hope that they would not carry out the threat. The consequentialist case could therefore go either way. The question is: is this the whole story, or is there some deeper reason for thinking that it would be wrong to send an innocent man to execution in order to save the passengers?)

Gewirth says of his own example that Abrams would *not* be responsible for the ensuing deaths if he refused to torture his mother to death. This, says Gewirth, is because of the 'principle of the intervening action'. Simplifying Gewirth's formulation somewhat, such a principle asserts the following:

If A's doing X will lead to C suffering harm Z, A's responsibility for Z is removed if there intervenes a further action Y performed by B, who intends Z.[11]

---

[11] Gewirth's full formulation is: 'when there is a causal connection between some person A's performing some action (or inaction) X and some other person C's incurring a certain harm Z, A's moral responsibility for Z is removed if, between X and Z, there intervenes some other action Y of some person B who knows the relevant circumstances of his action and who intends to produce Z or who produces Z through

In such a case, A is not responsible for Z, since B is responsible for it. So, in the example, it is the terrorists, not Abrams, who will be responsible for the deaths. If Abrams refuses to torture his mother to death, the deaths of the innocent inhabitants of the city will ensue only because the terrorists intentionally bring about those deaths. Abrams should abide by his absolute obligation.

The principle of the intervening action seems plausible when applied to Gewirth's example, but other examples may suggest that it is too simple. Gewirth makes it sound as though responsibility is primarily a matter of chronology – 'I am not responsible if someone else's contribution is subsequent to mine' – but if that is what he means it cannot be right.[12] We are not absolved from responsibility simply because someone else does the final deed. To say 'It's not my responsibility, because it's their responsibility' will in some cases be appropriate but in others it will be an evasion, a futile attempt to 'keep one's hands clean'. The phrase itself should remind us of the classic example: Pontius Pilate may have washed his hands of the matter, but he *was* partly responsible for the death of Jesus, even though it was the chief priests who played the more active part.

The idea that my responsibility for consequences is removed if someone else's contributory action comes after mine would, then, be too simple. What Gewirth's discussion does importantly bring out, however, is that moral responsibility is a *social* matter. What we are responsible for, and hence what we ought to do, depends in part on what other people are responsible for.

recklessness. The reason for this removal is that B's intervening action Y is the more direct or proximate cause of Z, and, unlike A's action (or inaction), Y is the sufficient condition of Z as it actually occurs' (ibid., p. 104).

[12] To be fair to Gewirth, I do not think he wants to say that it is *simply* a matter of chronology. When he introduces the principle of the intervening action, he does say that it is needed to *supplement* the principle of double effect and the 'acts and omissions' distinction (p. 104). And in his discussion of the Abrams example he does give weight to the fact that the deaths of the inhabitants of the city would be the 'foreseen but unwanted side-effect' of Abrams' refusal to torture his mother to death (p. 105). I think that Gewirth is right that an adequate account must incorporate all these considerations. Nevertheless it remains unclear exactly what is meant by the term 'intervening action', and whether 'intervening' itself is supposed to mean anything more than 'chronologically intervening'. (I am grateful to Susan Mendus for discussion of this matter.)

Responsibility is something which is shared, and depends on complex facts about the social relations between different moral agents. This is what consequentialism seems to ignore, and it is why the consequentialist model of moral responsibility is a deeply individualistic one. At its heart is a picture of the isolated moral agent face to face with the universe. Of course the picture will incorporate the recognition that there are other moral agents in the world. But my knowledge of what other people are likely to do, and what they are likely to see themselves as responsible for, will figure for me as just one more set of causal factors capable of affecting the likely consequences of my own actions.

What we need, in contrast to this, is a coherent *social* picture of moral responsibility. We need an account of where one person's responsibilities end and another person's begin – an account which will also recognise, of course, that different people's responsibilities overlap and that many of our responsibilities are shared. I shall come back later to a brief discussion of what this picture might look like, but for the moment I simply note that it will be complex. In Gewirth's example, the important relevant feature is surely not just that the terrorists' action intervenes between Abrams' refusal to torture his mother and the destruction of the city, but the fact that the terrorists are blackmailing Abrams, that they have put him in this position where he has to make this impossible choice; their responsibility does not just intervene, but overrides his because they are really responsible for whatever choice he makes. In the Pilate example, one of the reasons why his disavowal of responsibility is an evasion is that he is in a position of authority and it is his job to make such decisions. So an adequate social account of moral responsibility will have to take account both of the ways in which one person's responsibility may affect another's in virtue of the transitory relations between them in particular circumstances, and the ways in which people's responsibilities follow from their more fixed social roles and positions.

There are ways in which the consequentialist can make room for the social ascription of responsibilities. There are versions of utilitarianism in particular which acknowledge that we can, cooperatively, do more good in the world if we divide up our responsibilities between us, assume particular social and institutional roles and concentrate on these. Instead of everyone trying to do everything, it will be more efficient if each of us gives priority to working well at his or her own job and at meeting his or her particular social obligations. Though the consequentialist can say this, however, the place that is here given to social relations and responsibilities is a secondary one. Behind it still lies the original consequentialist model, and the assumption remains that it is from that standpoint that we should justify the secondary social division of responsibilities. I have suggested that in our account of moral responsibility, the social dimension needs to be present from the start.

CONSEQUENTIALISM AS INDETERMINATE

I turn now to the second, connected, criticism of consequentialism. Its account of moral responsibility has sometimes been objected to on the grounds that it is excessively demanding. On the consequentialist model it is not enough simply to go through life avoiding the most obvious kinds of wickedness and observing the standards of average decency. We have to widen our vision, we have to look for other possibilities that may be open to us to mitigate evils and to do good, and we have to assume responsibility for these. If we take this wider view, we may then recognise, for instance, that there is a great deal of suffering in the world resulting from poverty and starvation which we could help to prevent.[13] If I am an averagely affluent middle-class Westerner I could, by parting with some of my income, prevent people in other parts of the world from dying of hunger and illness and malnutrition. And this is indeed a demanding doctrine, for suppose that by conventional standards I donate quite generous amounts of money to the relief of famine and hunger: there remains more that I could do, to prevent more deaths and suffering, and this will continue to be

---

[13] For a very forceful presentation of the facts and the case for an obligation to assist, see Peter Singer, *Practical Ethics* (Cambridge, 1979), ch. 8, and his 'Famine, Affluence, and Morality' in *Philosophy and Public Affairs* vol. 1 (1972), reprinted in *International Ethics*, ed. Beitz *et al.*

true until my generosity reaches the point where the inroads on my own well-being begin to outweigh the further good that I can do for others. If I stop short of that point, my responsibility for the further deaths and suffering which I could have prevented is, according to the consequentialist, in principle no different from a willingness to commit murder.

Now if the only thing to be said about this account of moral responsibility were that it is very demanding, this would not be a convincing objection. The real objection is not that the account makes our responsibilities very great, but that it cannot provide any definite demarcation of them at all. As such, it is not a demanding doctrine; it is incoherent. Suppose that I take seriously my responsibility for combating hunger worldwide. I give away half my income, I devote all my spare time to campaigning and raising money. However, if I do this, I have done nothing to help combat the threats to the environment, and so I must regard myself as responsible for all the environmental destruction which I have failed to prevent. If I try to assume this responsibility, I will have done nothing for the plight of political prisoners, or the victims of racial prejudice or the mentally handicapped. The list is endless, and that is because the class of 'possible actions open to me' is entirely indeterminate. Consequently there is no way of saying what I am responsible for. Whatever I do, there is an indefinite number of other things which I could have done. To say that I am responsible not only for my 'acts' but also for my 'omissions' gives only the illusion of determinacy. Something can be identified as an omission only if there are prior reasons for picking out the corresponding action as the thing one should have done. We can describe the Halborough brothers as 'omitting' or 'failing' to save their father because of our prior belief that they should have saved him, but if we were asked to list all the other things which they were 'not doing', as a preliminary to deciding which of them they should have done, the question would be meaningless. The list of 'things I am not doing' is not set by the empirical features of my situation; it can be extended by every new action-description which I invent to describe a possible action which I am not performing. Bear in mind also that the consequentialist will have to say that when I look back on my past I must not only take responsibility for all the evils which I could have prevented, but must also take credit for all the good things which have happened which I could have frustrated. Therefore, as far as my past responsibilities are concerned, there is no way in which I can, as it were, look back over my moral record and assess it overall, for there is no way of identifying what it is that I have done or failed to do. And the same impossibility attaches to any attempt to identify in purely consequentialist terms a coherent set of responsibilities for the future.

It is instructive to consider how a consequentialist might reply to these criticisms. Jonathan Glover quotes from Dostoevsky's *The Brothers Karamazov* the statement by Father Zossima's brother that 'everyone is really responsible for everyone and everything'. He comments:

This view ... seems to have nightmare implications. There is so much misery in the world that, however hard one person tries, he cannot remove more than a fraction. Does rejection of the acts and omissions doctrine commit us to being responsible for all that is left? ... It is clearly absurd that a man who devotes his whole life to a campaign against poverty should reproach himself for, say, not having done any useful research into the causes of muscular dystrophy.[14]

Glover then tries to defend consequentialism against this imputation of absurdity:

In allocating our time between actions, we have to work out priorities. The moral approach advocated here does not commit us, absurdly, to remedying all the evil in the world. It does not even commit us to spending our whole time trying to save lives. What we should do is work out what things are most important and then try to see where we ourselves have a contribution to make. We should then be able to justify the pattern of our lives. This is still a very demanding morality, which hardly anyone succeeds in living up to, but it is not the totally impossible demand made by Father Zossima's brother.[15]

On the face of it, this looks reasonable: we cannot do everything, we have to make a selection. Notice however that Glover sees

---

[14] Jonathan Glover, *Causing Death and Saving Lives* (Harmondsworth, 1977), p. 104.
[15] Ibid., p. 105.

the problem only as being that consequentialism is too demanding, not that it is incoherent. There remains, therefore, the insoluble problem of how we can make the best selection from an indeterminate set of possibilities. But even setting aside that fundamental incoherence, what sense can a consequentialist give to the idea of 'working out priorities'? Identifying priorities ought to mean looking at who I am, what my relations are to others, what particular responsibilities I have to particular people or particular groups of people. For the consequentialist, however, 'working out what things are most important' must mean assessing importance from a purely abstract and external point of view, from the point of view of 'the universe', as it were, deciding what will 'do the most good on the whole'. The idea of 'particular responsibilities' has to be derived from that abstract, and again incoherent, calculation.

Likewise, what sense can the consequentialist give to the notion of 'the pattern of our lives'? Again this ought to mean recognising my particular social and cultural identity, working out who I am and where my loyalties lie. From the standpoint of a social model of responsibility, we could make sense of this. The pattern of my life might be set by my work, for instance, or my family responsibilities, or my loyalties to my country or to my community. If my priorities are wider than some conventional identification of social roles, this will still be because of my sense of the particular responsibilities which I incur by living at a particular time in a particular place. So, as a privileged Westerner, I may decide that I can no longer live by benefiting from the exploitation of other parts of the world, and I might then give up my career in order to become, say, a health worker in Sri Lanka. But it will still be my commitment to this work which gives a pattern to my life. For the consequentialist, however, such commitments and loyalties are perpetually liable to be subverted. Suppose I take up a career as a doctor, deciding that this is a way in which I can be useful to others. If I am a successful doctor and earn a good income, I may then come to discover that, however useful I am as a doctor, I could do more good in the world by donating half of my earnings to the cause of cancer research, at the expense of my family's prosperity; and this judgement will in turn be up for reassessment as my circumstances change. So the idea of a 'pattern' gives way to that of the endless calculation and re-calculation of possibilities. It is in the very nature of consequentialism to subvert the patterns in our lives, since every new piece of information about the potential consequences of our actions is liable to reveal new ways in which we could more effectively do good and prevent harm.

CONSEQUENTIALISM AS MORALLY QUESTION-BEGGING

I have said that consequentialism purports to be a purely causal view of responsibility. I also want to suggest, however, that that appearance turns out to be illusory. The idea that we are responsible for all the good and bad consequences of all our actions and inactions rests on a prior moral assumption: that our moral responsibility is a responsibility to *everyone*, to all the possible beneficiaries of and losers from our actions, now and in the future. Recall the sentence from Dostoevsky: 'everyone is really responsible for everyone and everything'. For Father Zossima's brother, the idea that each of us is responsible for everyone else gets its backing from Christian ethics, from the vision of all human beings as children of the one divine Father. Characteristically, however, consequentialism gets its plausibility from its association with the substantive moral theory of utilitarianism. Now consequentialism and utilitarianism are, in theory, supposed to be distinct. Consequentialism is held to be the wider doctrine, with utilitarianism as just one particular way in which it can be given a more specific moral content. Consequentialism is simply the claim that the rightness or wrongness of actions is determined by their good and bad consequences, whilst utilitarianism offers a more particular account of what we are to regard as good or bad consequences. I am suggesting, however, that consequentialism looks plausible only if the crucial moral work has already been done by a doctrine such as utilitarianism. As I have said, it does not have to be utilitarianism. A certain kind of Christian morality might play a similar role. There are other possibilities. But some such concrete morality is needed in order to establish the *moral relevance* of consequences. Typically, in the philosophical literature, the job has been done by the association of consequentialism with utilitarianism. Consequentialism then looks plausible because the crucial moral move has already been made, before the argument starts.

Consider any one of the myriad consequences which are supposed to be relevant. Someone, somewhere, is lonely, and is suffering from being lonely, and I could do something to help, so to that extent, it is said, I have a responsibility for the suffering which I could prevent (though my obligation to do so must then be weighed against all the countless other obligations with which it is in competition). Now to the initial fact, of someone's suffering, I can reply 'So what? What is that to me?' That question requires an answer. It can be answered, and various different kinds of answer are possible, but it cannot be answered simply by pointing to a causal relation between a possible action of mine and the possible relief of the suffering. Utilitarianism answers it with what I want to call its 'abstract universalism' – the idea that each of us ultimately stands in the same moral relation to everyone else. Everyone's moral relation to me is that of being the potential beneficiary of my actions, and therefore I have the same responsibility to everyone, the responsibility for the promotion of their happiness and the prevention of their suffering. That is why utilitarianism lends itself so readily to the support of consequentialism, for if my responsibility to everyone is of this same kind, then what I ought to do can be determined simply by the maximising calculation, the weighing up of the beneficial and harmful consequences. As I have argued, however, it is a mistake to suppose that all our responsibilities can be derived from this one universal relation, for this is to ignore the diversity of our social relations, and their complex implications for our moral responsibilities.

To revert, then, to the kind of example which is our primary concern in this chapter, suppose that, if I do not kill someone, thousands of people will die. For the consequentialist, the number of deaths is the crucial consideration. (Strictly speaking, of course, the benefits and harms likely to accrue to each life are the fundamental components in the calculation, but if the numbers are large enough we can assume that the larger number of deaths is likely to be the greater evil.) However, we can regard the number of deaths as clinching the moral argument only if we already assume that I have just the same responsibility to each of the potential victims. We cannot assume this. We can argue about it, but the argument will be a moral argument and it cannot be settled simply by establishing the causal relations between my possible actions and other people's deaths.

A SOCIAL MODEL OF MORAL RESPONSIBILITY

My three criticisms of consequentialism all point in the same direction. They indicate that the extent of my responsibility for the consequences of what I do depends on prior moral considerations, not just on causal considerations. They indicate also that those moral considerations will depend on the various kinds of social relations in which we stand to one another. In the light of these social relations we can understand how one person's responsibilities are limited by the responsibilities of others, and which of a person's responsibilities are shared with others. In the light of a determinate picture of specific social responsibilities, we can pick out which of the innumerable possible actions that are open to us count as significant omissions, and thus give a determinate content to questions about what we ought to do.

What I want to propose, then, is a social model of moral responsibility, in place of consequentialism's causal model. The consequentialist model *starts* from the assumption that we are in principle responsible for all the consequences of all the possible actions and inactions open to us, and that what we ought in principle to do is determined by the weighing up of these consequences, and *then* moves to the idea of social relations and responsibilities as a way of narrowing down our obligations in practice and enabling us to act more effectively. The alternative, social model which I am proposing starts from our relations to one another and the various particular responsibilities which these generate, and moves *from* there to an understanding of what we ought to do. Of course, in deciding what we ought to do, a knowledge of the likely consequences of our actions is relevant, but it is only in the light of a prior understanding of our responsibilities that we can consider *what* consequences are relevant and *how* they are relevant.

This social model will be a great deal more complex than the causal model. For the latter, complexity enters at the level of detailed causal calculations, but the concept of responsibility itself is a simple one. My social model will also lack the simplicity of absolutism. I cannot argue that certain kinds of action such as killing are always wrong, whatever the consequences. This would require the claim that our responsibility for the harmful consequences of our refusal to perform such actions is ruled out by some such principle as the 'acts and omissions' distinction or 'double effect'. I do think that those ideas have a role to play, but only as part of a wider and more complex picture.

In a sense, then, I do not have a general theory of moral responsibility. The task of working out what our responsibilities are is a matter for detailed moral argument. It is part and parcel of the business of arguing about what we ought to do, not a preliminary to it. Nevertheless I shall try to sketch in outline the kinds of social relation which will have to enter into the picture. This will draw on the sketch which I have already offered in chapter 1, but will emphasise the implications for our understanding of the idea of moral responsibility.

There are first, then, certain kinds of universal responsibility. I have criticised the abstract universality of utilitarianism. I have also argued, however, that there are indeed responsibilities which we have to everyone, and these are the general responsibilities to other human beings which are grounded in our capacities for respect and sympathy. I have previously linked the attitude of respect with the wrongness of killing. I have also suggested that it helps to ground a distinction between 'killing' and 'letting die'. Respect, I have suggested, is primarily a response to others as agents. I have linked it with a kind of distancing of oneself from others, recognising that they have their own lives to live and acknowledging their right to do so rather than ourselves engaging in helping others to live their lives or seeking to prevent their deaths. Our responsibilities to others to help to promote their well-being and to prevent their suffering or death derive from the distinct response of sympathy. This generalised sympathy is the basis for utilitarian moral considerations, but the mistake made by utilitarianism as a theory is to treat this one attitude as incorporating the whole of morality. We do indeed have general obligations to aid others and to prevent harm, but they occupy only a portion of our moral lives. Limits to that portion are set partly by the attitude of respect, the requirement not to live others' lives for them. Limits are set also by our more specific responsibilities arising out of our special relations to others, which compete for space in our lives. This is where we can agree with Glover that 'we have to work out priorities' in such a way that we are 'able to justify the pattern of our lives'. Detailed deliberation and argument has to take over here; no general theory can tell us what that pattern should be. In short, Father Zossima's brother is half right. We do have general responsibilities to others. We are, up to a point, responsible for everyone, but we are not responsible for everything, and to suppose that we are is to deny other people responsibility for their own lives.

These general responsibilities, then, deriving from sympathy and respect, are one element in my social model. A second class of considerations derives from relations of power and autonomy. This second category overlaps considerably with the first. Respect for others is, we have seen, respect for their autonomy if 'autonomy' is understood in an appropriately wide sense, as not just the ability to act on this or that particular desire but the ability to control one's life as a whole. A failure to respect the autonomy of others will characterisically consist in the exercise of power over them. Considerations of power and autonomy give some support to the 'acts and omissions' distinction and to the idea of 'double effect'. If I act in such a way as to affect another person, my relation to that person is, to that extent, different from what it would be if I left him alone, and the difference is typically a difference in our relative degrees of power and autonomy. If I and another person are in an open-ended situation, my acting will characteristically close off certain options for the other person, whereas my doing nothing will leave the options open. Even if I act in ways which are beneficial to the other person, my bringing about the valued outcomes for her will prevent her from *acting for herself* to bring them about. So if considerations of autonomy and of power-relations between people are morally important, the difference between action and inaction will likewise be important.

As it stands, however, that is too simple. As we have seen, refraining from action may itself sometimes be a way of deliberately bringing about a certain outcome (as in the Hardy example on p. 80). This is why intentions are also important, and the doctrine of double effect rather obscurely recognises this. My intentionally bringing about a certain outcome, whether by acting or by refraining from acting, will to that extent be a case of exercising power, and my bringing about a harmful outcome for another person amounts to exercising power over that person.[16]

The strength of the doctrine of double effect is that it recognises the positive importance of intentions, such that intentionally refraining may be morally equivalent to acting. The weakness of the doctrine on the other hand is, as we have seen, that it too easily exonerates people from responsibility for the unintended outcomes which they knowingly bring about. If relevant considerations are those of power-relations, of exercising control over others and imposing outcomes on them, then the plain fact is that, for example, dropping bombs on a military target and knowingly bringing about the deaths of the people in

---

[16] The doctrine of double effect is defended in these terms by Warren S. Quinn in his article 'Actions, Intentions, and Consequences: The Doctrine of Double Effect', in *Philosophy and Public Affairs* vol. 18 (1989). Quinn argues that what is especially wrong with the intended, as compared with the foreseen but unintended, harmful treatment of people has to be understood in terms of the special kind of relation between the harmer and the harmed. The latter falls under the power and control of the former in a distinctive way. The intentional harmer treats his victims 'as if they were then and there *for* his purposes', 'he sees them as material to be strategically shaped or framed by his agency' (p. 348). This is not true of someone who unintentionally harms others.

the vicinity is a classic case of exercising power over them, and no amount of playing around with the question of whether the deaths are intended or unintended can alter that fact.

Of course I do not want to say that all bringing about of outcomes for other people is an exercise of power over them and therefore bad. Some ways of intentionally bringing about a certain outcome for another will be ways of empowering the other person, for example if I offer my cooperation, or provide information or educate him and thereby enhance his autonomy.[17] Nor do I want to say even that all cases of bringing about *harmful* outcomes for others have the same moral status, and that the wrongness of doing so always takes precedence over the wrongness of an unintended failure to help others. For instance, the wrongness of telling lies and deceiving others is very much tied up with the relations of manipulation and control which this involves, and in this respect it is comparable to the bringing about of people's deaths, but I do not want to conclude that one may never tell a lie even to save another person's life. One cannot avoid taking account also of the scale of harms, and telling a lie, manipulative though it is, may be a trivial harm compared with the possibility of saving someone's life. So doctrines such as the 'acts and omissions' distinction and 'double effect' are too broad and simple for defining the relative importance of our different moral responsibilities, and it would be a mistake to look for any alternative doctrine which operates at the same level of generality. We cannot say in a general way that the wrongness of acts has a more fundamental status than the wrongness of omissions, or that intentional acts carry a greater weight than unintended consequences, or that obligations to refrain from bringing about harms to others take precedence over positive duties to provide aid and support.[18]

---

[17] But note the moral ambiguity even in such cases. Even in empowering another I am exercising power over his situation, for he may not want to be empowered, he may not want to be educated, he may not want to cooperate, he may not want to know. Relations such as that of teacher and pupil, or parent and child, always involve this ambiguity.

[18] This is why Philippa Foot's useful proposal of a classification into 'negative duties' and 'positive duties', though it has prompted some of the things which I have been trying to say, nevertheless seems to me to need breaking down into more specific

What we can say is that *certain kinds* of acts and intentions have a special status. In the light of considerations about the character of our moral relationships, I do want to claim that the wrongness of taking a human life has a fundamental place in the defining of our moral responsibilities. The bringing about of another's death, whether by active intervention or by intentional refraining, is the ultimate case of exercising power and control over another, of violating that person's autonomy and withholding the respect appropriate to him or her as a separate and unique individual with his or her own life to lead.

Considerations of power and autonomy, then, give a special importance to my responsibility to respect the lives of others. Beyond that, they set limits to my further responsibilities for others, at the point when my attempts to produce benefits or prevent harms to others start to become an exercise of control over their lives. A further significance of considerations of power and autonomy is in situations where other people's responsibility invades and overrides my own. I am referring here to cases like the Gewirth example. The relevant feature of such cases is that others, by their actions, deliberately put me in a situation where whatever I do will lead to an appalling outcome. They impose on me a 'forced choice'. Their doing so must then affect the judgement of my responsibility for the outcome. As I said when discussing Gewirth's example, this is not simply because their actions 'intervene' in a chronological sense. It is because, in exercising power over me and denying my autonomy, they must be seen as responsible for the outcome of the forced choice which they impose on me. If Abrams refuses to torture his mother to death, it is the terrorists who are responsible for the deaths of the inhabitants of the city. Abrams could have prevented the deaths, but only by doing something which would itself have been morally appalling, and since the terrorists have imposed the forced choice on him, their responsibility alters his. This idea that someone's imposing a forced choice on me affects my responsibility for the outcome is an idea to which

moral categories. See Philippa Foot, 'The Problem of Abortion and the Doctrine of Double Effect', in *Virtues and Vices, and Other Essays in Moral Philosophy* (Oxford, 1978), p. 27.

I shall return in the next chapter when I consider the problem of killing in self-defence.

So far I have considered two general kinds of relation between people which must feature in our social model of moral responsibility. They are the responses of respect and sympathy which ground our general concern for others, and the relations of power and autonomy which make a difference to how one person's responsibility affects another's. In addition to these two general kinds of social relation there is, thirdly, the category of all the specific responsibilities which we have in virtue of our various kinds of special relation. This is where a complete social theory is needed in order to give a full account, but obvious examples are the responsibilities which we have in our relations with family and friends, fellow workers and fellow citizens. These special responsibilities are not necessarily obligations to do more than we would do for everyone else. They may be – one's responsibilities to one's children may, for example, require one to make greater sacrifices to support them than one would make to meet the needs of others – but they may also be responsibilities of a different and distinctive kind. We owe it to our friends, for instance, to provide emotional support, and to those with whom we cooperate we have obligations to deal fairly and to share justly the products of our common endeavour.

Without going into details about the multiplicity of special relations and responsibilities, I want to make two points. Although I criticised the causal model of responsibility as 'individualistic', my own account so far may appear individualistic in another sense, for I have been emphasising the ways in which one person's responsibilities limit another's. That however is only part of the picture. To say that people have their own lives to lead does not mean that they live them in isolation. They live them as social beings, involved in various kinds of social cooperation, and this is where specific responsibilities arise from our membership of groups and communities. Many of our responsibilities are shared responsibilities, which we have in common as members of a group, and where what falls to me as an individual is the responsibility to 'do my bit'.

This is particularly relevant to our understanding of autonomy. I have discussed the case of one person's actions encroaching on another's autonomy, and suggested that this sets limits to our responsibilities for others. Equally important, however, is the role of social cooperation in *promoting* autonomy. I have mentioned briefly the importance of, for example, education in developing our ability to make informed choices about the direction of our lives. I would add that insofar as autonomy consists in our ability to exercise control over our lives, this is often something which we can do only in cooperation with others. Only through participation in shared social and political activity can I, for instance, have any effective control over the quality of my social and natural environment or over the economic institutions which profoundly affect my life.

The second point I want to make is to reiterate that our specific social relationships go to make up that 'pattern of priorities' within which we have to make sense of our responsibilities. If our general responsibilities for others are limited, this is partly because they have to take their place within a life structured by our specific roles and relationships. Organising our responsibilities in this way is, I have argued, not just a practical afterthought; only within such a context can we give any determinate content at all to the idea of 'responsibility'.

Here then are three categories of social relations which are relevant to our understanding of moral responsibility: those general responsibilities to others which are grounded in the attitudes of respect and sympathy; relations of power and autonomy; and more specific social roles and relationships. I do not want to claim that these give us a complete account of moral responsibility. They are parts of the picture, considerations which are important for the determination of our responsibilities.

TWO EXAMPLES

If my lack of a simple general theory still seems a defect, let me try to illustrate my approach by applying it to two examples. Consider first the example of action to combat world poverty and starvation. We have seen that, for the consequentialist, this must be a question of estimating how much good I can do by taking such action, and comparing it with the consequences of all the alternative actions open to me. This seems at first to give us overwhelming responsibilities, only for them to evaporate when we consider all our other overwhelming responsibilities. Can we offer a better account?

The consequentialist case for an obligation to assist gets its initial plausibility from the stark facts of human suffering. We are moved, for instance, by the suffering of the victims of drought and famine in sub-Saharan Africa, and we recognise their needs as urgent and as requiring emergency action on our part. That recognition is an expression of our basic human sympathy. As such, it may be limited, as an immediate response to an extreme situation. However, if we look more closely at the less dramatic but continuing economic hardship of the peoples of Africa and Asia and Latin America, we recognise that much of it is the product of economic relations from which we, in the affluent world, benefit. Present sufferings are in part the legacy of past colonialism, in part the consequence of unfair terms of trade and investment and the mounting burden of debt imposed by the rich countries. These facts create special obligations, to provide restitution for past injustices from which we still benefit, and to rectify existing relationships of exploitation. Causal judgements are involved here in two ways. First, they are necessary to establish how far world poverty really is a consequence of exploitation and of the economic activities of the rich nations. Second, they are necessary to establish which attempts to rectify the situation are likely to be most effective. If the aim of combating starvation is already established, then of course we have to determine which actions really will promote that aim and which will, for instance, merely reinforce existing relations of dependence, or encourage a population explosion. In other words, the investigation of consequences can be relevant if certain moral responsibilities are already pre-supposed. But this is quite different from supposing that we can calculate, in a moral vacuum, which course of action will have better consequences on the whole than all the other conceivable courses of action open to us.

Our more extended responsibilities, then, stem from the special relations in which we stand to the victims of poverty. As such, they are responsibilities which we share with others, with our fellow citizens of the rich countries of the world. It is not that I, as an individual, am morally obliged to shoulder the burden of responsibility for the whole world. My responsibility is more determinate than that, a responsibility both to urge the government of my country to fulfil its obligations, and to play my own part in the fulfilling of them. Finally, there is again the question of the place which this commitment has within the pattern of my life. How far my obligations extend is not just a question about the consequences of my actions, it is also a question about *my life*.

My second example is the question of active and passive euthanasia. I have, in the previous chapter, referred briefly to the euthanasia debate. I have agreed with the widely held view that there is an important difference between voluntary and involuntary euthanasia. Respect for life must also mean respect for a person's own considered decision that they wish their life to be ended, rather than to continue a pointless existence in unbearable pain. There are, I acknowledged, difficult practical problems concerning the legalisation of voluntary euthanasia, but a strong reason in support of voluntary euthanasia is that, other things being equal, a doctor who refuses a patient's considered wish to die is exercising an unwarranted degree of power over her and overriding her autonomy.

What, though, of the cases where euthanasia, if it is to be considered, cannot possibly be voluntary, because the person is in no position to have any wishes one way or the other? Consider the case of babies born with terrible physical and mental defects, such as severe spina bifida. The standard practice now, in this country, is that new-born babies suffering from spina bifida are operated on if the operation offers a reasonable prospect that the child can go on to live a satisfying life. If, on the other hand, the condition is too severe for there to be any such prospect, the operation is not performed, the baby is sedated to control its physical pain, it is fed on demand and made as comfortable as possible but infections are not treated with antibiotics, and the result is that most such babies die within a relatively short period. This practice is described as a decision 'not to prolong the baby's life', rather than actively terminating its life.

This is of course an application of the general distinction between killing and letting die. In the context of discussions of euthanasia the terms 'active euthanasia' and 'passive euthanasia' are standardly used. The distinction has been criticised, particularly by philosophers who argue that if someone's life holds out so little prospect of anything worthwhile and so certain a prospect of unbearable pain that passive euthanasia is justified, then active euthanasia is all the more justified. Passive euthanasia may still leave the patient or the baby to endure great pain for days, weeks or even years, and the period is cruelly and unnecessarily prolonged by the refusal to countenance active euthanasia.

I have argued that the distinction between killing and letting die does have a role to play in our moral thinking. The fact that the medical profession wishes to invoke it, and feels more comfortable with a code of practice which allows doctors not to prolong life but rules out killing, is testimony to its appeal.[19] Nevertheless I think we can see the force of the criticisms in this particular case if we bring to bear some of the other considerations which are relevant to our understanding of responsibility. Though it may in general be true that we are not responsible for people's deaths simply because we could conceivably have done something to prevent them, the fact is that in the case of passive euthanasia the doctor cannot disclaim responsibility. Two points are crucial. First, it is clear that in cases like that of the spina bifida babies, the *intention* is that they should die. They are allowed to die, and their infections are not treated, because it is felt that their death will be a merciful release from pain, and

---

[19] The conclusions formulated in 1988 by the British Medical Association's working party on euthanasia included the following: 'There is a distinction between an active intervention by a doctor to terminate life and a decision not to prolong the life (a non-treatment decision) ... An active intervention by anybody to terminate another person's life should remain illegal ... In clinical practice there are many cases where it is right that a doctor should accede to a request not to prolong the life of a patient' (*Philosophy and Practice of Medical Ethics* (British Medical Association, 1988), p. 91).

that is the intended outcome. It is worth noting that if the babies are demand-fed but are also sedated, they will demand less and the combination of the two practices will therefore hasten death. Again it seems difficult to deny that this is the intention. The second reason why a policy of 'not prolonging life' does not relieve the doctor of responsibility for the death is that saving lives is normally part of her job. The special responsibilities attaching to social roles enter into the picture here. We are not all responsible for saving the lives of everyone else, and there is normally a moral difference between 'not saving life' and 'killing', but doctors are normally responsible for trying to save the lives of their patients. I am not suggesting that it follows that doctors should always strive to prolong life and that all forms of euthanasia should be ruled out. What I am suggesting is that if, in a particular case, the doctor decides that it is better not to prolong life, then she cannot avoid responsibility for the death. The decision may well be the right one, but she is equally responsible, whether the decision is for active or passive euthanasia. The distinction between 'killing' and 'not saving life' does not carry its usual significance in this case, because of its interaction with the special responsibilities of the doctor's role. The case of euthanasia, then, provides another example of how we can make sense of moral responsibilities in terms of the interplay between the various factors I have identified. That complex approach is a workable alternative both to simple consequentialism and to simple absolutism.

CONCLUSION

The argument of this chapter reinforces the position which we reached at the end of the previous chapter and the claim made there about the special importance of the wrongness of killing. I have argued that that position cannot be undermined by consequentialist reasoning. On the other hand, it cannot be hardened into a pure absolutist position. We cannot rule out the possibility that in extreme circumstances it may be necessary to kill (or to kill the innocent) if the consequences of not doing so would be disastrous. We therefore cannot settle the question of whether war can ever be justified simply by invoking such an absolute principle. There nevertheless remains a very strong moral presumption against taking human life, which cannot be overturned simply on consequentialist grounds. War cannot be justified simply by arguing that the good consequences will outweigh the bad. Whether it can be justified in another way, we shall consider in the next chapter.

CHAPTER 4

Killing in self-defence

THE 'JUST WAR' TRADITION

Consequentialist arguments may be the ones which come most readily to hand to justify the waging of war, but the dominant intellectual tradition of thought about the morality of war has appealed to a different set of concepts. It is commonly referred to as the 'just war' tradition. It is an evolving tradition rather than a definitive set of principles, and the tradition has been especially shaped by Christian thinkers. The early Christian church rejected all participation in military activities, but when Christianity became the official religion of the Roman Empire it had to accommodate itself to the realities of political life, and thinkers such as Augustine tried to formulate the conditions under which the waging of war could be consistent with Christian morality. Over the centuries those conditions were more precisely formulated and codified into a body of doctrine which was the official teaching of the Catholic church. The broader tradition has been taken up also by some of the Protestant churches. Its secular development is reflected in modern international law, and it informs a great deal of public debate about the rights and wrongs of wars. Political leaders who seek to give moral legitimacy to acts of war will typically appeal to principles and concepts derived from the 'just war' tradition, and their critics often employ the same moral vocabulary.[1]

---

[1] There is an excellently clear and succinct summary of 'just war' theory in *The Church and the Bomb*, the Report of a Working Party of the Church of England Board for

The tradition distinguishes between two fundamental questions referred to by the Latin phrases *jus ad bellum* and *jus in bello*. The former is the question of what makes it right *to go to war*. The latter is the question of what it is right to do *in* war, that is, what means of fighting are permissible. The doctrine of *jus ad bellum* has traditionally specified the following conditions which must be satisfied if the decision to go to war is to count as 'just':

1. The war must be fought for a *just cause*. I shall consider shortly what this might mean.
2. The decision to go to war must be made with a *right intention*. It is not enough that there should as a matter of fact be a just cause; it is also necessary that the war should be declared for that reason, not with ulterior motives.
3. The decision to go to war must be made by a *legitimate authority*. It must be a decision on behalf of the community, not simply the act of private individuals.
4. There must be a *formal declaration of war*.
5. There must be a *reasonable hope of success*. Even if there is a just cause which defines the aim of the war, the evils which the war is bound to involve should not be incurred if there is no hope of achieving the aim.
6. The decision to go to war should be a *last resort*, taken only when the possibilities of achieving the same aim without war have been exhausted.
7. The decision must satisfy the requirement of *proportionality* – that the good to be achieved by the war must be of sufficient importance to outweigh the harms which will be produced.

Even if these conditions are satisfied, there remains a further question whether the conduct of the war is just. The doctrines of *jus ad bellum* and *jus in bello* are distinct, for a party which was justified in going to war in the first place might nevertheless

Social Responsibility (London, 1982), ch. 5, where it is brought to bear on the question of nuclear deterrence. Another useful book presenting the historical tradition and relating it to problems of contemporary warfare is James Turner Johnson, *Can Modern War Be Just?* (New Haven, 1984).

wage war by unjust means. The traditional conditions of *jus in bello* are two:

1. The requirement of *non-combatant immunity*: civilians, as non-combatants, must not be attacked or killed. The fighting must be directed solely against the armed forces of the enemy.

2. The requirement of *proportionality*, applied now to means rather than to ends: the means adopted in fighting the war must not be so harmful and destructive as to outweigh the good to be achieved.

Within this rather varied list of conditions, some are likely to appear more important than others. Two have in fact come to be especially emphasised: for *jus ad bellum*, the requirement of just cause, and for *jus in bello*, the requirement of non-combatant immunity. The traditional phrase 'just cause' is a vague one, and as it stands it might appear to give no guidance at all. Slightly more specific and more helpful is the formulation that war is permissible only if it is fought to right a specific wrong. This at least imposes the requirement that the ruler declaring war must be able to point to the wrong which the enemy has committed, and thus gives something less than carte blanche.[2] It also draws attention to another important assumption in much 'just war' thinking, namely that waging war can be compared with the imposition of legal punishment.[3] I shall return later to the problems with this comparison.

'Just war' thinking has increasingly, and especially in its secular versions, come to focus on one specific justification for war. The wrong which war should attempt to right is the crime

---

[2] See for example Anthony Kenny, *The Logic of Deterrence* (London, 1985), p. 9: 'War, then, must be waged in order to right a specific wrong: that is what gives one the right to go to war, the ius ad bellum.'

[3] Augustine, 'Contra Faustum', in R. N. Beck and J. B. Orr, eds., *Ethical Choice* (New York and London, 1970), p. 368: 'The real evils in war are love of violence, revengeful cruelty, fierce and implacable enmity, wild resistance, and the lust of power, and such like; and it is generally to punish these things, when force is required to inflict the punishment, that, in obedience to God or some lawful authority, good men undertake wars...' For a good critical discussion of the comparison between war and punishment, see Jenny Teichman, *Pacifism and the Just War* (Oxford, 1986), ch. 5.

of aggression, and the only justification for going to war is therefore as *defence against aggression*. This is the version of 'just war' theory encapsulated in modern international law, and regularly invoked by politicians. It has been presented and discussed at length in an extremely impressive modern restatement of just war theory, Michael Walzer's book *Just and Unjust Wars*, and in assessing it I shall in due course refer to Walzer's account.[4]

The core idea, then, is that war can be justified in self-defence. In this chapter I shall examine that claim. In the next chapter I shall turn to the most important requirement of *jus in bello*, that of non-combatant immunity, and we shall see that the idea of self-defence plays an important role there too. Since appeals to 'self-defence' in war are often thought to derive their moral legitimacy at least partly from the comparison with individual self-defence, I shall begin by looking at that case.

THE RIGHT OF SELF-DEFENCE

Do individuals have a right of self-defence? Note first that the question is indeed typically formulated in those terms, as a question about *rights*. The right that is asserted here is, more specifically, a right to *kill* in self-defence, and such a right is problematic because of its relation with another supposed right, the right to life. If people have a right to life, how can it be justifiable to kill them in self-defence? The standard answer is: if someone attempts to kill me, my right to life justifies me in killing him if necessary. In other words, the attacker's right to life is in some way overridden or negated by the defender's right to life.

This assumption is the starting-point for arguments in support of 'just war', and is epitomised in the classic question supposed to be put to conscientious objectors by tribunals: 'What would you do if someone attacked your sister (or mother or grandmother or some other favoured female relative)?' The implied answer is 'Defend her, of course, and so you ought also

[4] Michael Walzer, *Just and Unjust Wars* (Harmondsworth, 1980), hereafter referred to as *JUW*.

to be prepared to defend your country, and to kill in her defence.' Note also that the example points to a standard extension of the idea of self-defence: it is assumed that, if it is justifiable to kill one's attacker in self-defence, then it must also be justifiable to defend someone other than oneself by killing their attacker.

The claim that there is such a right of self-defence is often put forward as an assertion needing no further justification. It will be apparent from previous chapters that I regard such a position as inadequate. There are no self-evident rights. Rights-claims always need some further justification, they need to be defended by appeal to some moral concept more basic than that of rights. To those who make the dogmatic assertion that it is just obvious that there is a right of self-defence I can only offer the dogmatic counter-assertion that it is not obvious to me.

What further justification might be given? A standard approach, in philosophical discussions of the topic, is to look at the distinctive features of self-defence situations to see whether a justification can be found in these.[5] One important feature of such situations is that they involve a *forced choice between lives*. Whatever is done, someone will die. The only practical question for an agent faced with such a situation is therefore 'Who is it to be?' It might be suggested that this is in itself a justification for killing in self-defence; if someone is coming at me with a knife, then 'it's him or me', and I cannot be blamed for choosing my life over his. The only principle that can be appealed to here, it might be said, is 'Everyone for himself'.

This, however, offers no positive reason for thinking it right that I should kill the attacker rather than that he should kill me.

---

[5] Good discussions are: Judith Jarvis Thomson, 'Self-Defense and Rights', 1976 Lindley Lecture at University of Kansas, reprinted in Judith Jarvis Thomson, *Rights, Restitution and Risk*, ed. William Parent (Cambridge, Mass., 1986); Phillip Montague, 'Self-Defense and Choosing Between Lives', in *Philosophical Studies* vol. 40 (1981); Cheyney C. Ryan, 'Self-Defense, Pacifism, and the Possibility of Killing', in *Ethics* vol. 93 (1983); Jenny Teichman, *Pacifism and the Just War*, ch. 8; David Wasserman, 'Justifying Self-Defense', in *Philosophy and Public Affairs* vol. 16 (1987); Phillip Montague, 'The Morality of Self-Defense: A Reply to Wasserman', in *Philosophy and Public Affairs* vol. 18 (1989); B. J. Smart, 'Understanding and Justifying Self-Defence' in *International Journal of Moral and Social Studies* vol. 4 (1989); Judith Jarvis Thomson, 'Self-Defense', in *Philosophy and Public Affairs* vol. 20 (1991).

All that is being said is that I can hardly be expected to do otherwise. Many would claim, however, that there is more to be said of self-defence situations. The mere statement that 'it's him or me' fails to distinguish self-defence from other forced choices between lives, including cases where it would surely be wrong to kill in order to save my own life. Suppose that I am in hospital, desperately needing a kidney transplant, without which I will die, but no donor is available. In the next bed is an unconscious patient being kept alive on a respirator. If I pull out the plug when no one is looking, he will die and I can have his kidney. If I resist the temptation, he will survive and I shall die. 'It's him or me', but this hardly justifies me in killing him.

In contrast to such cases, what seems to be distinctive of self-defence situations is not just the forced choice between lives, but the *asymmetry* of the situation. Most people would say that, on the one hand, I am justified in killing the attacker to save my own life, but that, on the other hand, if I attempt to do so and his life is then at risk, he would *not* be justified in killing me to save his own life. The moral asymmetry seems to be created by the attacker's aggression. What account can we give of this?

I have already noted that self-defence is often justified in terms of rights. One possible account might therefore go like this: people normally have a right to life, but the attacker, by his aggression, has *forfeited* his right to life, and that is why his potential victim, who retains her right to life, has a right to kill in self-defence. In doing so, she would not be violating the attacker's right to life, since he no longer has such a right.

This idea of 'forfeiture of rights' looks attractively neat as an account of self-defence, but it has been convincingly criticised by a number of philosophers.[6] It seems to grant too much. Suppose that I can defend myself without killing my attacker, for example by simply running away. Presumably I ought to do that rather than kill him, but if by his aggression he has forfeited his right to life, it would seem to follow that I would have the right to kill him rather than run away. Or suppose that the danger has passed. I have disarmed the attacker. May I now kill

[6] See Thomson, 'Self-Defense and Rights'; Ryan, 'Self-Defense, Pacifism, and the Possibility of Killing'; and Wasserman, 'Justifying Self-Defense'.

him? Surely not, yet if he has forfeited his right to life what objection can there now be to my doing so? The trouble with the 'forfeiture of rights' idea is that it assimilates self-defence too closely to punishment. Some people might indeed think of it in that way: if the attacker is killed, he has met his just deserts. In fact, however, self-defence and punishment are importantly different. Punishment requires settled institutions, publicly fixed laws and penalties and impartial judgement. If I kill an attacker and call it 'punishment', I am 'taking the law into my own hands'. It is therefore neither genuine judicial punishment on the one hand, nor self-defence on the other. (The difference between self-defence and punishment will be important to bear in mind when we return to the case of war.)

Behind the idea of 'forfeiture of rights', and the tendency to assimilate self-defence to punishment, there may nevertheless be a sound point, namely that the moral asymmetry in self-defence consists in the fact of the attacker's *fault*.[7] I think that the best way to formulate this point is in terms of the account of 'responsibility' which I presented in the previous chapter. What is distinctive of self-defence situations is not just that there is a forced choice between lives, but that the attacker is responsible for forcing the choice. That, it may be said, is why, if someone has to be killed, it should be the attacker – because he is the one responsible. I discussed in the previous chapter Gewirth's example of the terrorists who threaten that, if Abrams does not torture his mother to death, they will blow up the city. The example illustrates, I suggested, that what we are responsible for depends in part on what other people are responsible for. That example is in important respects different from the case of self-defence. There, the terrorists' responsibility for creating the situation may make it permissible for Abrams to *refuse to kill an innocent person* even though killing would save other lives. In the self-defence case, the attacker's responsibility for creating the situation may make it permissible for me to *kill the*

---

[7] Various versions of this idea can be found in Montague, 'Self-Defense and Choosing Between Lives', Ryan, 'Self-Defense, Pacifism, and the Possibility of Killing', Wasserman, 'Justifying Self-Defense', and Smart, 'Understanding and Justifying Self-Defense'.

attacker in order to save my own life. But common to both cases is the feature that someone else's responsibility for forcing the choice between lives may affect my responsibility for the outcome, and hence my justification for what I do. It is not that the other person's responsibility simply removes my responsibility. That way of putting it would be objectionable just as the idea of 'forfeiture of rights' was seen to be. It suggests that because the attacker is responsible, 'anything goes' on my part. That is not so. I still have a responsibility to avoid killing him if I possibly can. And if I have to kill him to save myself, I am still in part responsible for his death. It was not my choice that someone should be killed, but it was my choice, albeit a justified choice, that *he* should be the one to be killed. I have had to do something terrible, and if I were to feel remorse at his death this would surely be appropriate. The most that I can say is that in one sense I was forced to do it, and that it is his responsibility in forcing the choice that justifies my action.

This line of thought does seem to me to be worth following. But how far will it take us? There is a range of possible cases to consider. The classic case which would most obviously come to mind would be of the following kind.

Case 1: I am walking along a quiet street. It is closing time. A man tumbles out of a pub, obviously the worse for drink and spoiling for a fight, and comes at me with a knife. We struggle, and it is obvious that he is too strong for me. He stabs me once and makes to do so again. In desperation I grab a brick lying on the ground and bring it down hard on his head – thereby killing him.

The important feature of this case is that the attacker is culpable in the strong sense that he acts with the deliberate intention of killing me. There are, however, lesser degrees of culpability, short of malicious intent, such as recklessness or negligence. Compare the following case.

Case 2: I am a hunter hiding in the bushes and watching for a deer. I realise that another hunter is approaching, and is recklessly firing into the bushes at everything that moves, in the hope of hitting something. There is no way I can warn him of my presence, for if I make any noise or movement he'll shoot immediately. The only way I can stop him shooting me is to shoot him. Would I be justified in doing so?

I doubt whether there is any clear consensus of moral attitudes which we can appeal to in considering this example. The case may come more clearly into focus, however, if we first consider some others. Examples which are offered in the philosophical literature in this area, like case 2 itself, tend to be rather artificial or fantastic, and that fact is not without significance, as I shall suggest in a moment. First, however, let me try to imagine some examples which have as much realism as I can muster.

Case 3: A criminal gang wants to kill me (perhaps I'm a shopkeeper who refuses to pay protection money). Rather than do it themselves, they force one of their other 'clients' to do it. They kidnap his wife and children and tell him that if he wants to see them alive again, he has to assassinate me. Am I justified in killing him in self-defence?

The problem here is that if we want to say that I am forced to kill to defend myself, we also have to acknowledge that he too is being forced to do what he does. If 'responsibility' is the relevant consideration, he is no more responsible for the situation than I am. As it is regularly put in the philosophical literature, he is an 'innocent aggressor', in contrast to the attacker in case 1 and the reckless hunter in case 2.

Case 4: Again, the gang is out to get me. I am hiding from them. A passer-by is about to stumble on my hiding-place, thereby exposing me and making it inevitable that I shall be killed. Only by killing him can I prevent this. Should I kill him?

In this case the passer-by is not responsible for the danger I am in, nor is he even an aggressor. He is however, in the standard terminology, an 'innocent threat'.

Again I doubt whether there is any consensus about what it would be permissible to do in these cases. Some would say that there is a right to kill in self-defence in cases 3 and 4. It is difficult, however, to identify a relevant difference between killing the innocent aggressor or killing the innocent threat in these examples, and killing the potential kidney-donor in my earlier example. It might be said that the man in the next bed whose kidney I need is not a threat, and that is why I cannot kill him, whereas the forced assassin in case 3 and the passer-by in case 4 are both a threat to my life.[8] But what does this amount

---

[8] This is the position which Thomson takes in 'Self-Defense'.

to? In the absence of any culpability on their part, their being a threat to me consists of no more than a causal fact: their behaviour is liable causally to contribute to bringing about my death. They would be responsible for my death only in that limited causal sense. It can however be said of the potential kidney-donor that if he survives, I'll die as a consequence, and thus his death or survival is a causal condition for my survival or death. The only difference seems to be that he is not *doing* anything which will causally lead to my death, whereas it is the *actions* of the innocent aggressor and the innocent threat which play the causal role. I have previously taken the view that in some contexts the distinction between action and inaction can make a moral difference, but I must say that it is difficult to see how the distinction can carry so much weight in these cases, where the actions of the innocent aggressor and the innocent threat are so minimally *theirs*.

I shall consider in a moment one other thing which might be said about these cases, but first I want to look at a further case, where responsibility in a strong sense *is* a relevant feature. 'Lifeboat' examples are popular in the literature. Here is one.[9]

Case 5: The ship has gone down, and there are twenty of us crowded into the lifeboat – too many to offer any reasonable chance of survival. Someone has to be thrown out. One of the twenty is the ship's navigator, who was responsible for the disaster (he was drunk while on duty and failed to spot the iceberg). Since he is the person responsible for our predicament, should he be the one whose life is to be sacrificed for the rest?

Although there is no doubt where responsibility lies in this case, many would see it as importantly different from our classic case 1. Maybe someone has to be thrown out of the lifeboat if anyone is to survive, but to choose the navigator on the grounds that he is responsible for creating the situation would be seen by many as simply vindictive, in contrast to the killing of the attacker in case 1. It looks like a reversion to the idea of punishment rather than self-defence – and again a 'punishment' without the judicial context which would make it a genuine and justifiable one. However badly the navigator has acted, and however

[9] For a similar example see Wasserman, 'Justifying Self-Defense', p. 367.

responsible he may be, that is now in the past, it might be said, nothing can now be done about it, and it should not determine the present decision.[10] This suggests that what justifies killing the attacker in case 1 is not just the fact that the attacker is responsible, but also the immediacy and urgency of the threat.

I suspect that this is reflected in the impatience which many readers tend to feel when they encounter the examples offered by philosophers to illustrate the permissibility of killing in self-defence. Of many such examples it is likely to be said, 'But there is always something else one can do – one doesn't have to kill the attacker.' A standard philosophical response will be, 'But suppose that there *isn't* any alternative.' As a defence of the use of extreme examples in philosophical argument in order to test a thesis, this is fair enough – but I must say that I have some sympathy with the non-philosophical reaction. In most cases where one's life is threatened, there are possible ways of trying to save one's life other than by killing the person who is a threat to it. The cases where this can most plausibly be said not to be so are those, like case 1, where the threat is so immediate that all alternatives are excluded. That is why killing in self-defence is most likely to be justifiable in cases like case 1; and insofar as there is any degree of justification for killing in cases 2, 3 and 4, in contrast to case 5, this will again be because of the immediacy of the threat.

I am led to the conclusion that the two relevant features of self-defence situations, in addition to their involving a 'forced choice', are 'responsibility' and 'immediacy'. Where the two features combine, as in case 1, the justification for killing the attacker is strongest. As the responsibility of the attacker, or of the person posing the threat, diminishes (as in cases 2, 3 and 4), so the justification for killing in self-defence diminishes. And as the immediacy diminishes, so again the justification diminishes (as in case 5).

Given this combination of 'responsibility' and 'immediacy', it can be said that one who kills in self-defence is 'forced' to do so in a fairly strong sense. I have noted that she still, in some

[10] The significance of the difference between present aggression and past aggression is discussed by Wasserman in ibid.

sense, has a choice, but the choice is drastically circumscribed by the attacker's action and by the immediacy of the threat. I am therefore inclined to say that the justification for killing in self-defence belongs more in the realm of *necessity* than in that of *justice*. Recall the point that it would still be appropriate for one who has killed in self-defence to feel great remorse at having done so. The more self-defence is separated from the idea of punishment, and from that of the 'forfeiture of rights', the less scope there is for thinking that, when someone has killed an attacker in self-defence, 'justice has been done'. The more fitting account for the self-defender to give of her action would be 'I had to do it – I couldn't help it.' (These doubts about the appropriateness of the language of 'justice' for self-defence obviously have implications for the idea of a 'just war', and I shall spell out those implications in due course.)

There remain two further questions to consider. First, can the justification for killing in self-defence be extended to include defending things other than one's life? Most people's answer would be, I imagine, to set pretty strict limits to this. Someone might be entitled to kill an attacker who threatens to rape her, or kidnap her, or enslave her, but I doubt whether the justification would be thought to extend much further than this. Note in particular that it is implausible to set up a general and undifferentiated right to kill in defence of one's *liberty*. 'Defending one's liberty' could cover a vast range of possibilities. Kidnapping or enslaving are extreme threats to a person's liberty, but there are many other freedoms which, though certainly desirable, are a great deal more trivial. A farmer who blocks a right of way across his field, and thereby prevents me from enjoying a favourite country walk, may be unjustifiably restricting my freedom, and I may find this intensely annoying, but to shoot him and declare that I am 'defending my freedom' would be absurd. The need to break down the general category of 'defending one's liberty', and to look much more closely at the different kinds of freedom which might be involved, will again be important when we turn to the case of war. The idea of a right to kill in defence of one's *property* is similarly problematic. I suspect that this would be the most contentious area, and some would insist that there is indeed such a right. Whether or not this is so, it would be extremely implausible to cast it very widely. To adapt my previous example, if there is no right of way across the farmer's field, and I am trespassing, he would have no right to shoot me to 'defend his property'.

This sense that there are strict limits to the right of self-defence, and that it cannot be extended very far beyond the right to kill in defence of one's life, is reinforced by the account which I have been giving of self-defence. I have emphasised the idea of a 'forced choice between lives'. In other supposed cases of self-defence, the element of 'forced choice' may indeed be present – I have to choose, say, between killing or losing my property – but it is not a forced choice between lives, and an analogous justification for killing can be sustained only if I am threatened with the loss of something which has a value of the same order as my life. Furthermore, in many of the possible cases to which I have referred, one would be faced with a 'forced choice' in a less strong sense, because the immediacy of the threat would be less. Cases where someone is about to be raped or kidnapped or enslaved are closest to the case of a threat to one's life, because the danger with which the person is threatened is, or may be, similarly final and irreversible. This is much less true of other cases, such as the defence of one's property, where the possibilities of future redress make it much less plausible to suggest that 'there is no alternative' to killing in order to meet the threat. Although, therefore, in all these cases of defending something other than one's life, the feature of the attacker's *responsibility* is present, this is not by itself sufficient to justify killing the attacker if the other relevant features of self-defence are absent.

It could be argued that if an attacker's attempt to restrict my liberty or seize my property is backed by a threat to kill me unless I comply, the case is converted into one of a threat to my life and thus generates a justification for me to kill in self-defence. Consider the following argument.

Suppose that one discovers a burglar in the process of stealing valuable possessions from one's home. Although this is perhaps controversial, most of us believe that it would not be permissible to *kill* the burglar to prevent him taking the possessions; for that would be a disproportionate response to the threat. One is, however, entitled to take certain steps to resist the theft. Suppose, however, that the thief threatens to kill one if one resists. In that case one is permitted to create the conditions of one's own lethal defense. For the thief's threat does not nullify one's right to resist. Indeed, it seems that, as soon as the thief structures the situation in such a way that the attempt to defend one's possessions automatically creates a need for self-defensive killing, one's right to self-defense is immediately activated. One is permitted to kill the thief even without first provoking him to attack by attempting a non-lethal defense of one's possessions.[11]

This argument seems to me to depend on a conflation of the two distinct rights – the right to resist the theft, and the right to defend one's life. The conflation may seem plausible, for if, once I have resisted the theft and the thief tries to kill me, I am justified in killing in self-defence, why should I wait for him to start? If I am justified in killing in self-defence at the second stage, and if I will be put at a disadvantage by waiting till the second stage, and if the second stage will be created by my legitimate exercise of my rights at the first stage, then why not say that I have a right to kill in self-defence at the first stage? The trouble is that this conflation of the two rights obscures the crucial question of whether and to what extent I am faced with a forced choice. The fact is that I am not forced to choose between killing the attacker or being killed. I can avoid both options by sacrificing something else. We therefore have to consider what it is that I would have to sacrifice, and how important it is in comparison with the alternatives. If someone approaches me in the street and asks for money to buy a cup of coffee, and then, when I refuse, whips out a knife and demands the money, it would be absurd to suppose that I am then justified in killing him to defend my property. If I can avoid the choice between his life and mine by parting with 50 pence, then of course I should do so. The choice facing me at that point is not 'his life or mine', it is 'taking his life or parting with 50 pence'. When we are considering whether killing is justified in defence

---

[11] Jeff McMahan, 'Innocence, Self-Defense, and Killing in War', in *Journal of Political Philosophy* vol. 2, no. 2 (July 1994).

of something other than one's life, we cannot avoid the question of *what* is being defended, and whether it is of sufficient importance to justify killing. That remains the case even if the attacker's demand is backed up with a threat to one's life.

The other remaining question is whether the justification for killing in self-defence can be extended to a justification for killing an attacker in order to defend *someone else's* life. The two kinds of justification would seem to stand or fall together; if I am justified in killing to save my life, then surely also someone else is justified in doing the same thing on my behalf. I think that this is basically right, but the relation between the two cases is slightly more complicated than that. In both cases, there is a forced choice between lives in the sense that either the victim or the attacker will have to be killed, and in both cases the attacker is responsible for creating the 'forced choice' situation. To that extent it can plausibly be claimed that a third party, like the victim, has a *right* to kill the attacker in defence of the victim's life. A further question which arises, however, is whether a third party positively *ought* to defend the victim against the attacker, whether indeed the third party has not just a right but also an *obligation* to do so. If I am a bystander the situation is not a 'forced choice' in quite the same sense as it is for the victim; the choice is not forced on *me*. The immediacy of the threat, which creates the necessity for the victim to act, does not impose the same necessity on me. To that extent it might be thought that some further reason is needed why I should *intervene* in a situation which affects someone else. As we saw in the previous chapter, it cannot be automatically assumed that there is always an obligation to help anyone who is in need. However, if there is ever an obligation to aid, there is surely such an obligation in a situation of extreme emergency where someone's life is threatened and I am the person best placed to defend it. A further difference between self-defence and other-defence which might be thought to support the idea of a third-party obligation to assist is this: if my life is threatened, then, although I may have a right to kill the attacker to defend my life, it is up to me whether I choose to exercise the right. It is my life, and therefore, if I choose to sacrifice my life rather than kill the attacker, I am entitled to do so. I have a right but not an obligation to kill in defence of my own life. For a third party it is different; it is not her life that is threatened, and therefore she is not in the same way entitled to sacrifice it. To that extent it may be said that she has an obligation to try to defend me if she can, even though I do not have an obligation to defend myself.

A further complication would be created if she could defend my life only by risking her life. Rather than a forced choice between two lives, we would then have a complex set of relations between the risks to the three lives. I will not try to spell out the complexities, but common sense suggests that someone else's obligation to kill the attacker in order to defend my life is lessened if her doing so would pose a threat to her own life.

My discussion of the right to kill in self-defence has been in some ways inconclusive, but the main conclusion which I do want to draw is that that right is severely circumscribed. The only cases where I think that such a right can unproblematically be recognised are those situations where there is a 'forced choice', the attacker is morally responsible for creating that 'forced choice' situation and the threat has an immediate urgency. Even in such situations the attacker has not forfeited his own right to life, the act of killing him is not a punishment and to that extent it is more appropriately seen not as an act of justice but simply as an inescapable necessity. Though the right to kill in self-defence is not limited to the defence of one's life, it does not extend much beyond that case, and it extends only to cases where what is being defended is of broadly comparable importance. In the light of this discussion let us now turn to the case of war. Can the limited justification for killing in self-defence also provide a justification for killing in war?

DEFENDING THE POLITICAL COMMUNITY

The possibility of such a justification depends on drawing an analogy between an individual's right of self-defence and a political community's right to defend itself. This analogy is explicitly presented by Walzer, and is central to his restatement of 'just war' theory.

Over a long period of time, shared experiences and cooperative activity of many different kinds shape a common life. 'Contract' is a metaphor for a process of association and mutuality, the ongoing character of which the state claims to protect against external encroachment. The protection extends not only to the lives and liberties of individuals but also to their shared life and liberty, the independent community they have made, for which individuals are sometimes sacrificed ... Given a genuine 'contract', it makes sense to say that territorial integrity and political sovereignty can be defended in exactly the same way as individual life and liberty. (*JUW*, p. 54)

Walzer's analogy is carefully crafted. Self-defence, by the individual or the community, is justified as a defence of rights. The most fundamental rights of individuals are the right to life and the right to liberty. The collective analogues of these are the right to territorial integrity and the right to political sovereignty. (Sometimes he speaks of these as the rights of the state, sometimes as the rights of the political community, which it is the state's job to protect.) The right to territorial integrity is the community's right to life, its right to go on existing as a community, defined by its borders. The community can of course survive minor violations of its borders, but if the territory is overrun the community dies. The right to political sovereignty is the community's right to liberty, its right to control its own political life. Internally the community may be markedly authoritarian, but if it is a genuine community whose political life is shaped by its own distinctive shared traditions and shared culture, then it has the right to go on working out its own political destiny in its own way.

Just as the individual right of self-defence entails also the right of other individuals to defend the victim of an attack, so also, according to Walzer, a community's rights of territorial integrity and political sovereignty can be and should be defended by other states. States are themselves members of an international society, defined by the recognition of those rights. Any act of aggression against an individual state is also a crime against the international order, and as such it should be resisted and punished. Notice that Walzer uses the traditional judicial language of 'just war' theory: war against an aggressor is the punishment of a crime. This leads him to a strong conclusion: resistance to aggression is not only morally permissible but also, normally, obligatory. There is a

presumption in favor of military resistance once aggression has begun. Resistance is important so that rights can be maintained and future aggressors deterred. The theory of aggression restates the old doctrine of the just war: it explains when fighting is a crime and when it is permissible, perhaps even morally desirable. The victim of aggression fights in self-defense, but he isn't only defending himself, for aggression is a crime against society as a whole... All resistance is also law enforcement. (*JUW*, p. 59)

This, then, is Walzer's extended analogy between the rights of the individual and the rights of the political community. Can it provide a justification for war as self-defence?

The first thing to be said is that it is, as it stands, *only* an analogy. As such, I do not think it can do the work of justification. The right of individual self-defence, if it justifies anything at all, justifies the killing of the attacker to defend the life of the victim. In attempting to justify a war of self-defence, what we have to justify is, again, *literal* killing, the taking of hundreds, thousands or even millions of human lives. According to the self-defence analogy, however, what are being defended are not literally lives, but their collective analogues, the life (and liberty) of the community.

Suppose we take the analogy seriously and follow it through consistently. This will mean substituting the collective analogue for the individual case throughout the argument. Therefore, just as the defence of the individual's right to life and liberty will justify overriding the attacker's right to life and liberty, so also the defence of the community's rights to territorial integrity and political sovereignty will justify overriding the aggressor community's rights to territorial integrity and political sovereignty. That, however, is not, of course, what we were supposed to be arguing for. We needed a justification for *killing* to defend the community. The analogy, understood strictly as an analogy, cannot provide one.

Suppose, instead, that we go beyond a mere analogy. Individual self-defence is supposed to justify killing the individual attacker. Collective self-defence is supposed to justify killing large numbers of people in the aggressor community. What is being defended would therefore have to be, literally, the lives of people in the victim community. Only something like a defensive war of resistance to genocide could be justified in this way. If we are looking for a direct rather than merely analogical parallel with individual self-defence, the protection of lives on a massive scale would have to be invoked to justify the equally wholesale killing which military resistance entails. I noted in the discussion of individual self-defence that the right of self-defence could be extended to include defence against the threat of other extreme harms such as rape or kidnapping or enslavement (though not just any threat to one's liberty or property). Certainly, military aggression does sometimes take the form of the threat of mass enslavement or other such atrocities, and the individual right to kill in self-defence could then be directly invoked, but this is different from a right of military resistance to invasion as such.

It might be said that the reality is likely to be somewhere between these two extremes, combining elements of both literal and analogical self-defence. The aggressors may not be embarked on a war of genocide, but in invading a country and violating its territorial integrity they are also engaged in attacking and killing its defenders, and therefore, it may be said, the defenders are justified in killing in return in order to defend their country. However, this attempt at a justification would beg the question. In some cases the aggressors will kill only because they are resisted. If there were no resistance, they could invade without having to take any lives. It is precisely this resistance that has to be justified. As I argued in discussing individual self-defence, the fact that unjust demands are backed up by lethal threats does not by itself justify killing in response; it depends on the importance of what is defended. In other cases the aggressors may be an undisciplined army, running amok and pillaging and looting. Or the invasion may be a product of long-standing ethnic rivalries, and the invaders may be keen to settle old scores. Or it may be an attempt to impose a new political regime, and the invaders may see it as their task to round up political opponents for summary execution or interrogation and torture. In all such cases it may be said that the defenders have a right to kill in self-defence. But the collective analogy, the appeal to rights of territorial integrity and political sovereignty, plays no role here. The appeal is to individuals' rights of self-defence (albeit on a large scale), and the moral questions are then whether the right to kill in defence of one's life can be extended to killing in defence of one's property, or to protect oneself against unjust imprisonment and torture, or whatever.

I suggest that if ideas of territorial integrity and political sovereignty are to play a significant role in the moral argument, we would have to move beyond the self-defence analogy. What would have to be shown is that the life of a political community is itself, *in its own right*, something worth defending, and indeed so valuable as to justify killing in its defence. That, I suspect, is what Walzer would, in the end, want to say, and the parallel with individuals' rights to life and liberty would then become relatively incidental. In the passage from which I have already quoted, Walzer says:

> The moral standing of any particular state depends upon the reality of the common life it protects and the extent to which the sacrifices required by that protection are willingly accepted and thought worthwhile. If no common life exists, or if the state doesn't defend the common life that does exist, its own defense may have no moral justification. (*JUW*, p. 54)

Part of what is being said here is, I think, that the citizens' willingness to sacrifice their own lives for the life of the community is itself a measure of the value and importance which they attach to it, and an indication that they are justified in defending it. But what has to be shown is, of course, not just that the political community is worth dying for, but that it is worth killing for. Walzer and others might say that the one follows from the other: if the common life is felt by its citizens to be worth dying for, that itself shows that it is of sufficiently great value to justify them in killing in defence of it. This might do as a start. Negatively, at least, if the life of the community is not worth dying for, it could hardly be worth killing for. The stronger positive claim, however, does not automatically follow. Further argument is needed. I want now to consider what form that argument might take, and whether it is good enough. Why does the life of a political community matter, and does it matter enough to justify killing in its defence?

It will be as well to note at the start just how much that argument would have to do. I have tried to establish in previous chapters the central place occupied in our moral thinking by the idea of respect for life. The wrongness of taking human life may not be an absolute principle, but it is one which can only very rarely and exceptionally be overridden. Perhaps it can be overridden in cases of literal self-defence, but any other case would have to be of the same order. So, although we have set aside the appeal to a formal analogy between individual and collective rights to life, the 'just war' theorist would have to show that the life of a political community has a value comparable to that of human life itself, and that a threat to the one is of the same magnitude as a threat to the other, in order to override the very strong principle of the wrongness of killing.

Next we have to note an obvious dissimilarity between the two cases. I have referred previously to the idea of the uniqueness and irreplaceability of an individual human life. There is truth in the cliché of the finality of death: once you're dead, you're dead, and nothing further can then compensate for the loss. This is why a threat to one's life is such as to justify exceptional measures. A threat to the life of a political community is not like that. If a country is invaded and conquered, this may in some sense spell the 'death' of the community, but such a death does not have the same 'all or nothing' character.[12] In extreme cases the conquering forces may set out to obliterate the culture of the conquered. Even then the community's traditions and way of life may be revived, perhaps in exile. Or they may go underground, preserved in secret. What is more likely is that the indigenous community's political, social and cultural life will persist after the conquest,

---

[12] In this respect it is different also from the death of the species – the threat posed by nuclear war, which Jonathan Schell calls 'the second death' in his book *The Fate of the Earth* (London, 1982).

but in an attenuated form. Political life in particular may be severely restricted, people may engage in it at great risk to themselves, but there remains the hope of a future revival and flourishing. As we shall see, I certainly do not want to suggest that these things do not matter. Nevertheless, the conquest of a community is in these ways importantly different from the death of a person, and to that extent killing in defence of the community will be that much harder to justify.

One other initial caveat is necessary. There is no doubt that an attachment to the life of the political community can assume an enormous importance for its members. People do identify fiercely with national and other communities; the very history of warfare over the centuries is testimony enough to that. We also know, however, that such loyalties can take distorted and inauthentic forms. Notoriously, the historical record provides numerous examples of monarchs, dictators, revolutionary leaders and governments facing re-election who deliberately create an external threat in order to counter internal divisions and cement the loyalty of their subjects. The relation between communal loyalty and military defence is then reversed, and the latter gives rise to the former instead of vice versa. Political leaders can create an enemy. They can deliberately provoke a conflict with another country, declare that the community is under threat, and exploit their subjects' fear and ignorance in order to generate a communal loyalty.

Admittedly such loyalties cannot be created out of nothing. They can be created only if, in some way, they answer to real psychological needs. There are, however, both authentic and inauthentic ways of meeting such needs. There is, in particular, the phenomenon which psychologists call 'bonding by exclusion' and existentialists call the need for 'the Other'. People often 'need' an enemy. The underlying need is for confirmation of one's identity, and this need can in part be satisfied by the sense of security which comes from belonging to a group. The strongest confirmation of this belonging comes from the sharing of a common enemy. 'We' are defined in opposition to 'them'. The enmity, however, may well be spurious. There may well be no objective grounds for hostility; the hostility may be imagined simply because it meets the need for an enemy. And that need arises only because the need for a sense of identity is not met in more genuine ways, through a positive sense of achievement in the active pursuit of a common purpose. This kind of communal loyalty, then, I call 'inauthentic'; it rests on illusion, rather than on any real participation in and appreciation of a common life.

Our task, then, is to consider what is authentic in the value attached to the life of a community, and in particular of a national community. It will be authentic only if it is not undermined by a true understanding of its nature. Some of our desires and attitudes are ones which we have only because we are mistaken about the real nature of our beliefs and motivations; other desires and attitudes are not like that. The question is how far communal loyalties come into the latter category. And if we can make progress in answering that question, we shall be in a better position to estimate how important the life of a political community is, and whether it can justify war and killing in its defence.

THE LIFE OF A POLITICAL COMMUNITY

We have seen that Walzer sometimes uses the language of the 'social contract' to describe people's attachment to an authentic communal life. 'Contract,' he says, 'is a metaphor for a process of association and mutuality, the ongoing character of which the state claims to protect against external encroachment' (p. 54). It is, however, a very limited metaphor, and I think Walzer would acknowledge that it does not properly capture the status which he thinks that a community has for its citizens. The 'social contract' theory in its classic form sees the community as an instrumental good, something which its members accept as a means to the protection of their individual lives.[13] The 'state of nature' would be replete with disadvantages. In the absence of social restrictions, each individual

---

[13] Classic versions of 'social contract' theory are Thomas Hobbes, *Leviathan* (1651), John Locke, *Second Treatise of Civil Government* (1690) and Jean-Jacques Rousseau, *The Social Contract* (1762).

would be constantly prey to the threats posed by others, and would live in perpetual fear and distrust; therefore it is in each individual's interests to agree to accept such restrictions. Implicit in this account is the assumption that the things worth living for, and therefore needing to be protected by the social contract, would already be identifiable in the state of nature, prior to any acceptance of community membership.

The contract theory makes it difficult to see how people could ever rationally regard their loyalty to a community as something worth sacrificing their lives for. If the point of participating in communal life is simply to protect one's own individual life, then the only acceptable sacrifices would be ones which furthered that good. In that case it would seem to be irrational to give up one's own life in order to protect the communal life. The most that could be said is this: that people's individual lives can be protected only if they enter into membership of the community and accept the obligations which it imposes, and that these obligations must include an obligation to give one's life in defence of the community if necessary, for only if everyone accepts the possibility of having to do this can the community protect its members. The risk that you may have to give your own life is the price that you pay for the probability that your life will be protected. In that case, however, the thought of someone who, as it turned out, had to sacrifice his or her life for the community could not be 'This is something worth dying for' but only 'It's the luck of the draw.' And it is debatable whether contract theory can really treat even that thought as rational. Given the assumptions of the theory, it could be argued that the only rational response for the individual in that situation would be 'This is where my allegiance ends. I agreed to accept the obligations in order to protect my own life, but if those obligations now require me to sacrifice my life, there is no good reason why I should keep the agreement.'

To defend a position such as Walzer's, then, we should, as I think Walzer does, move beyond contract theory to an alternative perspective, that of what has been called the 'communitarian' tradition. With philosophers such as Aristotle and Hegel, we should have to say that 'a human being is a political (social) animal'.[14] One's membership of a community enters into, and is partly constitutive of, one's identity as an individual. The things that are worth living for include things which one can recognise and value only as a member of a community, and to lose them would be to lose part of what makes one the person one is. As I argued in the first chapter (pp. 14–19), only by means of a shared language can we give meaning to our experience, creating a picture of the world and of what is of value in it. So in acquiring the language of a community we acquire values, we acquire a way of thinking about our lives and what is important in them. To identify ourselves with those values is to identify ourselves with the linguistic community from which we derive them and with which we share them. Equally important for our sense of identity are our various particular relationships and allegiances. Each of us exists within a network of relations to parents and children, to friends, colleagues, and neighbours, to social groups and political and cultural movements, and these relationships make up the distinctive texture of one's life and make it a life worth living. Even the hermit, or the lone embattled artist or thinker, can do what he or she is doing only within a religious or cultural tradition.

All of this is true and important, and it repeats things that I have maintained previously in this book, but it does not yet give the 'just war' theorists what they need. They have to assert the importance not only of communal allegiances in general, but of one particular kind of community: the nation, a community defined by its territorial boundaries. The kind of self-defence which they are concerned to justify is the defence of borders, and they have to show that the community identified by its borders is of such a kind as to justify killing in its defence. Can this be done?

A first suggestion might be that, since the nation is defined by its territory, the inhabitants' allegiance to the nation grows out of an attachment to the land itself, the 'homeland'. It is, perhaps, a love of place which makes people attach an

---

[14] Aristotle, *Politics*, I.2.

importance to the nation. That, however, cannot be the whole story, for it immediately raises the question: which place? Where are the borders to be drawn? What kind of place constitutes the territory of a nation? Not just any location will do, as the following exchange from James Joyce's *Ulysses* demonstrates:

– But do you know what a nation means? says John Wyse.
– Yes, says Bloom.
– What is it? says John Wyse.
– A nation? says Bloom. A nation is the same people living in the same place.
– By God, then, says Ned, if that's so I'm a nation for I'm living in the same place for the past five years.[15]

At this point we might combine the idea of territory with the idea, already mentioned, of the importance of language. Perhaps what makes a particular geographical area the territory of a nation is its being the land of a people who are united by a shared language. The stress on language is to be found in the classic theorists of nationality such as Herder. Language assumes this importance for reasons which we have previously noted. A language is the repository of shared ideas and a shared way of apprehending the world. Each language has its own literature, embracing not only 'high' culture but also popular literature of all kinds. The possessors of a language thereby inherit a cultural tradition which shapes their thoughts and feelings. Finally, the very fact of being able to communicate is a bonding mechanism. People who can understand one another are thereby enabled to empathise with one another and to feel united, people who do not share that understanding feel excluded. This is negatively attested to by that deep sense of alienation which will be recognised by anyone who has ever been in a country where they knew nothing of the language.

I want first to acknowledge the power of these two ideas, of the importance of shared territory and the importance of shared language. It is undeniable that people can feel a strong sense of attachment to a place. This is to be distinguished from the feeling of enjoyment or appreciation of a beautiful or impressive

---

[15] James Joyce, *Ulysses* (London, 1960), p. 430.

landscape, for such an appreciation is something which anyone can feel about any landscape, it is not specifically a response to a place which is *one's own*. The English can enjoy the Alps, visiting Americans can admire the Cotswolds and so on. What is quite different from this is the sense of a particular landscape as one's home, as a familiar environment imbued with associations which make it one's own, the place where one belongs. When people strive to defend their country, such feelings may well be in play.

However, though this is part of what goes into the making of attachment to a country, there is no reason why the locality which one feels to be 'home' should coincide with the locality enclosed by the boundaries of a nation-state. It is quite likely to be much more localised. Such feelings of 'attachment to place' are at least as likely to be regional attachments, produced by a relatively small area with a distinctive 'feel' and character of its own, such as Wessex or the Lake District, the Downs or the Fen country. Even more particularised, and equally typical, would be one's attachment to the particular town or village in which one was brought up, whose buildings and streets are intensely familiar and are intimately associated with events and phases of one's life. It may be that these various more particularised attachments may combine into a sense of attachment to the distinctive natural and human environment of a whole country. Thus the traveller returning from abroad may recognise again the particular 'feel' of England, the scale of the landscape, the characteristic interrelation of town and village and country. Still, this does not furnish any special and unique status for 'the nation' in contrast to narrower or wider localities. There is no reason why loyalty to a nation, insofar as it is built on attachment to a place, should be any greater than loyalty to other localities.

Turning now to the case of language, we find also that the match between languages and nations is highly imperfect. This is most blatantly true of those nations which are ex-colonies. The territorial boundaries of many of the countries of Africa, for instance, are simply the arbitrary creations of colonisers, lines drawn on a map, which do not coincide at all with the linguistic divisions. An earlier generation of ex-colonies, the countries of Latin America, are with the exception of Brazil all Spanish-speaking and therefore not differentiated by language. But even among the older-established nations, such as those of Europe, there are polyglot nations and there are languages shared by different nations. Switzerland, to take but one example, has three languages, one of which is shared with Germany (now one nation again after having been two) and with Austria. Therefore, though the bonds created by the sharing of a language may be important, they do not coincide with loyalty to a nation.

It might be counter-argued that where the territory of a language fails to coincide with the territory of a nation, this simply shows that the national borders are in the wrong place. 'Real' nations, it might be said, are linguistically homogeneous, and if some of the existing 'nations' do not have one distinctive language, they cannot after all be real nations. Perhaps Belgium is really just a bit of France and a bit of the Netherlands cobbled together. Perhaps Wales is not really a part of the United Kingdom but a separate nation, since it possesses its own language. Certainly this is an influential line of thought, which has inspired various bids for nationhood. It is, however, a line which is doomed to impracticality, for the fact is that languages and nations could never properly coincide. Languages cannot possibly have the precise boundaries which a nation has to have. Where are the territorial boundaries of the Wales which is defined by the Welsh language? We should have to settle on a fuzzy boundary vaguely separating rural north and mid-Wales from the industrial south, and since many Welsh-speakers are fully bilingual, the boundary would also have to go through the middle of their heads.

The relation between a language and a culture is also highly imprecise. As I have noted, certain forms of cultural tradition are closely tied to a language, and this is most obviously true of literary traditions. There is a tradition of English literature, and people whose literary experience is primarily within the English language could be said to inherit, with that tradition, a range of attitudes and sensibilities which may contribute importantly to their sense of their cultural identity. Even in the case of literature, however, there are problems. Are 'the English novel' and 'the American novel' two separate traditions, or one? Is James Joyce an 'English' novelist? What about the Anglophone literatures of former British colonies? These are familiar conundrums, and for the literary theorist they may not in the end greatly matter, but they are fatal to the case for equating national identity with cultural identity. When we move beyond literature the case becomes even weaker. Other artistic forms, such as music and the visual arts, may include national schools (the Italian renaissance, French impressionism, the various 'national' composers of the late nineteenth and twentieth centuries) but they have also always been resolutely inter-national. And when it comes to 'culture' in the wider sense, the equation with nationality is even less tenable. I have argued in chapter 1 (pp. 8–19) for the importance of language as the repository of moral criteria. This certainly does not mean, however, that the members of a nation or even the speakers of a common language will typically share the same practical moral attitudes. The moral criteria contained within a language are always variously interpreted and applied. Thus people who in one sense share the same moral language can use it as much to disagree as to agree with one another, disputing for instance whether abortion is or is not 'murder', or whether inequalities of wealth are or are not 'unjust'. Within any nation there will always be conflicting moral views about sexuality, or the taking of life, or the proper balance between freedom and restraint. Certainly in the modern world the cultural diversity within nations is immediately visible, not only in people's moral attitudes but in other aspects of their way of life. Every nation contains different sub-cultures, and the precise mix is constantly changing in consequence of modern patterns of immigration and labour mobility. Some would say, of course, that this is itself objectionable – that the emergence of new sub-cultures in Britain, for instance, formed by communities with West Indian or Asian origins, constitutes some kind of disruption of the 'unity' of the 'nation'. This is nonsense. There never was a unified British culture. The newer kinds of diversity have merely replaced older kinds, regional diversities, for instance, which have been eroded by modern forms of mass communication. In short, the identity of a nation cannot be constituted by its culture.

My general point is, then, that though attachments to a place, and to a language and a culture, are important elements in people's identity, they cannot justify any ethically privileged status for the defence of territorial boundaries. Nobody would suggest that people should fight and kill for the sake of the Cotswolds or the Fen country, however deep their attachments to those localities; why, then, should they fight and kill for Britain? It is an important part of my sense of who I am that I speak and think in English, the language of Shakespeare and the Authorised Version, but this linguistic and cultural inheritance is one which I share with the inhabitants of other countries including most of North America; why should it justify me in fighting and killing to maintain the existing territorial boundaries of Britain? Attachments to place and to language and culture might reinforce people's sense of national identity, but they cannot be primarily constitutive of it. If we could identify some more fundamental reason why people should and do set very great value on their membership of a nation, we could then recognise how this could be given greater emotional force by their affection for the land, the language and the culture of their nation. But we have not yet done so. We have not yet, therefore, found any satisfactory reason to justify the taking of life in defence of a nation.

POLITICAL SOVEREIGNTY

We saw that Walzer identifies two rights of political communities, the right to territorial integrity and the right to political sovereignty. Communities are said to be justified in defending themselves insofar as they are defending these rights. My argument so far has emphasised the former of the two, and I have been suggesting that the territorial borders of nations do not necessarily demarcate the kinds of shared life which are of value. At this point we should perhaps turn from territorial integrity to political sovereignty. The two cannot be entirely separated, for the kind of self-defence which we are discussing is the defence of borders, but perhaps what is important about borders is simply that they protect political sovereignty. Perhaps we just have to accept that the location of the borders is relatively arbitrary, but wherever they are, it may be said, they make possible the existence of a self-governing community, and this is what ought to be defended. Let us look further at this idea.

The idea of sovereignty is essentially the idea of an ultimate authority. In the modern political world, nation-states are sovereign, that is, they are not bound by any higher authority. This may not last; the European Community already has certain powers over its member countries, and in due course all countries might become subject to the authority of, say, a strengthened United Nations, but this is only to say that nation-states may yield the sovereignty which has until now been theirs. Internally, the sovereignty of the nation-state means that all the other bodies within it are ultimately bound by its authority. There may be innumerable other sources of authority, in workplaces and in voluntary organisations and in local or regional governments, but all of these are in turn subject to the government of the sovereign nation-state.

One aspect of political sovereignty is that the sovereign authority has a monopoly on the use of force. This suggests one possible way of appealing to the idea of political sovereignty within 'just war' theory. It is not Walzer's argument, which I will turn to shortly, but it is an argument worth considering. Its starting-point is the recognition that if everyone had the right to use force and to injure or kill in pursuit of their own interests, there would be chaos. Therefore, it is argued, the right has to be confined to those entrusted with the job of using the threat of force to keep the peace within their societies and, as far as possible, between societies. This is why the ruling authorities of nation-states have a monopoly on the use of force, and why it is therefore permissible to fight and kill on behalf of the nation-state but not as an individual or on behalf of any other social group.

Note that this argument does not have to provide any special reason why it has to be the nation-state, rather than any other body, that exercises the monopoly on the use of force. The argument is only that, to make social life tolerable, that monopoly has to be located somewhere, and for historical reasons the sovereign authority which exercises that monopoly in the modern world happens to be the nation-state.

The important feature of the argument is the linking of *internal* force and *external* force. The idea is that if the sovereign authority legitimately exercises force within the society to maintain order, then it is also legitimate for it to exercise force externally, against other states, in order to maintain the international order. It is, however, this merging of internal and external force that needs to be questioned. The legitimacy of the second does not follow from the legitimacy of the first. On the contrary, we could as well draw the opposite conclusion. If the monopolisation of internal force is needed to prevent anarchy, should there not likewise be an international authority, with a monopoly of force at the global level, to prevent the anarchy of individual states using force against one another? The most that the argument from internal force to external force can amount to is a negative argument. There is, it could be claimed, a special reason why individuals and groups within the nation-state should not use force in their dealings with one another, namely that this is incompatible with the monopolisation of force by the nation-state to keep the peace (assuming that it does so). The negative argument would then be that there is no corresponding special objection to the external use of force by the state. Nation-states exercising sovereignty are not beholden to any higher authority, and therefore their use of force externally is not a flouting of any such authority. From this, however, it does not follow that it is *right* for nation-states to use force in their dealings with one another; it is merely that one special objection to the use of force does not apply to them.

Sovereignty justifies the internal use of force insofar as this preserves a civil order, the rule of law, incorporating impartial judicial processes and institutions of political representation, and these institutions themselves set strict limits on the use of force even by the sovereign authority. It may be expedient for nation-states to threaten military resistance against one another in order to preserve whatever international peace they enjoy, but that is not the argument we are considering. Their possession of *sovereignty* gives them no *right* to do this. The right to use force at the international level could be exercised only by an international authority possessing a sovereignty over individual nations which was genuinely parallel to the sovereignty exercised by the nation-state internally.

SOVEREIGNTY AND COMMUNAL SELF-DETERMINATION

I have said that the way in which Walzer's argument appeals to the idea of political sovereignty is different, and I want now to look at his position. For Walzer the important feature of political sovereignty is not the formal entitlement of the sovereign authority to use force, but the right of the political community to work out its own destiny without outside interference. What needs to be protected is the authenticity of the political process. Its outcome should reflect the configuration of forces within the community, and outsiders should not tip the scales. That is why wars of intervention cannot normally be justified, and it is the justification for wars of self-defence to protect the community against invasion and uphold its right of self-determination.

Walzer is attempting to tread a fine line here. On the one hand, he says that the community to be defended must be a genuine community. This is why he uses the language of 'contract'. To say that a community rests on a genuine contract is to say that there is a genuine common life, a 'process of association and mutuality' (*JUW*, p. 54). On the other hand, Walzer does not want to specify particular kinds of political institutions as the only ones worth defending. It is up to each community to shape its own institutions in the light of its accumulated historical experience and its inherited culture and traditions. That, I take it, is what political sovereignty amounts to for Walzer. In particular, he wants to resist the idea that the only communities possessing the rights of self-determination and self-defence are those with liberal-democratic institutions, or those which guarantee the rights of individuals. To say this would be to invite the response that, if communities lack such institutions or violate individual rights, outside military intervention should be permissible to create the institutions and protect the rights. Walzer argues against this. He maintains that, with certain very limited and extreme exceptions, wars of intervention are not permissible.[16] The only normal justification for war is to defend borders against aggression, so that within those borders communities can carry on their own political life, whatever form it may take, and thereby exercise their right to political sovereignty.[17]

I am not convinced that Walzer can establish an identifiable position in this middle ground, maintaining both that there has to be a real common life and that it does not have to take any particular institutional form in order to create the right of self-defence. The difficulty is apparent in two examples which he discusses, one real and one imaginary, in an article written as a reply to critics.[18] The first example, put to him by David Luban, is that of the Sandinista revolution against the Somoza regime in Nicaragua. In August–September 1978 the Sandinistas led an insurrection, which received widespread popular support,

---

[16] The exceptions are: (i) cases of secession, where intervention across borders is to help what is really a separate political community struggling for independence; (ii) counter-intervention in a civil war, to redress the balance if a foreign power has already intervened on one side; (iii) humanitarian intervention, 'when the violation of human rights within a set of boundaries is so terrible that it makes talk of community or self-determination ... seem cynical and irrelevant, that is, in cases of enslavement or massacre' (p. 90). See *JUW*, ch. 6.

[17] Walzer does not, as far as I am aware, ever clearly define the term by saying what the difference is between territorial integrity and political sovereignty. They tend to be merged into a hybrid 'right to territorial-integrity-and-political-sovereignty'. Cf. *JUW*, p. 89: 'the legal doctrine of sovereignty ... defines the liberty of states as their independence from foreign control and coercion ... The recognition of sovereignty is the only way we have of establishing an arena within which freedom can be fought for and (sometimes) won. It is this arena and the activities that go on within it that we want to protect, and we protect them, much as we protect individual integrity, by marking out boundaries that cannot be crossed, rights that cannot be violated.' Sometimes the hybrid right receives the label 'communal integrity'.

[18] Michael Walzer, 'The Moral Standing of States: A Response to Four Critics' (hereafter MSS), in *International Ethics*, ed. C. R. Beitz, M. Cohen, T. Scanlon and A. J. Simmons (Princeton, 1985). The article originally appeared in *Philosophy and Public Affairs* vol. 9 (1980).

especially in the form of strikes, but was brutally put down by the National Guard. The Sandinistas regrouped, negotiated an alliance with other anti-Somoza forces, and successfully over-threw the Somoza regime in July 1979. Luban argues that the 1978 insurrection demonstrated that the government enjoyed 'neither consent nor legitimacy'. An illegitimate state, he says, cannot possess sovereign rights, and this, he thinks, undermines the moral position of those other states which 'continued to recognize the sovereignty of the Somoza regime and thus committed themselves to a policy of non-intervention in the state's war against its nation' (p. 206). Walzer replies:

> had there been a foreign intervention at the time of the first campaign, aimed at rescuing the rebels from defeat, as Luban believes there should have been, this internal process of bargaining and commitment [with other opposition forces] would have been cut short. And then the character of the new regime would have been determined by the intervening state together with whatever faction of rebels it chose to support. It is my claim that such an intervention would have violated the right of Nicaraguans as a group to shape their own political institutions and the right of individual Nicaraguans to live under institutions so shaped. (MSS, pp. 227–8)

That right, he says, is not, as his critics would have it, a worthless right to live in 'a civil society of almost any sort'; it is 'the right to live in a civil society of a Nicaraguan sort'.

A similar phrase recurs in Walzer's imaginary example. He asks us to imagine 'a country called Algeria' in which a revolutionary movement comes to power. Though initially committed to the establishment of democracy and social justice, it creates

> a military dictatorship and a religious 'republic', without civil and political liberties, and brutally repressive, not only because a new political elite has established itself and resists all challenges but also because women have been returned to their traditional religious subordination to patriarchal authority. It is clear, however, that this regime (in contrast to the one the revolutionaries originally had in mind) has deep roots in Algerian history and draws importantly upon Algerian political and religious culture. It is not a democratic regime; its popularity has never been tested in a democratic way; but there can be no doubt that it is an Algerian regime. (MSS, p. 233)

Walzer again claims that it would be wrong for another country to intervene in 'Algerian' politics in support of democratic institutions and civil liberties.

It can hardly be the case that the relevant consideration in these two examples is simply that the society or the regime has a distinctively national character, that it is 'Nicaraguan' or 'Algerian'. Consider another example. Haiti was for many years under the dictatorship of the infamous Duvalier family. Their power rested almost entirely on the secret police, the Tontons Macoutes, and the island became a by-word for unrestrained brutality. Democratic elections have subsequently been held, but the democratically elected president has been ousted by the military, who are closely linked to the old regime. The outcome of the struggle between the military and the democratic forces is, at the time of writing, still in the balance. If the military win, there is no doubt that their regime will be characteristically 'Haitian', one which can most pointedly be said to have roots in Haitian history and tradition. I do not see that this would be any evidence whatever for the existence of a real 'common life', or for the ability of the Haitian people to shape their own political institutions. Why should such a regime enjoy any right of self-defence? Walzer's position seems to me to depend, in the end, on the optimistic assumption that provided secure borders exclude outside intervention there will be an authentic political culture and an authentic process of political self-determination. For that to be the case, more is needed than simply that the society or the regime should have distinctively national characteristics. I agree with Walzer that we should not automatically equate self-determination and a common political life with the existence of democratic electoral processes, but at least we would have to be talking about a society where the political authorities enjoyed widespread support and where the political institutions were rooted in a genuinely shared popular culture. A relevant example might be that of Iran under the domination of the Ayatollah Khomeini in the period after the 1979 revolution, a country with many of the features of Walzer's 'Algeria', ruled by a repressive regime which disregarded the civil rights of individuals and minority groups, but which did seem to enjoy genuine popular support and to be rooted in a shared religious culture.

The conclusion which I want to draw from all this is that, in deciding whether a community ought to be defended, we cannot escape the need to make *qualitative* judgements about its cultural and political life. We cannot short-cut the argument by appealing to the concept of political sovereignty.

Nations do not have an automatic right to be defended. I agreed, earlier, that membership of certain kinds of community may be of very great importance to people. We may identify with a community through sharing its language, through inheriting its culture, and in virtue of our attachment to a place. A threat to this communal life may be experienced as a threat to our very identity, a threat to something which is as precious to us as life itself. Nevertheless it is not necessarily threatened or destroyed by an invasion of a nation's territory, and it is not necessarily protected by the defence of the nation's borders. Likewise, underlying the talk of 'political sovereignty' is the truth that authentic political processes, whereby people actively shape their lives and institutions, may be of very great value; but they too are not necessarily protected by keeping a nation immune from outside intervention. The possible justification for war has to be a matter of judgements about how important these things are, how they are threatened and how they can be secured or defended in a particular case, and whether they are of sufficiently great value to override the very strong moral presumption against the destruction of human lives. The judgement is in principle of the same kind, whether the possible military struggle that is being contemplated is against an external or an internal enemy. Which way the decision should go is of course the great moral dilemma, but it cannot be resolved by invoking rights to territorial integrity and political sovereignty.

Walzer's critics have tended to claim that his conception of just war is too restrictive: it does not make sufficient allowance for other kinds of war, in addition to wars of defence against aggression, which might be justified. My own criticism is that it is too permissive: he has not successfully shown even that wars of defence against aggression will be justified, either in particular cases or in general. I agree with him, against some of his critics, that it would be extremely difficult to justify wars of intervention. However, because he wants to tie this to a general right of political sovereignty, he is led to overstate the case against intervention with some dubious empirical claims, as though to suggest that the political life of a national community ought to be a self-contained and insulated process on which outsiders can never intrude. To counter the view that governments may lack legitimacy, and hence have no standing in international society, no right of self-defence or immunity to intervention, Walzer makes the following assertions:

> The state is constituted by the union of people and government, and it is the state that claims against all other states the twin rights of territorial integrity and political sovereignty. Foreigners are in no position to deny the reality of that union, or rather, they are in no position to attempt anything more than speculative denials. They don't know enough about its history, and they have no direct experience, and can form no concrete judgements, of the conflicts and harmonies, the historical choices and cultural affinities, the loyalties and resentments, that underlie it.[19]

This is sometimes true, but it depends very much on the particular case.[20] I do not see why, in at least some cases, outsiders should not be able to build up a reasonably accurate and objective picture of the condition of a society and the relation between its government and its people. They may draw on the accounts of eye-witnesses, of reporters, perhaps, and of exiles, and the various political movements in the country, and though all these accounts may be slanted one learns how to assess evidence and whom to trust, as one has to even in one's knowledge of one's own country. Sometimes indeed outsiders may have a more balanced overall picture than insiders, if the latter are confined to a limited perspective, or their knowledge

---

[19] MSS, p. 220. Cf. p. 229: 'In most civil wars, it just isn't possible to determine whether the government or the rebels (or which faction among the rebels) has majority support.'

[20] One case in which it was true was that of the American involvement in Vietnam from 1954 to 1973. This may well be a case which Walzer has in mind; his *Just and Unjust Wars* was in large part prompted by debates about the legitimacy of the United States' involvement in the Vietnam War.

is affected by censorship or by wishful thinking. (One sometimes had the impression, for instance, that some white South Africans, who had never moved outside their own area, who had never seen the townships, who read a censored press and believed that 'our blacks are perfectly happy', were the people least well-informed about the condition of their own country under apartheid.) On the basis of such knowledge, outsiders will regularly and rightly engage in various kinds of intervention, organising economic boycotts or pressing for economic sanctions, mounting campaigns of protest or solidarity. All this is of course intended to influence the outcome of the political process within the country, that is to say, the interveners are not content for the process to be entirely shaped by internal forces. I can see no objection to such intervention; I do not think that Walzer has provided any convincing objection to it, and I am not sure whether he has intended to. What is not justifiable is military intervention, and it is objectionable not because it is *intervention* but because it is *military* intervention. The case against it is that it is bound to be coercive, that one cannot create a free society by means of coercion, and that the likely product of military interference is internal oppression. A free society can be created only as people acquire, over time, habits of self-organisation and build up the institutions with which they take control over their own lives. As Walzer himself says, agreeing with Mill and with Marx, 'the (internal) freedom of a political community can be won only by the members of that community' (*JUW*, p. 88). Outsiders, I would add, can help them, and that is why some kinds of intervention are acceptable, but military intervention is not.

It may now seem that the practical implications of my position are not so very different from Walzer's. I have agreed with his rejection of wars of intervention. I have said that military interventions, even if well intentioned, are likely to turn into internal oppression. It seems to follow that if armed resistance to internal oppression is ever justified, then armed resistance to invasion is equally justifiable, for why not resist invasion immediately, before it ever becomes internal oppression? Why not stop it at the borders? Without invoking rights to territorial integrity and political sovereignty, it would seem that we still have a good case for resisting invasion and defending borders.

The important word in that paragraph remains the 'if'. *If* armed resistance to internal oppression is justified, armed resistance to invasion is also likely to be justifiable. It remains an open question whether armed resistance is ever justified at all, in either case. Given the very strong moral presumption against it, we still have to consider how if at all that presumption could be overridden, and that means also looking at the possibility of other kinds of resistance. But even if my practical conclusions were in the end to be not all that different from Walzer's, they are importantly different from a great deal of contemporary received wisdom, especially the received wisdom of those in power. Not surprisingly, governments tend to be very keen on the idea of political sovereignty. They tend to assume that they have an automatic right of military resistance to any violation of national sovereignty, and, again unsurprisingly, they tend to regard armed resistance to internal oppression as much less justifiable. I want to conclude this chapter with a pair of examples which show how my argument runs directly counter to that received wisdom.

TWO EXAMPLES

On 2 April 1982 Argentine forces invaded the Falkland Islands, a British territory in the South Atlantic which the Argentinians claimed had been wrongly taken from them in 1833. The invasion was denounced by the British government as an act of aggression and a violation of sovereignty. Invoking rights of self-determination and self-defence, the government dispatched a naval task force to recover the Islands. The ensuing war re-established British sovereignty in the Islands, at the cost of the lives of 255 Britons and 652 Argentinians.

It has been claimed that it would have been possible to safeguard the way of life of the Falkland Islanders without a war. They could have retained their cultural and linguistic affinities with Britain, and political arrangements enabling them to continue running their own affairs. Not only could this have been compatible with the Argentinian government's intentions, it could also have been guaranteed by the Peruvian peace plan, which was close to being accepted until it was aborted (some say deliberately) by the British sinking of the Argentinian cruiser *General Belgrano*. Whether or not this was possible, however, was not the central question for the British government. Its principal reason for fighting was not for the sake of preserving a way of life, but for the sake of formal sovereignty.

I want to compare the British decision to go to war to recapture the Falkland Islands with the decision of the African National Congress in South Africa to resort to armed struggle. The latter was not a decision to employ military resistance against an occupying regime. Although there would have been a case for presenting it as such, the aim of the ANC was not the expulsion of the white population but a democratic non-racial South Africa in which full citizenship would be enjoyed by all, black and white. The achievement of that goal meant the destruction of the system of apartheid, which exploited and degraded the black majority in every area of life, economic, cultural, social, legal and political. The system was maintained by means of the banning of organisations and the imprisonment of their leaders, extensive police powers, censorship and all the other paraphernalia of a police state. For many years the ANC followed a policy of non-violent struggle, until the shooting of peaceful protesters at Sharpeville in 1960 dramatised the fact that so long as they confined themselves to non-violent actions their protests and campaigns would be simply disregarded and crushed. They turned to armed struggle because, they said, they had no alternative. I do not know whether that was the right decision (and I will return later to the idea that there was 'no alternative'), but if military resistance can ever be justified, I think it could be justified in this case.

Many people who instigated or supported the war to recapture the Falkland Islands, including the British Prime Minister, also criticised the ANC for the campaign of armed struggle and called on its leaders to 'renounce violence'. That

combination of judgements seems to me to depend on a moral
distinction which cannot be sustained. Agreed, by the standards
of 'just war' theory, the British government was in the right in
recapturing the Falklands. The Argentinian invasion was an act
of aggression against British territory. Whatever the strength of
the Argentinian claim that the territory was wrongly taken from
them in the past, British sovereignty in the islands was desired
by the Islanders and was internationally recognised, and the
invasion was a violation of that sovereignty. I have argued
however that the appeal to the rights of territorial integrity and
political sovereignty cannot by itself justify a resort to war. The
Falklands War was a classic example of a situation where a
formal concern with sovereignty had little to do with any
substantial threat to a way of life worth defending. Given the
possibility which existed of reaching an acceptable settlement
by diplomatic means (and the invaluable precedent which this
would have set), the attempt to justify the resort to war had to
rest heavily on the appeal to 'sovereignty'. I do not see that this
was in itself a sufficient justification. (By the same token, of
course, the Argentinian invasion was not justified by its own
appeal to rights of sovereignty.)

   I have argued that the question of whether military resistance
can be justified is in principle the same, whether what is being
contemplated is resistance to internal or external oppression. In
either case the question is whether the substantive evils that
would otherwise have to be suffered by the community are so
great as to override the moral presumption against the taking of
human lives. Judged from that point of view, the case for
resorting to armed conflict against apartheid was at least as well
founded as the case for resorting to armed conflict to recapture
the Falkland Islands, and an appeal to rights of territorial
integrity and political sovereignty cannot by itself make a
decisive difference between the two cases.

CHAPTER 5

Killing the innocent

NON-COMBATANT IMMUNITY

We saw that the 'just war' tradition distinguishes between the questions of *jus ad bellum* and *jus in bello*. The latter is concerned with identifying the morally acceptable modes of conduct in war, and the moral restrictions on how wars should be fought. Even if one is justified in resorting to war, there are, according to the theory, limits on what it is morally acceptable to do in order to achieve victory. Traditionally the most important of these limits has been set by the principle of non-combatant immunity – the principle that it is wrong to attack or kill non-combatants. The distinction between combatants and non-combatants is the distinction between members of the armed forces and the civilian population. What has standardly been said within the tradition is that the killing of non-combatants is wrong because, unlike combatants, they are innocent.

Whether a clear and morally relevant division can be made between the two categories of people is, as we shall see, a matter for debate. Undoubtedly there will be grey areas. Some members of the armed forces, such as cooks and drivers and musicians, perform tasks which do not have a specifically military character. Some members of the civilian population, such as those who work in munitions factories, contribute much more directly to the prosecution of the war, and it has been argued that, within the terms of the non-combatant immunity principle, they should be regarded as permissible targets. By the same token, the politicians who direct the war, though they are not strictly military personnel, would have to be regarded as coming on the combatant side of the line if the division is to be at all plausible. But the assumption behind the principle is that, whatever the grey areas, some such broad division can be made, and can be regarded as a morally significant distinction between two classes of people.

The principle of non-combatant immunity is not just a component of a moral tradition, but is also embodied in modern international law. It is reflected in the Hague Conventions of 1907 and the Geneva Conventions of 1949, and most explicitly in the 1977 Protocols amplifying the Geneva Conventions. Articles 48 and 51 of Protocol 1 state:

In order to ensure respect for and protection of the civilian population and civilian objects, the Parties to the conflict shall at all times distinguish between the civilian population and combatants and between civilian objects and military objectives and accordingly shall direct their operations only against military objectives ... The civilian population as such, as well as individual citizens, shall not be the object of attack ...

The form of warfare most obviously excluded by such rules is the bombing of cities, towns and villages. The German, British and American bombing of cities in the Second World War, the dropping of atomic bombs on Hiroshima and Nagasaki and American area bombing in Vietnam would all, for instance, have been contrary to the principle. As I noted in chapter 3, virtually all uses of nuclear weapons would violate it. Clearly, governments which have accepted these international conventions have all too often failed to observe them in their military policies and practices, but the fact that they feel the need to make special excuses and exceptions to justify violations of the principle is itself testimony to its persuasiveness. Britain, for instance, has signed but not ratified the 1977 Geneva Protocols and has declared that it does not regard them as ruling out the use of nuclear weapons – an admission that without such a proviso they *would* naturally be regarded as carrying that implication.

Though the question of *jus in bello* is distinguished from that of *jus ad bellum*, there are close connections between them. Some people have argued, for instance, that modern techniques and conditions of warfare make it almost inevitable that non-combatant immunity will be violated. Or it is argued that since modern armed forces tend to consist largely of conscripts, since even professional soldiers are only doing a job, and since both classes of combatants are therefore, in the relevant sense, innocent, modern wars cannot be conducted without the wholesale killing of the innocent. Both arguments claim that since the requirement of *jus in bello* cannot be met, it cannot be right to go to war in the first place.[1] *Jus ad bellum* and *jus in bello* are also connected at a deeper level. To assert that the killing of non-combatants is wrong, because they are innocent, is also to assert that the killing of combatants is permissible, because they are not innocent. The assertion thus purports to answer the pacifist who says that war cannot be justified because it involves the taking of human life. The reply of the 'just war' theorist would be that the taking of life in war *can* be justified, because those who are killed are combatants and therefore not innocent. The conflict between 'just war' theory and pacifism has been starkly asserted by Anscombe:

> Now pacifism teaches people to make no distinction between the shedding of innocent blood and the shedding of any human blood. And in this way pacifism has corrupted enormous numbers of people who will not act according to its tenets.[2]

Turning this on its head, the pacifist might respond that 'just war' theory, by emphasising the distinction between killing

---

[1] Richard Wasserstrom, 'On the Morality of War: A Preliminary Inquiry', in Wasserstrom, ed., *War and Morality* (Belmont, Calif., 1969), p.101: 'in war, no less than elsewhere, the knowing killing of the innocent is an evil that throws up the heaviest of justificatory burdens. My own view is that in any major war that can or will be fought today, none of those considerations that can sometimes justify engaging in war will in fact come close to meeting this burden. But even if I am wrong, the argument from the death of the innocent does, I believe, make it clear both where the burden is and how unlikely it is today to suppose that it can be honestly discharged.'

Robert L. Holmes, *On War and Morality* (Princeton, 1989), p. 211: 'modern war inevitably kills innocent persons. And this, I contend, makes modern war presumptively wrong. What I consider the strongest arguments to defeat that presumption, by way of trying to defeat the presumption against the killing of innocent persons, also do not succeed. If that is the case, then war has not been shown to be justified, and if it has not been shown to be justified, then it is unjustified.'

[2] G. E. M. Anscombe, 'War and Murder', in *Collected Philosophical Papers* vol. III, *Ethics, Religion and Politics* (Oxford, 1981), p. 57.

combatants and killing the innocent, has blinded people to the fact that all war is killing and as such is wrong.

In this chapter, then, I want to examine the idea of non-combatant immunity from both points of view. Does it create a distinction between classes of acts which are permissible in war and those which are not? And does it point to a justification for some kinds of killing, and thus a justification for war itself?

It is doubtful whether we can get very far by appealing to people's immediate intuitions to answer these questions, for those intuitions are likely to vary and to conflict. To some people the deliberate killing of civilians in war seems obviously barbaric and inhumane, to others it does not seem essentially different from other kinds of killing in war. A good example of these differing responses is provided by the controversy over the British and American bombing campaign against German cities in the Second World War. The British campaign began in the autumn of 1940. The first dropping of German bombs on London was followed immediately by a retaliatory attack on Berlin, and the campaign continued throughout the war, culminating in the fire-bombing of Dresden in February 1945. Although the bombing was initially intended for precise military and industrial targets, it soon became apparent that the bombers lacked the technical means to achieve that degree of precision, and the strategy quickly developed into the carpet-bombing of German cities. In February 1941 Bomber Command was ordered: 'The new aiming points are to be the built-up areas, not for instance the dockyards or aircraft factories.'[3] By 1943 the Allied strategy was for American day-time raids to dislocate economic and military activity, and for British night-time area-bombing to destroy civilian morale. There were those who criticised the strategy at the time, and one of them was Vera Brittain, a prominent pacifist who believed that if a pacifist has failed in the main purpose of preventing war, 'that does not exonerate him from any attempt to mitigate war's worst excesses'.[4] In her pamphlet *Seed of Chaos* she claimed that

---

[3] John Keegan, *The Second World War* (London, 1989), p. 421.
[4] *Testament of a Generation: the Journalism of Vera Brittain and Winifred Holtby*, edited by Paul Berry and Alan Bishop (London, 1985), p. 244. The quotation is from a reply

'owing to the R.A.F. raids, thousands of helpless and innocent people in German, Italian and German-occupied cities are being subjected to agonising forms of death and injury comparable to the worst tortures of the Middle Ages'.[5] George Orwell, taking issue with her in his regular column in *Tribune*, asked 'Why is it worse to kill civilians than soldiers?' He suggested that it made no sense to try to pick and choose between more and less 'barbarous' or 'legitimate' forms of warfare. So-called 'legitimate' warfare in fact 'picks out and slaughters all the healthiest and bravest of the young male population'.[6] Orwell was even inclined to welcome civilian bombing as something which brought home to everyone the full horror of war. 'War is not avoidable at this stage of history, and since it has to happen it does not seem to me a bad thing that others should be killed besides young men.' Nevertheless we also find Orwell himself conceding in the same article that 'obviously one must not kill children if it is in any way avoidable'. He thus appears to allow, after all, that even in war some deaths are worse than others. Is there any coherent way of making such distinctions? Many of us, I would suppose, can feel the intuitive force of both sides of this argument; we may at first agree with Vera Brittain that the deliberate killing of civilians is barbaric, but a moment's reflection reminds us of the horror of all killing in war and the differences may then come to seem less significant. We therefore need to look for some deeper account of why the distinction between different kinds of killing in war may have a genuine moral importance.

CONVENTIONS

The simplest, and least theoretically demanding, account of non-combatant immunity would be that it is a *useful convention*. Like other agreements to restrict the conduct of war, such as

to the article by George Orwell cited in fn. 6 below, and was originally printed as a letter in *Tribune* on 23 June 1944.

[5] Vera Brittain, *Seed of Chaos* (London, 1944), p. 8.

[6] George Orwell, *Collected Essays, Journalism and Letters* vol. III (Harmondsworth, 1970), pp. 179–81. The article originally appeared in *Tribune* on 19 May 1944.

agreements not to use gas or other chemical weapons, it reduces the amount of suffering created by the fighting of wars. This account of non-combatant immunity is put forward by George Mavrodes in an article 'Conventions and the Morality of War'.[7] He emphasises that the point of such conventions depends on their being agreed and observed by both sides in a war. One's reasons for abiding by the convention will apply only if the other side also abides by it. Those reasons are themselves broadly utilitarian in nature. Mavrodes says of the non-combatant immunity convention that it will probably, if followed, 'reduce the pain and death involved in combat – will reduce it, that is, compared to unlimited warfare' (p. 85).

The question which I want to raise is: why pick on non-combatant immunity as a principle which should be adopted as a convention? If possible conventions were to be judged by the utility of their being observed, one might suppose that an even more useful convention would be one which prohibited war altogether, and required all disputes to be settled by negotiation. Mavrodes plays with the idea of a convention that all disputes which are in danger of leading to war should be settled by single combat between the chosen champions of each side. As he says, the costs of war in terms of human death and suffering 'would be reduced by several orders of magnitude' (p. 83). He quickly adds, however, that the 'single combat' convention 'cannot be made practical, and nations just will not consent in the end to abide by this convention'. No doubt he is right, but why? Why is it that some restrictions on warfare stand some chance of being accepted (as they have been in the Hague and Geneva conventions) whereas others such as the 'single combat' convention do not?

In the case of restrictions of a specific kind, for instance banning specific kinds of weapon, we can identify correspondingly specific and pragmatic reasons for their acceptance. For example, gas and other kinds of chemical weapons are particularly horrific and if they are not yet a standard feature of

---

[7] George I. Mavrodes, 'Conventions and the Morality of War', in *International Ethics*, ed. C. R. Beitz, M. Cohen, T. Scanlon and A. J. Simmons (Princeton, 1985). The article appeared in *Philosophy and Public Affairs* vol. 4 (1975).

warfare there is some chance of reaching an agreement that may stick. Non-combatant immunity, by contrast, is not a specific prohibition but a general principle. If, however, general principles are being offered for agreement on the grounds of their utility, the tendency will be for such principles to collapse into the utilitarian principle itself. This is well illustrated in a discussion by R. B. Brandt of 'Utilitarianism and the Rules of War'.[8] He suggests that the following general rule for the conduct of war might be adopted on utilitarian grounds: 'a military action ... is permissible only if the utility ... of victory to all concerned, multiplied by the increase in its probability if the action is executed, on the evidence ... is greater than the possible disutility of the action to both sides multiplied by its probability' (p. 157). This principle amounts to little more than saying that military actions should be judged by utilitarian standards. It is far removed from the principle of non-combatant immunity, as is evident from Brandt's proposing the following more specific proposals for 'serious wars' (i.e., presumably, wars where victory would have great utility): 'substantial destruction of lives and property of enemy civilians is permissible only when there is good evidence that it will significantly enhance the prospect of victory' (p. 156). In other words, pointless and gratuitous destructiveness is ruled out. From a practical point of view this would be a not inconsiderable achievement, given the way that most wars in history have been fought. But if we are trying to get clear about the moral status of non-combatant immunity, Brandt rightly indicates that it cannot plausibly be seen as a convention which might be adopted simply on grounds of utility. If, as Mavrodes claims, the principle is one which people could agree on, this must be because it has some independent moral weight. In other words, there must be something independently wrong in killing non-combatants, or at any rate it must be plausible to suppose that there is. We still have to consider, therefore, what gives the principle its moral plausibility.

[8] R. B. Brandt, 'Utilitarianism and the Rules of War', in *Philosophy and Public Affairs* vol. 1 (1972). (Reprinted in *Today's Moral Problems*, ed. R. Wasserstrom (New York and London, 1975).)

INNOCENCE

Let us look more closely at the idea of 'innocence'. Does it offer any help here? Is there any appropriate sense in which the killing of non-combatants is 'the killing of the innocent', and as such is wrong?[9] Clearly what is meant here cannot be moral innocence in any general sense. There is no reason to suppose that civilians are in general morally superior to members of the armed forces. The bombing of a town may kill all sorts of morally disreputable individuals. Babes-in-arms may perhaps be morally innocent (if we do not believe in original sin), and people do sometimes talk of attacks on civilians in war as being especially wrong because they involve killing 'innocent children'. We know, however, that such innocence, if it exists, does not last long, and cannot be ascribed to the civilian population in general.

What must be meant is that non-combatants are in some sense innocent *in respect of the war*. This notion however is still not terribly clear. Two points in particular may bring out the difficulties.

(i) The 'combatant'/'non-combatant' distinction is supposed to be a distinction between those who are and those who are not innocent, whichever side they are on and whatever the cause for which they are fighting. However, in any particular war, the armed forces of one side may be fighting for what is, in the terms of 'just war' theory, a just cause. It is difficult to see why, in virtue of their fighting for a just cause, they should be thought to have lost that 'innocence' which would make it wrong to kill them.[10] In ordinary language 'innocent' is usually contrasted with 'guilty', but if people are fighting in a just cause, what are they supposed to be guilty of? Let us suppose

---

[9] The difficulties which I proceed to explore are well stated in Mavrodes, 'Conventions and the Morality of War' (see fn. 7), and in Jeffrie G. Murphy, 'The Killing of the Innocent', *The Monist* vol. 57 (1973).

[10] Jeff McMahan, in 'Innocence, Self-Defense, and Killing in War', *Journal of Political Philosophy* vol. 2, no. 2 (July 1994), regards this as a principal ground for criticism of what he calls 'the Orthodox View' of non-combatant immunity. Against it he defends 'the Moral View', one element of which is that 'a combatant's moral guilt or innocence is determined in part by whether or not he is fighting in a just war'.

that, in the Second World War, the British were fighting in a just cause and the Germans were not. From the point of view of *jus ad bellum*, then, the Germans were wrong to fight at all; but from the point of view of *jus in bello* and of non-combatant immunity, it was wrong for German soldiers to attack British civilians but morally acceptable for them to attack British soldiers. The distinction cannot be accounted for by saying that British civilians were 'innocent' but British soldiers were 'guilty'.

(ii) If 'innocent' were to be contrasted with 'guilty', it is not even clear that soldiers fighting for an *unjust* cause could properly be described as 'guilty' rather than innocent. To talk of 'innocence' and its absence in this way would seem to invoke a 'punishment' model of killing in war, but if we were to take that model seriously it is doubtful whether it would lead to the conclusion of non-combatant immunity. Combatants, whether they are conscripts or professional soldiers, are acting under orders. They did not decide that the war should be fought, or how it should be fought. This does not necessarily exonerate them from guilt if they are fighting for an unjust cause, but it does at any rate raise questions about whether they are the most appropriate targets of punitive action. Many people in the civilian population are likely to carry a much greater burden of guilt for an unjust war. Take again the case of the Second World War, and the Allied bombing of German cities. Many of the German civilians who were killed could more appropriately have been regarded as 'guilty' than many members of the German armed forces. The civilians would have included many people who had helped to bring the Nazi party to power, had fostered German belligerence and had enthusiastically supported the war effort. Many German combatants, especially towards the end of the war, would have been young conscripts who had grown up when the war was already in progress, who perhaps had little idea what it was about or why it had started and who could not convincingly be regarded as morally responsible for it. Above all, of course, the burden of guilt must lie with the politicians. They are the people who must be held primarily responsible for the decision to go to war in an unjust cause. If, therefore, we were to take seriously the 'punishment' model for understanding 'innocence' in war, it would lead to practical conclusions very different from the standard interpretation of non-combatant immunity. It would imply that the most clearly legitimate targets in war would be not the combatants, but the politicians.

Defenders of the traditional principle of non-combatant immunity would at this point suggest that 'innocence' in this context does not carry the usual connotation of a contrast with 'guilt'. The term 'innocent', they would say, is being used in a technical sense. According to Walzer, when we account for the immunity of civilians by calling them 'innocent' this is 'a term of art which means that they have done nothing, and are doing nothing, that entails the loss of their rights'.[11] However, if 'innocent' is simply a term of art, its use here becomes question-begging. We want to know *why* it should be thought that combatants have lost their right not to be killed whereas civilians retain that right. It is not explained by describing civilians as 'innocent' if this simply *means* that civilians have not lost their rights.

An explanation has sometimes been offered by referring to the etymology of the term 'innocent', as the negative of the Latin word *nocens*, which means 'harming'. Kenny, for instance, says:

> The most important of the traditional conditions for a just war was that it should not involve the deliberate killing of non-combatants. This was sometimes called the prohibition on 'killing the innocent', but the innocence in question had nothing to do with moral guiltlessness or lack of responsibility: the 'innocent' were those who were not *nocentes* in the sense of engaged in harming one's own forces.[12]

The distinction is, then, between civilians who are 'harmless' and combatants who are engaged in an activity of 'harming' others. We still need some further explanation, however, of why their engaging in that activity should render them liable to be killed. The distinction which is made between combatants and

---

[11] Michael Walzer, *Just and Unjust Wars* (Harmondsworth, 1980), p. 146.
[12] Anthony Kenny, *The Logic of Deterrence* (London, 1985), p. 10.

non-combatants has to be not just any distinction, nor even just one which seems to have some moral relevance; it has to be one which will carry sufficient moral weight. It has to be capable of explaining how the fact of someone's being a combatant, even in a just cause, can overcome the strong moral presumption against killing. Can the fact that someone is engaged in 'harming' provide such an explanation?

The question could usefully refer us back to the discussion of 'killing in self-defence' in the previous chapter. In the context of individual self-defence it may sometimes be morally permissible to kill in order to prevent harm to oneself, but we also saw that not just any threat of harm can justify killing. The analogy with self-defence has sometimes been invoked by the advocates of the principle of non-combatant immunity. Let us see whether it can help.

SELF-DEFENCE

Robert Fullinwider argues for the idea of non-combatant immunity by appealing to the analogy with self-defence in the following terms:

> a nation may justifiably kill in self-defence. From the point of view of self-defence, only those are justifiably liable to be killed who pose the immediate and direct jeopardy. In the case of war, it is nations' armed forces which are the agents of the jeopardy ... To intentionally kill non-combatants is to kill beyond the scope of self-defence.[13]

I have argued in the previous chapter that the comparison between war and self-defence is a great deal more problematic than is often supposed. 'Nations' do not, as Fullinwider has it, 'kill in self-defence'. In war, people kill people. They may do so in individual self-defence, to save their own lives. They may also do so because they see themselves as defending their nation. Which of the two do we mean here? If Fullinwider's suggestion were that killing in war is morally permitted only in individual

---

[13] Robert Fullinwider, 'War and Innocence', in Beitz *et al.*, *International Ethics*, p. 94. The article originally appeared in *Philosophy and Public Affairs* vol. 5 (1975). For another discussion of the link between non-combatant immunity and self-defence, see Murphy, 'The Killing of the Innocent', p. 538, but note also his scepticism about self-defence on p. 539. Cf. also Walzer, *Just and Unjust Wars*, p. 137.

self-defence, in the literal sense, then the implications of this suggestion would be a great deal more restrictive than the principle of non-combatant immunity. It would imply that combatants could kill enemy combatants only when it was necessary to save their own lives (or perhaps the lives of others). If this principle were followed (even only by the defending side), wars would never begin. The attackers need never fire a shot, and the defenders would themselves then have no justification for opening fire. Even when a war had already started, the practical implications of such a principle would be extremely restrictive. It could perhaps be stretched to allow not just immediate defence against direct attack but also pre-emptive strikes against the enemy to prevent further attacks, but all such actions would have to be limited to what was necessary for protecting the lives of one's own people, and that would probably amount to something very different from what would be necessary to win the war.

Presumably what Fullinwider and others have in mind is not literal self-defence but an analogy between this and the defence of the nation. The problem is then, as we have seen, that there is no clear way of deciding how far to take the analogy. The most permissive version would be that if nation A attacks nation B, nation B may engage in activities analogous to self-defence against nation A, but this does not imply any restrictions on which individuals within nation A may be killed; it implies only that the activities of self-defence must be directed *against nation A*. The most restrictive version would be that nation B may do something against nation A *analogous to* killing in self-defence, but this does not yet provide any justification for the *literal killing of anyone* in nation A. It might, for instance, be held to justify non-violent resistance but no more, or violent resistance which stops short of the taking of life.

Fullinwider of course wants something between these two extremes. He wants to say that it is the *armed forces* of nation A who are doing the attacking and may therefore be killed. Some further argument is needed, however, for that conclusion. This is where we need to refer back to my earlier discussion of self-defence. Although it was difficult to specify clear-cut criteria determining who may legitimately be killed in self-defence, an essential consideration seemed to be that of *responsibility*. If, in the extreme case, someone is faced with an immediate threat which forces her to choose between her life and that of her attacker, then the fact that the attacker is responsible for the situation is what justifies her in taking his life in order to save her own.

The relevance of responsibility can be brought out by looking at the examples with which Fullinwider elaborates the analogy between killing in war and in individual self-defence. He first imagines Jones walking down a street, being fired on by Smith, and killing Smith in self-defence. He then adds other possibilities. Suppose that Smith's wife has a grudge against Jones and has falsely told him that she has been raped by Jones; she instigates his attack and is egging him on. Or suppose that Smith is being blackmailed by gangsters, who will financially ruin him or kill his children unless he kills Jones. (The wife and the gangsters are presumably analogous to sections of the civilian population in an aggressor nation.) Still, says Fullinwider, Jones' self-defence must be directed only at Smith, who is the direct and immediate threat.

Suppose that Smith's wife was standing across the street egging Smith on as he fired at Jones. Jones, though he justifiably shot Smith in self-defence, could not justifiably turn his gun on the wife in self-defence. Or suppose the mobsters were parked across the street to observe Smith. After killing Smith, Jones could not turn his gun on them (assuming they were unarmed). (pp. 92–3)

These, I suggest, are loaded examples. If the only way Jones can save his own life is by killing his immediate attacker Smith, then perhaps he is justified in killing Smith. I am not certain that this follows – the situation is comparable to my case 3 in the previous chapter, much will depend on the precise detail of the case and even then people's moral responses to the example are likely to vary. Certainly, if Jones does kill Smith, he is not then justified in killing the wife or the gangsters as well, if this is not necessary to save his life. Suppose, however, that he has a choice, and that he can equally effectively defend himself by killing Smith or by killing the wife/the gangsters: then surely he should kill the wife or the gangsters rather than Smith himself, since they are the ones who are primarily responsible for the attack.[14] Analogously, in war, if a nation can defend itself by killing enemy combatants *and* can do so by killing enemy non-combatants, it is as yet an open question which should be killed. We have to raise the question of moral responsibility, and ask whether it is the combatants or the non-combatants of the aggressor nation who bear the greater moral responsibility.

There is unlikely to be any easy answer to that question. Combatants must presumably always bear some responsibility for the prosecution of the war, but the extent of their responsibility can vary considerably. They may well be unwilling conscripts. If their country allows them no right of conscientious objection, and if the only alternative to serving in the armed forces is punishment by imprisonment or death, their responsibility for carrying on the war may be minimal. Alternatively, they may be willing conscripts, or they may be volunteers. If they are volunteers, they may have joined the armed forces simply in order to get a job (perhaps with few other options), or they may have joined up enthusiastically, as eager supporters of the war. A further question would then be how far they know what they are doing, and how far they have been duped by their government. To the extent that the latter is the case, their responsibility will be less. It is therefore debatable whether the responsibility even of volunteer combatants is ever comparable to that of the individual attacker who can permissibly be killed in self-defence. Almost certainly, in any actual war, the combatants who will be killed fighting for an aggressor nation will include many who cannot be held sufficiently responsible for the prosecution of the war.[15]

---

[14] Cf. the criticism of Fullinwider in Lawrence A. Alexander, 'Self-Defence and the Killing of Noncombatants: A Reply to Fullinwider', in Beitz *et al.*, *International Ethics*.

[15] Cf. McMahan, 'Innocence, Self-Defense, and Killing in War': 'nonculpable ignorance may be a powerful excuse available to Unjust Combatants. And there is ... the additional excuse of duress. Either singly or in combination, these considerations may be sufficient to excuse an Unjust Combatant's participation in an unjust war, thereby giving him the status of an Innocent Attacker.' McMahan suggests that a possible response is to maintain that in any particular case there is a strong presumption that an Unjust Combatant will be a Culpable Attacker and may therefore permissibly be killed; he notes however that this still leaves the problem of

Even more certainly, there will be many non-combatants who bear a greater responsibility for the war than many combatants. Recall my earlier discussion of the Second World War. What was said there about 'guilt' and 'innocence' is equally applicable to the present discussion of 'responsibility'. Civilians who had actively supported the Nazi regime and its expansionist policies must surely be regarded as having carried a greater responsibility than many German combatants. Their position, and that of innumerable non-combatants in other wars, is like that of the gangsters in Fullinwider's Smith-and-Jones example. I said that if Jones can choose between killing Smith and killing the gangsters to save his own life, he ought surely to kill the gangsters. Analogously, then, considerations of responsibility cannot support any clear principle of killing combatants rather than killing non-combatants in wars of defence.

Finally we must remember two other points which further undermine the 'self-defence' account of non-combatant immunity. One is that, as I have previously argued, the whole analogy between individual and collective self-defence is in any case highly suspect. The other point is that, as with our earlier discussion of 'innocence', the 'self-defence' account cannot justify the traditional principle of non-combatant immunity, one which is supposed to apply equally to both sides in any war. Even if killing the combatants of an aggressor nation could be justified on the grounds that they are the people responsible for doing the aggressing, the same distinction cannot be made between the combatants and the non-combatants of a nation which is fighting a defensive war. The most that could possibly be said is that the combatants of the aggressor nation might be justified in killing enemy combatants in individual self-defence.[16]

how it can ever be permissible for a Just Combatant to kill a *group* of Unjust Combatants knowing that it is statistically certain that the group contains both guilty and innocent attackers.

[16] And as McMahan notes in ibid., even this justification would be available only to those combatants of the aggressor nation who are themselves innocent attackers (e.g. unwilling conscripts). Those who are culpable attackers do not even have a right to kill in individual self-defence.

PERSONS AND THINGS

I want to look at one other way of trying to make sense of non-combatant immunity – the one which seems to me to be the most promising. This is the account put forward by Thomas Nagel in his article 'War and Massacre'.[17] Nagel's starting-point is one with which I have agreed in previous chapters: that the rightness or wrongness of actions is not just a matter of their effects, but also a matter of the kinds of relations with others which they involve (p. 63). In warfare we are concerned especially with relations of hostility between people, and this leads Nagel to formulate

the principle that hostile treatment of any person must be justified in terms of something *about that person* which makes the treatment appropriate. Hostility is a personal relation, and it must be suited to its target. One consequence of this condition will be that certain persons may not be subjected to hostile treatment in war at all, since nothing about them justifies such treatment. (p. 63)

What is wrong with attacking civilians in war, then, is that the attack on them cannot be justified in terms of *what they are doing*. An attack on a civilian, says Nagel, is not 'aimed at him as a subject' (p. 66). It manifests not an attitude to *him/her* but simply an attitude to his or her *situation*, a response to his or her vulnerability and the use which can be made of it. Nagel illustrates this with a pair of examples. 'To fire a machine gun at someone who is throwing hand grenades at your emplacement is to treat him as a human being', it is to respond to him as a dangerous adversary (p. 68). In contrast, to 'stop him by machine-gunning his wife and children, who are standing nearby, thus distracting him from his aim of blowing you up and enabling you to capture him' would be to treat the wife and children simply as means. Such treatment of them, Nagel adds, 'is just Hiroshima on a smaller scale', and all attacks on civilian populations are morally objectionable in a similar way (p. 69).

Nagel attempts to accommodate these ideas to the traditional

---

[17] Thomas Nagel, 'War and Massacre', in Beitz *et al.*, *International Ethics*. The article originally appeared in *Philosophy and Public Affairs* vol. 1 (1972), and is also reprinted in Nagel, *Mortal Questions* (Cambridge, 1979) and in *Consequentialism and its Critics*, ed. S. Scheffler (Oxford, 1988).

language of 'innocence', in ways which I have just been considering. In this context, he says, 'innocent' does not mean 'morally innocent' but 'currently harmless' (p. 69), and 'we must distinguish combatants from noncombatants on the basis of their immediate threat or harmfulness' (p. 70). Accordingly he says of the machine-gunning of the soldier about to throw a hand grenade that 'the attack is aimed specifically against the threat presented by a dangerous adversary', and is a response to the 'directness' of the threat (p. 68). This looks like an appeal to the idea of killing in self-defence, and would raise the difficulties which I have already discussed. If the idea is that the machine-gunner is justified in killing the hand-grenade thrower in order to counter the direct and immediate threat to his own life, this will apply to only a very limited range of cases. If we were to try to extend it more widely, we should have to raise the wider questions of responsibility for the prosecution of war, and this is unlikely to lead to the conclusions which Nagel wants, given that many civilians are morally more responsible for the waging of war than many combatants.

Nagel's use of the language of 'innocence', then, is no more successful than other such attempts, and I suggest that we should abandon it. What is more appropriate, I believe, is Nagel's use of Kantian moral concepts. He speaks, as we have seen, of one's attitude to someone 'as a subject', of treating someone 'as a person'. He says that 'in attacking the civilian population, one treats neither the military enemy nor the civilians with that minimal respect which is owed to them as human beings' (p. 69). Such language clearly invokes Kant's concept of 'respect for persons' and his distinction between treating human beings as persons and treating them as mere objects, mere means to an end. The essential characteristic of treating someone as a person is that one is responding to him or her as an *agent*. The objection to attacking civilians is not so much that what they are doing poses no threat, but that attacking them is not really a response to what they are doing at all. It is also in this sense that we can relevantly describe attacks on civilians as 'indiscriminate'. The point is not that such attacks fail to discriminate between the innocent and the non-innocent, it is that they fail to discriminate between human beings as persons, as agents engaged in various kinds of activities.

The point is connected with one which has been made by Barrie Paskins and Michael Dockrill, using a similarly Kantian perspective.[18] The moral standpoint of treating people as ends, they say, leads to 'a very important distinction between two kinds of death in war':

> Some people, in virtue of what they are doing, can regard death in battle as, however terrible, neither more nor less than suffering the consequences of their own actions. Some other people who might be killed in war do not have this thought open to them. The distinction coincides pretty closely with that between combatant and non-combatant. For the combatant must recognise that death in war would be a fate internally connected with the activity in virtue of which he is a combatant. But, except in very special circumstances, this does not apply to the noncombatant. (p. 224)

And again:

> Because of the internal connection between combatancy and being killed, a combatant has the option and opportunity to regard the prospect of death in war as meaningful: written into what he is doing is a connection with being killed that gives his own death a meaning ...But the death in war of a noncombatant does not have any such guaranteed meaning ... (p. 225)

The phrase 'guaranteed meaning' overstates the case. There is no such guarantee. If combatants are simply 'cannon-fodder', treated as expendable by their own leaders, thrown into a futile and pointless attack and simply mown down by the enemy, it may be difficult to see their deaths as anything other than meaningless slaughter (and I shall say more about this in a moment).[19] But the more cautious wording employed by Paskins and Dockrill seems to me to make the right point:

---

[18] Barrie Paskins and Michael Dockrill, *The Ethics of War* (London, 1979). I am grateful to Susan Mendus for drawing my attention to the connections between their account and the ideas which I am considering here.

[19] Paskins and Dockrill, ibid., also make their account less plausible than it might be by running together the idea of a 'meaningful death' with that of a 'good death'. Though I do not want to dismiss the idea of a combatant 'dying well', I suggest that this is a different matter, and what is to count as 'dying well' will bring in importantly different considerations.

combatants have at least the *possibility* of a meaningful death, because the prospect of being killed is internally connected with the activity of soldiering in which they are engaged. For non-combatants who are killed in war, there is normally no such possibility; their deaths have no meaningful connection with what they are doing.

Once we embark on this line of thought, however, two other important points follow. One is that, having abandoned the distinction between those who are and those who are not innocent, we are no longer dealing with a simple moral dichotomy at all. The contrast between treating human beings as persons and treating them as things is (whatever Kant may have thought) a matter of degree, and in war in particular there is a continuum of degrees of depersonalisation. Consider the following sequence of cases.

(a) Nagel's example of machine-gunning the soldier who is about to throw a hand-grenade at you.

(b) Sniper fire in the trenches, directed at anything which moves in the enemy lines.

(c) The bombardment of an enemy position, as when, in the First World War, an assault on enemy trenches was preceded by a blanket bombardment of the part of the line to be attacked.

(d) The bombing of an enemy airfield, intended to make it inoperable and therefore destroying indiscriminately the airfield itself, the equipment, and the personnel, both air crew and ground crew.

(e) The obliteration-bombing of a city.

I would describe these as successive stages in the deperson-alisation of killing. This is apparent in the relevant descriptions of those who are killed. In (a), the soldier is killed because he is attacking the person who kills him. In (b), the soldiers are killed not because of anything specific which they are doing as individuals, but because, as soldiers in the enemy lines, they are in a general way engaged in the activities of a front-line soldier. In (c) they are in an even more general way occupying an enemy position, but they may not be doing anything at all; they may, for example, be asleep. In (d), those who are killed are people who engage in any of the range of activities which make them members of the armed forces; they may not be doing them at the time, and their activities may not have any distinctively hostile character, if for instance they maintain equipment or cook food. In (e), those who are killed are simply members of the enemy nation. Even that depends on the minimal performance of at least some activities; they must for instance reside in a certain place and go about their daily lives there, and their doing so may well contribute at least something to the war effort. Those activities, however, do not distinguish them from millions of other people.

I noted earlier that any version of the combatant/non-combatant distinction would inevitably involve some grey areas, and that this is admitted by those who maintain the moral relevance of the distinction. It turns out however that we have to recognise more than just a grey area. What we have is a continuum, a progressive depersonalisation of those who are attacked. In the sequence from (a) to (e), the attack is less and less a response to what people are actually doing, and increasingly a response to them simply as belonging to a certain category of people. The extreme of depersonalisation is the use or threatened use of nuclear weapons, which by their very nature do not admit of any more discriminate use than the destruction of a whole area.

The second point which follows is closely connected with the first. If we are to think of non-combatant immunity in Kantian terms rather than in terms of 'innocence', we not only have to recognise a continuum. We also have to recognise that all killing is, to some degree, a violation of respect for persons. If the sequence from (a) to (e) is one of progressive stages of depersonalisation, that sequence has already begun with the act of killing as such. I have argued that the wrongness of killing is grounded in the attitude of respect for human beings as persons with their own lives to lead. To kill someone is to violate that requirement of respect. Moreover, most killing in war is already at a further stage of depersonalisation. As we have seen, killing in direct and immediate self-defence, as in case (a), is the exception. Combatants are rarely killed because of what they are doing, then and there, to the person who kills them. They are killed because they are 'the enemy', killed not as individuals but as members of the armed forces of a particular nation. We therefore have a problem. If the underlying objection to the indiscriminate killing of non-combatants is that it dehumanises them and fails to respect them as persons, and if this is only a more extreme version of the objection to all killing in war, then it might seem that the logic of non-combatant immunity leads us back to the position of pacifism. Perhaps we should morally rule out not only the killing of non-combatants but also the killing of combatants.

Nagel recognises the difficulties here. He acknowledges that 'it may seem paradoxical to assert that to fire a machine gun at someone who is throwing hand grenades at your emplacement is to treat him as a human being' (p. 68). If this is so, 'if hostile, aggressive, or combative treatment of others always violated the condition that they be treated as human beings', then indeed, he says, 'it would be difficult to make further distinctions on that score *within* the class of hostile actions' (p. 64). Nevertheless, as we have seen, Nagel does want to hold that 'extremely hostile behaviour towards another is compatible with treating him as a person' (p. 64). He claims that we recognise this in the everyday distinctions we make between 'fighting clean' and 'fighting dirty'. His example is that of standing for public office, where ways of 'fighting dirty' would include spreading scandal about your opponent, blackmailing him, flattening the tyres of his supporters, stuffing the ballot boxes and assassinating him. The example is fine. Undoubtedly these are ways of 'fighting dirty' and undoubtedly fighting a campaign by making speeches, putting forward policies, canvassing and appealing to the good sense of the voters would be 'fighting clean'. The question remains: can *killing*, in any conflict, ever be a way of 'fighting clean'? Again, there certainly are forms of 'hostile behaviour' which are compatible with treating someone as a person. One may lose one's temper with someone because of what he or she has done, one may argue with them, shout at them, perhaps even physically fight them. The question is: can one respect

someone as a person and yet *kill* them? And, more prob-
lematically still, can one kill someone in war, simply because he
is a member of the armed forces of the enemy, whilst also
respecting him as a person?

The difficulties emerge most clearly in a further argument of
Nagel's. He suggests that his approach can also justify prohibitions on the use, even against combatants, of

certain particularly cruel weapons: starvation, poisoning, infectious
diseases...weapons designed to maim or disfigure or torture the
opponent rather then merely to stop him. It is not, I think, mere
casuistry to claim that such weapons attack the men, not the soldiers.
(p. 71)

For the same reason, he says, the use of flamethrowers and
napalm is 'an atrocity in all circumstances'; their effects are
'both extremely painful and extremely disfiguring'. With
admirable candour, however, he then adds the following
footnote:

Beyond this I feel uncertain. Ordinary bullets, after all, can cause
death, and nothing is more permanent than that. I am not at all sure
why we are justified in trying to kill those who are trying to kill us
(rather than merely in trying to stop them with force which may also
result in their deaths). (p. 71)

Nagel's uncertainty here is entirely appropriate. Killing an
enemy combatant is, if anything is, a case of attacking 'the man,
not the soldier'. It does not just put an end to his soldierly
activities, it puts an end to all his activities. To kill someone in
war, by whatever method, is to abstract from the wider reality
of the life which was his to live and is now destroyed; it is to
respond to him simply in virtue of his existence as 'the enemy'.

Conversely, the appeal of pacifism is characteristically
achieved by reminding us that the soldier who is killed is not just
a soldier but a human being, an individual who had a life of his
own. A classic example is the passage which is the emotional
climax of Remarque's novel *All Quiet on the Western Front.*[20] Paul,
the narrator, has stabbed a French soldier who has stumbled
into the shell-hole where Paul is sheltering in no-man's-land. He

---

[20] Erich Maria Remarque, *All Quiet on the Western Front*, trans. A. W. Wheen (London,
1987).

then has to watch the Frenchman die. He looks through the dead man's papers and learns that he is 'Gerard Duval, printer'. He looks at photographs of Duval's wife and children. He says:

Comrade, I did not want to kill you ... But you were only an idea to me before, an abstraction that lived in my mind and called forth its appropriate response. It was that abstraction I stabbed. But now, for the first time, I see you are a man like me ... Forgive me, comrade; how could you be my enemy? (p. 147)

When Paul returns to the line, however, he puts the experience behind him. His friends tell him 'You can't do anything about it. What else could you have done? That is what you are here for' (p. 150). He watches as a sniper shoots an enemy soldier in the distance. He tells himself 'It was only because I had to lie there with him so long ... After all, war is war.' Remarque nevertheless leaves us in no doubt that Paul's words to the dead Frenchman are the more honest expression of his experience.

DEPERSONALISING AND DISTANCE

Cheyney Ryan, in a sympathetic discussion of pacifism, recognises that its moral appeal takes this form.[21] He illustrates it with an example similar to the passage from Remarque, this one being not fictional but an actual experience, recounted by George Orwell in an essay on the Spanish Civil War. Orwell tells how he had approached the enemy trenches.

At this moment, a man presumably carrying a message to an officer, jumped out of the trench and ran along the top of the parapet in full view. He was half-dressed and holding up his trousers with both hands as he ran. I refrained from shooting at him. It is true that I am a poor shot and unlikely to hit a running man at a hundred yards ... Still, I did not shoot partly because of that detail about the trousers. I had come here to shoot at 'Fascists'; but a man who is holding up his trousers isn't a 'Fascist', he is visibly a fellow-creature, similar to yourself, and you don't feel like shooting him.[22]

[21] Cheyney C. Ryan, 'Self-Defense, Pacifism, and the Possibility of Killing', in *Ethics* vol. 93 (1983).
[22] Ibid., p. 521. The original is in George Orwell, 'Looking Back on the Spanish War', in *Homage to Catalonia* (Harmondsworth, 1966), pp. 230–1. It is also quoted to support the idea of non-combatant immunity in Walzer, *Just and Unjust Wars*, p. 140.

As Ryan says, Orwell was not a pacifist, but the pacifist's refusal to countenance any killing in war is a generalised version of Orwell's reluctance to shoot on this occasion. 'The problem, in the Orwell case, is that the man's dishabille made inescapable the fact that he was a "fellow creature", and in so doing it stripped away the labels and denied the distance so necessary to murderous actions' (Ryan, p. 521). When generalised this becomes what Ryan describes as 'the pacifist's problem', namely 'that he cannot create, or does not wish to create, the necessary distance between himself and another to make the act of killing possible'.

Ryan does not, however, endorse this attitude on the part of the pacifist. He implies that 'the pacifist's problem' may sometimes be based on a misconception.

If the pacifist's intent is to acknowledge through his attitudes and actions the other person's status as a fellow creature, the problem is that violence, and even killing, are at times a means of acknowledging this as well, a way of bridging the distance between oneself and another person, a way of acknowledging one's *own* status as a person. (p. 523)

This is similar to Nagel's claim that 'extremely hostile behaviour toward another is compatible with treating him as a person'. Again I want to say that though we can think of cases where this may be so, they are very different from the standard cases of killing in war. Forms of hostility outside a military context may indeed be a response to the other as a person. Even in the context of war, hand-to-hand combat in which each combatant acknowledges and respects the motivation and the prowess of the other may perhaps be 'a way of bridging the distance between oneself and another person'. (Aerial combat, it is said, has retained something of that character in modern times.) But, in modern war especially, most of the killing is literally done at a distance, by bombing, shelling, guided missiles and the like. When, in the Falklands War, the *General Belgrano* was sunk by a British submarine, and when *HMS Sheffield* was destroyed by an Exocet missile, these acts were in no sense a bridging of the distance between persons. Moreover, the distancing is psychologically necessary; those who are engaged in the activity of killing would find it much more difficult to do it face to face. The hardened combat veteran can perhaps kill with equanimity, but the hardening process is necessary. An important part of military training is breaking down the psychological inhibitions against killing. And these are not *just* psychological inhibitions, they are, as I have argued, the basis of our moral inhibitions. To overcome those moral inhibitions it is necessary to resort to the kind of distancing which blinds killers to the humanity of the killed.

Ryan's way of answering the pacifist, then, seems unconvincing.[23] There is, however, another approach which we must consider. We might agree that killing in war does involve distancing and depersonalising the enemy, but we could then ask, 'Is there necessarily anything wrong with this?' Perhaps such distancing is something that has to be done, and is sometimes not objectionable but even right and appropriate, in war and in other spheres of life.

I do think that some kinds of 'distancing' are appropriate, but the term is a vague one and we should be clear what kind we are talking about. I have suggested previously that the attitude of 'respect' itself involves a kind of distance. It is a matter not only of identifying with, and responding sympathetically to, the hopes and fears and desires of others, but also of standing back and letting them live their own lives instead of trying to live them for them. It involves recognising not only the 'humanness'

---

[23] Note also, in the sentence quoted from Ryan, the assertion that 'violence and even killing' may be 'a way of acknowledging one's *own* status as a person'. This may be true, but does not thereby support the claim that killing is a way of acknowledging *the other's* status as a person. There are other ways of asserting one's own personhood and self-respect, and these must always be morally preferable unless violence and killing can somehow be shown not to violate the personhood of the other. Ryan invokes 'Hegel's account of conflict in the master-slave dialectic'. In that account Hegel describes the primitive encounter between two combatants, each striving to assert his personhood by killing the other. What Ryan forgets is Hegel's demonstration that this fight to the death is self-defeating because the victor, in asserting his own personhood through conflict, obliterates the personhood of the other and is thus unable to obtain from the other the recognition which he sought.

Ryan further confuses things by asserting that fighting may be a way of acknowledging the personhood of *those whom we defend*; 'the willingness to commit violence is linked to our love and estimation for others' (p. 523). Again this is no answer to the pacifist's refusal to 'defend our loved ones' by obliterating the personhood of others.

of the other, that he or she is a human being like oneself, but also the 'otherness' of the other. This however is not the kind of 'distance' we are now discussing. We are concerned with the distancing exemplified in the Remarque passage, in Paul's movement away from the encounter with the French soldier as a person with a life of work and family, interests and affections, back to the view of the French as an impersonal category, 'the enemy'.

It is not absurd to suggest that this kind of distancing is sometimes necessary and desirable. An example would be the attitude which has to be adopted by juries and judges in courts of law. They have to set aside any personal sympathy for, or hostility towards, the person on trial, and pay attention simply to the question of the guilt or innocence and the appropriate penalty. If the defendant is guilty, the court must set aside the thought that he or she may also be someone with a wider life of interests and feelings and commitments, perhaps someone who would be crushed by the sentence and whose family and friends would be devastated; the court must respond to him or her as a criminal, ignoring the other aspects of his or her identity. Again, to take a rather different case, a teacher will need to avoid becoming too personally involved with his or her pupils. Of course a friendly and informal manner is valuable, and an understanding of and sympathy for difficulties in the pupil's personal life may be an important part of sensitive teaching, but there has also to be the element of distance, the acceptance that too close an emotional involvement may jeopardise the teacher–pupil relation and stand in the way of the teacher's impartial judgement of the pupil's work. Likewise, doctors and other members of the medical profession have to maintain a certain distance from their patients. Again this is not to deny the value of the human touch, but if they allowed themselves to be fully sensitive to the sufferings of their patients, and to respond to every one of them at the personal level, the work would become unbearable and they would become incapable of performing it properly. In these cases, then, it is quite proper to shut off a whole range of human responses and react to the other person simply as the occupant of a particular limited category. Why then should a similar distancing not be just as acceptable in war? Can one not argue that war-fighting, like these other institutionalised activities, involves a necessary depersonalisation? Perhaps in order to do the job you have to forget about the complex human identity of the people against whom you are fighting, and think of them simply as the enemy.

Are the cases really analogous? Notice some important differences. In the case of the doctor and the teacher, their distancing is done partly in the interests of the patient or the pupil. This makes it crucially different from distancing in war. One could say that in these cases there is depersonalisation at the surface level but not at a deeper level: the patient or pupil is being respected as a person, for it is in the light of a full recognition of their needs and interests that the distanced attitude is adopted.

The judicial case is more difficult. The distancing is not straightforwardly in the interests of the person on trial. That might be so. It might be in the interests of an innocent defendant that the judgement should not be influenced by any personal prejudices or antipathies of the jury members or the judge. On the other hand the opposite might be the case. It might be that if the court took full account of the personal situation of the defendant and were swayed by his or her predicament and by the thought of how his or her life would be ruined, they would be reluctant to pass the judgement which they nevertheless have to pass in order that justice may be done. Although it can be said to be in the interests of the community as a whole that courts should distance themselves in this way, it cannot in such cases be said to be in the interests of those who are sentenced. Perhaps here, then, we have a more plausible analogy with the case of war, of which something similar might be said. In war too, perhaps, the distanced attitude has to be adopted so that justice may be done.

Here too, however, there are crucial differences between the two cases, and the most important point is once again that the judicial 'distancing' is sustained by a strong notion of 're-sponsibility' which, as we have seen, cannot be applied to combatants in war. In the courts, distancing is necessary in reaching a verdict of 'guilty' or 'innocent' because what is at issue is solely the question of fact, on which other considerations should not intrude. If a verdict of 'guilty' is reached, the question of sentencing then arises. Here judges will distance themselves in the sense that, if they are impartial, they will not be distracted from passing sentence by the thought of the suffering it will cause and by sympathy for the defendant. This however is not because they ignore those considerations, it is because they can regard the suffering as in some sense deserved. The defendants are not strictly speaking 'depersonalised' or 'dehumanised'. On the contrary, they are treated as they are because of what they have done, because of the actions for which they are responsible. That is why Kant himself insisted that 'respect for persons' is shown by punishing criminals, since that punishment involves treating them as responsible for their own actions.[24]

Two other points are worth noting. The first is that judges can take account of mitigating circumstances. For example, a woman may be found guilty of shoplifting but she may have been under great pressure at home, perhaps her family is breaking up and her action is an expression of anxiety rather than of any criminal intent. The fact that mitigating circumstances can be considered indicates that the judicial process does not involve a completely depersonalising attitude towards the defendant. It also reinforces the point about responsibility. That point was that the punishment may be justified by the criminal's responsibility for the crime. Accordingly, if the judgement of personal responsibility is modified by the consideration of mitigating circumstances, it may be appropriate for the punishment to be correspondingly modified.

The second additional point to note is that though punishment as such may be compatible with respect for persons, certain kinds of punishment may not be. That claim could in particular be made about the death penalty. Other kinds of punishment, even a term of imprisonment, in some sense leave

[24] Immanuel Kant, *The Metaphysics of Morals*, Part I, 'The Metaphysical Elements of the Theory of Right', para. 49, section on 'The Right of Punishment and the Right of Pardon'.

the rest of the criminal's life intact, they respect him or her as a person whose life goes on beyond his or her status as a criminal. The criminal is punished in proportion to what he or she has done and his or her responsibility for it, but it is not the case that his or her whole life is engulfed by the punishment. That however is precisely and literally the case with the death penalty. Even the criminal condemned to life imprisonment retains the possibility of activities through which he can give a sense to his situation, can make some meaningful response to what he has done and what has been done to him (he can show penitence, he can try to reform, he can rebel and so on). The executed criminal of course has no such possibilities. We are therefore returned to the question whether respect for persons is ever compatible with killing them, even when the killing would be punishment for a deed for which they are responsible. Kant thought that the two things could be compatible. He argued for the death penalty as the only punishment for murder which fully recognises what the murderer has done.[25] I am not convinced by this. Hostile treatment of another may be compatible with respect insofar as it is a response to what the person has done, but the death penalty, and killing in general, submerges the person in the particular deed for which he or she is killed. It is difficult to see how the death penalty or any other killing can be compatible with respect for that person as an agent with a range of aims and aspirations and projects.

In all these ways, then, the analogy between the distancing of the judicial process and the distancing of war breaks down. Killing, whose place in the judicial process is of doubtful validity, is precisely what the distancing in war makes possible. The idea that killing in war could be inhibited by a knowledge of 'mitigating circumstances' is of course ludicrous. And that in turn points to the central difference. The majority of the combatants who are killed in war are killed not because of what they have done, not because of actions for which they are in any strong sense responsible, but because they are the enemy. That is where the dehumanisation resides, and it is quite different

---

[25] Ibid.

from the necessary distance which is maintained in the judicial process and in other spheres. In the light of that difference it would seem that the distancing of the enemy in war is of a distorting and falsifying kind which cannot be defended as necessary or desirable.

WAR AND INDISCRIMINATE KILLING

I began this chapter with the idea of non-combatant immunity. I suggested that this idea, if it has any validity at all, must be more than just a useful convention. Such a convention could stand a chance of being adopted only because the idea of non-combatant immunity has its own independent moral appeal. I argued that the wrongness of killing civilians cannot be equated with the wrongness of killing the innocent, for there is no morally relevant sense in which non-combatants can be contrasted with combatants by being described as 'innocent'. I also argued that no valid idea of non-combatant immunity can be derived from that of self-defence.

The most plausible interpretation of non-combatant immunity, I suggested, is that which gives it a broadly Kantian basis. What is especially wrong in killing civilians, on this view, is that they are not killed because of anything they are doing. They are treated simply as things, instruments of military strategy, and are not respected as agents, as persons. However, I argued that this objection to the killing of civilians in war is only a more extreme case of the objection to all killing in war. There is indeed a difference between killing non-combatants and killing combatants, but it is a difference in degree, not a difference in kind. The reason why the killing of human beings in general is normally wrong is that it is a failure to respect the lives of persons, active beings with their own hopes and aspirations. And the killing even of combatants in war is most often a depersonalised killing which reduces individual human lives to the status of 'the enemy'.

I conclude that the principle of non-combatant immunity does point to something important, but it does so only imperfectly. Some kinds of killing in war are worse than others.

Indiscriminate attacks on the civilian population are worse than attacks on the armed forces of the enemy. Certain forms of warfare, such as the use of nuclear weapons, or any obliteration bombing of cities or other populated areas, are a moral atrocity. They are extreme cases of reducing people to the status of objects which can simply be used or destroyed for other people's purposes. The contrast is not, however, between the killing of non-combatants which is impermissible and the killing of combatants which is morally legitimate. If the killing of non-combatants is as unthinkable as 'just war' theory maintains, then the justifying of war itself must be, to say the least, deeply problematical.

CAN THERE BE A 'JUST WAR'?

In this and the previous chapter I have been considering the two main components of modern versions of 'just war' theory. In attempting to sum up our assessment of the theory, we should recall the task which it needed to perform. In chapters 2 and 3 I tried to establish the special status of the moral prohibition against the taking of human life. I argued that justifications for killing cannot be subsumed within a utilitarian calculation of costs and benefits, or even within a narrower calculation of lives lost and lives saved. On the other hand, I was not able to defend a strict absolutism. We cannot rule out the possibility of exceptions to the prohibition of killing. Any such exceptions, however, would need a justification of a special, non-utilitarian kind. The two main components of 'just war' theory, taken together, are an attempt to supply this.

The attempt is made in the moral vocabulary of *rights*. The strength of the principle that it is wrong to kill can be expressed by talking of a 'right to life'. Killing in war, as a defence against aggression, can then be identified as an exception by claiming that because the aggressors have violated the rights of others, their own rights to life are in some way negated. The moral conflict can thus be presented as a problem of clarifying the relations between competing rights. The resulting claim is a strong one: war may be required for the sake of justice. War may be not merely a terrible but unavoidable necessity, it may be positively just if it is fought in defence of rights.

I noted that the strongest version of this approach consists in assimilating a just war to the imposition of *punishment*. The analogy with punishment is problematic on various counts. Essential to the institution of punishment is the existence of an independent and impartial judicial authority. If private persons 'take the law into their own hands' and retaliate against those who they think have wronged them, this cannot be properly described as the operation of penal justice. For war against an aggressor to count as punishment, therefore, there would have to be an independent judicial authority at the international level, empowered to impose such punishment, and its mode of operation would have to incorporate the essential features of due legal process (such as allowing the accused the right to make a full legal defence). Such an international authority does not exist. A country which goes to war on the grounds that it is the victim of aggression is therefore acting as judge in its own cause, and combining the roles of plaintiff, prosecutor, judge and executioner. Other countries which come to its aid against its alleged aggressor are, though not judges in their own cause, still combining all but the first of those four roles, and the accused country cannot plead its case as it would be able to do in a court of law.

An international authority may one day come to exist. Some would say that the United Nations is already an embryonic version of such an authority; its Security Council did, for instance, authorise the war against Iraq in 1991 to reverse the invasion of Kuwait. However, if any such body is to act as a judicial authority, meting out punishment, its mode of operation will have to be very different from war in its present form. The judicial body would have to be genuinely independent of the vested interests of any particular country. The most important point, however, is that the conception of a just war as a form of punishment would have to depend on a strong notion of guilt and innocence. My argument in this chapter has been that such a basis is not available. We have seen the difficulties in making any relevant distinction between those who are and those who are not 'innocent' in war, and making it in a way which would enable one to say that combatants are not innocent. Such a distinction can be made only by using the word 'innocent' in a special and looser sense. Though I have rejected such a use of the word, one might defend it, as Walzer, Kenny and Nagel do. But it would not be sufficient to support the idea of punishment. War, even if fought solely against combatants, involves punishing people who are 'innocent' in any relevant sense.

If the punishment model fails, there remains the possibility of employing the wider comparison with self-defence in an attempt to present war as a just exercise of rights, overriding the right to life of those who are killed. In civil life one may in extreme circumstances, if one's life is at stake, kill in self-defence without having to claim that one is acting as a properly constituted judicial authority meting out punishment. The claim that war is justified as self-defence need not, therefore, involve the stronger claim that it is justified as punishment. My argument in these two chapters has, however, been intended to show that the self-defence model is equally flawed. The first objection, developed in chapter 4, is that the analogy between individual and collective self-defence breaks down. At the individual level, if one is to rebut the prohibition against the taking of life, one has to show that killing in self-defence is a necessary response to a threat to one's own life, or to some comparable threat. At the collective level, however, military aggression, to which a war of self-defence is supposed to be a response, is not necessarily a threat to the lives of those who are attacked. The analogy is therefore inadequate to justify the literal killing which a war of self-defence entails. If we go beyond the analogy, to emphasise what is literally being defended when a nation is attacked, we can recognise that the goods which aggression threatens may be important. Military aggression which threatens to destroy a nation may thereby be a threat to a culture which is rooted in the lives of people who share a territory and a language and traditions. It may threaten to destroy an authentic political community which enables its members to participate in political self-determination. These may be things of great value. Whether they are at risk, however, will depend on the particular case, and the mere fact that borders are violated does not settle the issue. Even if they are at risk and worth defending, we still have to show that the protection of such things can justify killing on a massive scale. The self-defence analogy purported to supply that justification, but we have seen that the analogy collapses.

My second line of argument against the self-defence model emerges from the present chapter. I suggested in chapter 4 that the justification for killing in self-defence, no less than the justification for punishment, depends crucially on claims about responsibility. The idea is that the attacker is responsible for creating a situation which poses an inescapable choice of lives, and consequently if someone must be killed it is appropriate that he should be the one. Like the punishment model, then, the self-defence model needs to rest on a fairly strong notion of individual moral responsibility. Those who are killed in a war of self-defence are justifiably killed only if they bear some degree of individual responsibility for the attack. We have seen that this condition can, at most, be only imperfectly satisfied. Therefore the self-defence model of war is as untenable as the punishment model.

There remains the possibility of appealing not to the idea of collective self-defence, or to an analogy between individual and collective self-defence, but to individual self-defence itself as a direct justification for war. Sometimes people have literally to fight for their lives. Military aggression may sometimes be a direct attack on the lives of the members of a community; it may sometimes involve extreme threats of other kinds which, we have seen, are thought to justify killing in individual self-defence, such as rape or torture or enslavement. At the time of writing, the situation in former Yugoslavia provides an example, particularly in Bosnia-Herzegovina where policies of 'ethnic cleansing' have motivated the military operations of Serbian and Croatian forces engaged in the slaughter of rival ethnic groups and in systematic rape and torture. If military resistance is ever justified, it surely is in such cases.

Though such examples of atrocities may be all too familiar, they are not necessarily characteristic of military aggression and invasion as such. If there is a moral justification for lethal resistance in such cases, it is not a justification of a kind specific to *war*. It appeals to more basic considerations about the lives of individuals. What we are talking about here is not war understood in terms of the 'self-defence' model, it *is* self-defence. (It is worth noting, of my example, that the typical language of justifications for war, the language of territorial integrity and invasion and the violation of borders, is not much help in trying to understand the rights and wrongs of the fighting in Yugoslavia, where the system of territorial boundaries has simply broken down.)

Direct appeals to individual self-defence, then, are not characteristic of 'just war' theory. I noted when introducing the theory at the beginning of the previous chapter that the idea of 'just cause' has not always been focused so specifically on the issues of territorial invasion and defence against aggression. That is a relatively recent development. It is no accident, however, that the theory has acquired this focus. The primary (though not exclusive) institutions of war in the modern world are the armed forces of nations. Unlike dynastic regimes, founded on systems of personal loyalties, nation-states define themselves by their territory. The archetypal injustice which one nation can inflict on another is invasion of its territory. It is therefore in keeping that nations should seek to legitimate their possession of armed forces, and their willingness to use them, by reference to the injustice of territorial aggression. As Walzer puts it, 'aggression is the name we give to the crime of war … it is the only crime that states can commit against other states' (*JUW*, p. 51).

My critical discussion of 'just war' theory has, then, been concentrated entirely on two of the traditional criteria for a just war: in the theory of *jus ad bellum*, the criterion of 'just cause' interpreted as the right of defence against aggression, and in the theory of *jus in bello*, the criterion of 'non-combatant immunity'. I have concentrated on these two not only because they are the two criteria most frequently cited and discussed, but also because they are, I suggest, the two which are essential to any attempt to see war as a matter of *justice*. If that is so, and if I am right that these two criteria do not stand up to critical scrutiny, it must follow that war cannot be 'just'. I shall attempt to back up this claim by looking very briefly at the other traditional criteria. If 'just cause' and 'non-combatant immunity' cannot do the job, can any of the other criteria be used to show that a war can sometimes be just?

I shall argue that each of the other criteria is either tied to that of 'just cause' and unable to provide any independent justification for war, or, if it can stand independently, must then take on a rather different meaning. Consider first the criteria of 'legitimate authority' and 'formal declaration of war'. It is clear that these do not carry any independent *positive* weight. If a war is not being fought for a just cause, it cannot be rendered just by the fact that it has been formally declared, and by a legitimate authority. They are simply additional conditions which have to be met. A war fought for a just cause may still be unjust if it fails to satisfy these conditions, but it cannot be made just by them alone. All that they do is to formalise the idea that wars are the activities of societies, not of private individuals. If the 'just cause' criterion worked, it would be a way of showing that there can be special justifications for taking life in war, in the name of a legitimately governed society, which would not be available to justify the taking of life by a private individual. 'Legitimate authority' and 'formal declaration of war' would then simply spell out the requirement that the action really is that of an organised society. Conversely, if 'just cause' fails to stand up to examination as an adequate criterion, the other two criteria fall with it.

The criteria of 'rightful intention' and 'reasonable hope of success' are likewise tied to that of 'just cause'. They simply indicate ways in which, even if the 'just cause' condition is satisfied, this may not be enough. It is not enough if that condition is satisfied only incidentally, and the real objective of the war is something different. Suppose that nation A has invaded nation B, and nation C seizes the opportunity to intervene on behalf of nation B as an excuse to damage the economy of nation A, its economic competitor. Though nation C formally had a just cause, its action would still be wrong. But of course 'rightful intention' cannot carry any positive weight independently of 'just cause', for the rightful intention must be precisely an intention to wage war for a just cause. Similarly 'reasonable hope of success' must mean a reasonable hope of succeeding in a just cause, and if there is no just cause 'reasonable hope of success' becomes irrelevant.

The two interesting cases are those of 'proportionality' (a criterion both of *jus ad bellum* and of *jus in bello*) and 'last resort'. The idea of proportionality has been variously interpreted. Insofar as it suggests the need to weigh the goods and harms of prospective action, it has sometimes been thought to be an essentially consequentialist requirement, implying that a war, or any other action, can be justified if it will on balance produce more good or less harm than the alternatives. That, however, is not how the idea was traditionally understood within 'just war' theory and the wider context of Christian ethics from which the theory grew. 'Proportionality' was not a matter of weighing up all the possible goods and harms of an action and all its alternatives – the sort of consequentialist approach which I criticised in chapter 3. Rather, it was a matter of proportionality between a specific action and the specific good aimed at by the action, that is to say, a proportionality between ends and means.[26] Applied to the case of war, the question would be whether the waging of war, and the form which this was likely to take in the particular circumstances, would be disproportionate to the specific good which the war was intended to achieve. Understood in this way, 'proportionality' is not independent of 'just cause'. In order to decide whether the requirement of proportionality can be satisfied, one would have to look at the just cause for which it is proposed that the war should be fought, and at the likely course which the war will follow, and one would then have to ask whether the harms which the war is likely to produce will be such as to undermine or frustrate the specific good which constitutes the just cause.

[26] See John Finnis, *Fundamentals of Ethics* (Oxford, 1983), p. 85. I have also found very helpful the discussion of proportionality in Jeff McMahan and Robert McKim, 'The Just War and the Gulf War', in *Canadian Journal of Philosophy*, vol. 23, no. 4 (December 1993).

Consider an example. Suppose that, at the height of the Cold War, Warsaw Pact troops had cut off all Western access to West Berlin, with a view to incorporating the city into the German Democratic Republic. The NATO countries would then have considered whether to go to war to reverse this action. There would have been a strong possibility that any such war would turn into a nuclear war. There is no knowing what level of escalation such a war might have reached and to what devastation it might have led, but let us suppose, for the sake of argument, that a likely consequence would have been the almost complete breakdown of organised social life in both Germanies and in several other countries of Europe – the deaths of the majority of those populations, the wholesale destruction of buildings and property, and the disintegration of cultural life and political life to such an extent that it would take at least a generation for those societies even to begin to recover. The question of proportionality could then be formulated as follows. The intended good which was supposed to be the just cause for the war would presumably be something like the preservation of an independent political society and free institutions. However, will not a war which is conducted in this manner and with this outcome be in effect an assault on the very same good for which it was supposed to be fought? It may in some sense achieve the goal of a 'free West Berlin', but all the characteristic objects of free political life will have been drastically curtailed in the process. Put like that, 'proportionality' has affinities with 'reasonable hope of success', insofar as it points to the way in which the conduct of a war may be self-defeating. 'Proportionality', however, is a broader notion since it recognises the possibility that success might be nominally achieved, but only by sacrificing things of the same kind for which the war is being fought.

Understood in this way, then, 'proportionality' cannot provide an independent justification within the 'just war' perspective. It refers to proportionality between the conduct of the war and the specific good at which it is aimed. Therefore there must already be a good to be aimed at which satisfies the requirement of 'just cause'. One cannot appeal to 'proportionality' to justify a war simply on the grounds that the good it achieves will outweigh the harm. Suppose that one country (call it 'America') were to invade another (call it 'Cuba') which had itself committed no injustice, on the grounds that American intervention would change Cuba in ways which would be better for Cuba and better for the world. Even if that claim about the likely outcome were correct, it would not make the war a just war.

There remains the possibility that we could employ something like the idea of proportionality outside the context of 'just war' theory as a way of independently assessing the moral case for war. It would then, however, mean something importantly different. On the one hand, it would not necessarily be a reversion to simple consequentialism. In particular, it would have to incorporate the recognition that the taking of life in war is a distinctive evil which cannot be reduced to utilitarian terms. Nevertheless, accepting the fact that there are such qualitatively distinct goods and harms, we might then be able to use something like a 'proportionality' argument to justify a war in terms of the weighing of genuinely comparable evils. For instance, it might be argued that the evil represented by Nazi policies of genocide and the concentration camps was so radical a denial of the value of human life as to be worse even than the slaughter of war which might therefore have been a necessary price to pay. This would not be a utilitarian argument. The argument would be that the very same good, the valuing of human life, which normally rules out the waging of war, might in this case require a resort to war. There might in that sense be a kind of proportionality between the waging of war and its intended end. I shall look at the possibility of this kind of argument in the next chapter. For the moment I want to note that though such an argument might be mounted as a way of showing that war could be 'the lesser evil', it would not be a demonstration of the *justice* of such a war.

Why does this matter? It may appear that I am being simply pedantic. If a war can somehow be shown to be morally permissible, does it make any difference whether or not this is expressed in the language of 'justice'? Yes, I think that it does.

There is an important distinction between possible moral defences of war as a 'lesser evil' and as an act of 'justice'. One way of putting the difference would be this: if one can say of an action which perhaps inflicts great suffering or harm on some human beings that it is an act of justice, then, despite the harm that is done, it is not normally an action for which the agents should properly feel guilt or remorse. The point here is not merely a psychological one – that if people can describe their action as 'justice' they are less likely to feel guilty about it. The point is a moral one – that these are not *grounds* for remorse. This is why the proposed criteria for a 'just war' have to take the specific form that they do, and why the ideas of 'just cause' and 'non-combatant immunity' are so central. If the infliction of great harms, and in particular the taking of life, is to count as an act of justice rather than as a matter for remorse, it must be because those on whom it is inflicted are culpable in some way. The most clear-cut case is that of punishment, where the infliction of harm is justified in the vocabulary of 'guilt' and 'innocence', and we have seen that 'just war' theory is accordingly drawn towards the 'punishment' model. I have argued that that model cannot be sustained. The other relevant model, we have seen, is that of 'self-defence'. This too depends, if not on notions of guilt and innocence, at any rate on ascriptions of moral responsibility, in some fairly strong sense, to those who are harmed or killed. I suggested when discussing individual self-defence that there are difficulties in seeing even a permissible act of self-defence as an act of justice. More importantly, I have now argued that the model of 'just war' as collective self-defence cannot be sustained, both because what is being defended is not necessarily comparable to the defence of an individual's life, and because those against whom it is being defended are not necessarily morally responsible in the requisite sense.

Suppose, in contrast, that a moral case for war could be made which was not an argument in terms of 'justice' but a 'lesser evil' argument. I have said that the appropriate attitude on the part of those who have acted in this way, and who see what they have done in these terms, would be different from a sense of having acted justly. The appropriate response *would* be one of remorse. It might take something like the following form.

I think that after the war there will have to be some great penance done for the killing. If we no longer have religion after the war then I think there must be some form of civic penance organized that all may be cleansed from the killing or else we will never have a true and human basis for living. The killing is necessary, I know, but still the doing of it is very bad for a man and I think that, after all this is over and we have won the war, there must be a penance of some kind for the cleansing of us all.[27]

The war in question is the Spanish Civil War, and the character to whom Hemingway assigns these thoughts is Anselmo, an old man, a peasant, fighting for the Republic. If we compare such sentiments with the usual attitude of those who consider that their winning of a war has been an act of justice, we can perhaps see what is at stake in distinguishing between arguments from justice and other possible kinds of moral defence of war.

Finally (appropriately!) we come to the idea of 'last resort'. I think it is clear that within 'just war' theory this too is a criterion which cannot itself add anything to the case for war, but is simply a further requirement to be satisfied. The bullying dictator with designs on neighbouring territory who, having for a year or two attempted unsuccessfully to acquire that territory by means of a combination of threats and diplomacy, declares 'My patience is exhausted' and launches an invasion, can hardly claim that the military offensive is any the more justified because it is a last resort. Within 'just war' theory, 'last resort' presupposes that there is a just cause, and requires that, even so, all the alternatives must have been exhausted before there is resort to war.

If something like the idea of 'proportionality' were to be developed outside the context of 'just war' theory as a way of defending the resort to war, it is possible that some version of the idea of 'last resort' could take on a new significance in combination with it. What I have in mind can perhaps be illustrated by referring again to the comparison with individual self-defence. It is not exactly that killing in self-defence is a 'last

---

[27] Ernest Hemingway, *For Whom the Bell Tolls* (Harmondsworth, 1955), p. 190.

resort' in the sense that one must first try all the other options, but rather that there *is* no other option – one is, as it were, already landed in a situation of 'last resort'. In a similar way the resort to war might seem the only option available as a means of resisting an even greater comparable evil, and one might then feel that in that sense one has 'no choice' but to fight. This again is an idea to which I shall return in the next chapter, and of which I want to say for the moment that it is very different from the idea of war as 'just'.

THE STRENGTHS AND LIMITATIONS OF 'JUST WAR' THEORY: AN EXAMPLE

Both the attractions and the difficulties of 'just war' theory are illustrated by the Gulf War of 1991, in which an international force headed by the United States, invoking resolutions passed by the United Nations Security Council, reversed the Iraqi invasion of Kuwait.[28] The Allies' motives for resorting to war seem to have been mixed. Almost certainly a significant consideration was that Iraqi control of the Kuwait oilfields would give Iraq an unacceptable amount of influence over world oil prices. This concern was at first made explicit, but was subsequently played down. More strongly emphasised was the callously authoritarian nature of the Iraqi regime under the leadership of Saddam Hussein. What most effectively generated support for the war, however, was the straightforward fact of aggression; the Iraqis had invaded Kuwait, had refused to withdraw and must therefore be forced to do so. President Bush condemned the Iraqi action as 'naked aggression'.[29] That this motive was decisive for the Allies appears to be confirmed by events in the aftermath of the war. After Iraqi forces had been evicted from Kuwait, the Allies encouraged the Iraqi people to overthrow their regime, but when certain sections of the population (the Kurds in the north, and Shi'ite groups in the

---

[28] For a range of discussions of this war in the light of 'just war' theory, see David E. Decosse, *But Was It Just?* (New York, 1992). Also McMahan and McKim, 'The Just War and the Gulf War' (fn. 26 above).

[29] *The New York Times*, 3 August 1990.

south) tried unsuccessfully to do so, the Allies declined to help them; this, they said, was an internal matter in which they could not intervene. Only reluctantly did they send troops into the Kurdish areas for a limited time, in order to prevent the massacre of the Kurds and to cope with the refugee problem.

In all this, then, the Allies appeared to be following 'just war' theory: a war of intervention was unacceptable, but a war to reverse aggression was justifiable. The example well illustrates the pros and cons of taking this to be the decisive consideration. There is no doubt that the borders were there, and that the Iraqis violated them. On the other hand, the borders of Kuwait were artificially defined (by the British, at a conference convened by them in 1922), they were relatively arbitrary and did not coincide with any clear divisions between distinct cultural groups or nationalities. It could be cláimed that the borders, though in a sense arbitrary, did make possible the life of a political community. Kuwait was not a democracy. Power was in effect monopolised by a single family, the al-Sabahs. Nevertheless their rule was less repressive than that of many other regimes in the area (including Iraq itself), there was an authentic political movement within Kuwait pressing for democratic reforms and Kuwait could therefore reasonably be described as, in Walzer's terms, a genuine political community, one which had the right to work out its own future. It was an odd sort of political community, since most of its inhabitants were foreign workers who had no political rights at all, but its problems were ones to be resolved by the interplay of internal forces, and there is no doubt that the effect of the Iraqi invasion was to destroy, not to enhance, the limited political life of Kuwait.

The theory of *jus ad bellum*, then, could be said to have some plausibility in this case, and by its standards the Allies' military action to secure an Iraqi withdrawal from Kuwait could plausibly be described as 'just'. From the point of view of *jus in bello*, however, the Allies' conduct of the war must, by any plausible criterion, be described as the killing of the innocent. The main feature of the war was a 43-day intensive bombing campaign against Iraq. This was said to be directed at 'military targets', but the phrase was given a broad interpretation, to include command and control centres (located in or near major cities), and those elements of the economic infrastructure which were particularly important for Iraqi military operations, such as the transport system and power supplies. 'Legitimate' targets were therefore taken to include bridges and roads, electrical power stations and oil refineries. The bombing of such targets inevitably involved large numbers of civilian casualities. Longer-term effects on civilian life appear to have been even more catastrophic. Loss of electrical supplies meant that water purification plants and sewage plants, both entirely dependent on electricity, could not function. This resulted in epidemics of gastroenteritis, cholera and typhoid. The child mortality rate increased to more than double its normal level as a result of the spread of these diseases together with the effects of malnutrition, and hospitals and health centres, also affected by the loss of electricity supplies, were quite unable to cope.

After the bombing campaign, the land war was a rout. The Iraqi army disintegrated in a chaotic retreat from Kuwait, and were mown down by Allied air strikes as they retreated. Iraqi military casualties were estimated by the US Defense Intelligence Agency to be between 50,000 and 150,000.[30] Most of these were suffered by the conscript army, which had already been devastated by the war with Iran and had by now conscripted a large proportion of the adult male population. The elite Republican Guard, the principal prop of Saddam Hussein's regime, survived with relatively light casualties, and of course the regime stayed in power, intact and unharmed. Therefore, even if we employ less strict notions of guilt and innocence than would be required for the punishment model of war, the fact is that most of the Iraqi civilian and military victims of the war were not people who could be held primarily responsible for Iraqi aggression.

[30] The figure was an imprecise estimate, and has subsequently been questioned by some experts. See Roland Dannreuther, *The Gulf Conflict: A Political and Strategic Analysis*, *Adelphi Papers* no. 264, published for the International Institute of Strategic Studies (London, 1992), pp. 56–7. He suggests that 'a more realistic figure of Iraqi soldiers dead might be in the region of 25,000 to 40,000'. All such figures remain controversial.

What does all this tell us about 'just war' theory? It is not necessarily a criticism of the theory. At least in the case of the civilian victims, the theory may itself furnish a basis for criticism of what happened. It could be held that the bombing of Iraq violated the traditional requirements of *jus in bello*. Whether we reach this conclusion will largely depend on what we make of the phrase regularly used by the Allies to refer to the civilian casualties of the bombing, as 'collateral damage'. The phrase is clearly intended to perform a similar function to the doctrine of double effect, excusing the civilian casualties as unintended but foreseen side-effects. Could the theory of *jus in bello*, when coupled with the doctrine of double effect, allow a bombing campaign of this kind? It could be argued that this would in fact be a misuse of the 'double effect' idea. The doctrine is not supposed to give *carte blanche* for any amount of unintended civilian loss of life, on however large a scale. Unintended side-effects must still meet the requirement of proportionality, and it could be maintained that the destruction of civilian life in Iraq, even if not directly intended, was out of proportion to anything positive that might have been achieved by the bombing, and was therefore illegitimate.

In part the difficulties which we encounter here are created by the vagueness of the 'double effect' doctrine, as we saw in chapter 3. It is not clear what is to count as the 'intended aim' and what are to count as 'unintended side-effects'. In the present case, was the destruction of Iraq's economic infra-structure the intended aim or the unintended side-effect? We have also seen in the present chapter that a similar vagueness surrounds the attempt to distinguish between 'civilian' and 'military' targets. What should we say, for instance, of a bridge which has strategic military importance but is also regularly used by civilians? Or of an air-raid shelter which is used both by civilians and by the military? Are they civilian or military targets? The examples bring out the lack of clarity in the very idea of non-combatant immunity.

It is a matter for debate, then, whether the combination of the ideas of 'non-combatant immunity' and 'double effect' could be used to defend the bombing of Iraq. However, I think it also has to be said that if that combination of ideas lends itself to such a conclusion, it is to that extent discredited. To describe several thousand civilian deaths as 'unintended', even if it is true, is an evasion of responsibility. I have allowed in chapter 3 that intentions must carry some weight in determining moral responsibility, since a failure to act, if it is intended to secure someone's death, may be morally equivalent to killing. It does not follow, however, that we are necessarily any less responsible for deaths which we bring about, simply because they are unintended. In some cases we *may* be less responsible, for instance, if other people's deliberate actions intervene to bring about the unintended effect. In cases such as the one we are now considering, however, we are talking about deaths which are directly, actively and knowingly brought about. It seems to me that in such cases the doctrine of double effect puts altogether too much weight on the description of the agents' intentions.

Without back-up from the doctrine of double effect, the principle of non-combatant immunity must entail moral criticism of the bombing of Iraq. Could the war have been fought in any other way? This raises the wider question: can modern wars in general be fought in any other way than by the bombing of targets of economic importance and the consequent sacrifice of civilian lives? No doubt they *sometimes* can. In the previous chapter I mentioned the example of the war to re-take the Falkland Islands. This was a war fought with almost no loss of civilian life. Such wars, then, are possible. However, a war fought over a few sparsely inhabited islands in the South Atlantic, hundreds of miles from any major urban or industrial centre, is hardly typical of modern warfare. The Gulf War is much more typical. Military campaigns fought with modern technology depend on the strength of economic support, and the chances of success are likely to be enhanced by an ability to destroy the enemy's economic resources. Lines of communication and supply will assume a vital importance, but these cannot be cut off, nor can disputed territory be fought over, without carrying the war into populated areas, and the immense destructiveness of modern weapons is then likely to mean heavy civilian casualties. However, though modern conditions make it very tempting to fight a war in this way, and though we can predict that the temptation will not often be resisted, the fact is that things *could* be done differently. The Gulf War *could* have taken the form of a land war with the limited objective of dislodging Iraqi forces from Kuwait, and with air support playing a strictly subsidiary role. The traditional criteria of *jus in bello* can be observed, if not completely, at any rate more fully than is normally the case or than was the case in this instance.

Finally, however, the fact remains that even if the war had been fought in that way, it would still have been a case of 'killing the innocent' in any natural sense of the word. It would still have been fought against Iraqi conscripts who could not be held personally responsible for the invasion of Kuwait. Almost all modern wars are likely to be like this. They are almost bound to involve conscript armies. Even modern professional armies are likely to consist of volunteers who will have had little idea of what they might be volunteering for, and who are more likely to have joined up because of their need for a job than because of any real commitment to the political and military policies of their government. A war to prevent or reverse aggression, if fought against such an army, will not be fought against those who should be held responsible for the aggression.

The example of the Gulf War, then, though it lends some plausibility to the criteria employed by 'just war' theory, seems to me on balance to illustrate the inadequacy of the theory. It reminds us that the invasion of a country, even a country whose institutions are undemocratic and repressive, will more often than not be a great evil, which ought if possible to be rectified. It reminds us also, however, that war can rectify that evil only by killing those who are not responsible for it, and that analogies with 'self-defence' and 'punishment' fail to provide sufficient justification for this. It illustrates the moral plausibility of 'just war' theory in criticising a war fought against innocent civilians, though that criticism becomes less incisive when the theory is joined with the doctrine of double effect. It illustrates also, however, the implausibility of any sharp distinction between innocent civilians and combatants who can legitimately be killed.

In the light of this example, can anything positive be retained from 'just war' theory? What can be said, I think, is that *if* war can ever be justified at all, then the theory points to certain morally relevant distinctions which can be made between some wars and others. There is a pragmatic case for thinking that wars of resistance to aggression stand a better chance of being justifiable than any other kind of war. Although there is nothing sacrosanct about rights of territorial integrity and political sovereignty, the fact is that invasions are rarely benign. Usually they will crush and exploit the people who are invaded, they will impose an authoritarian rule on them, they will be likely to destroy the shared culture and the shared political life of the community. Even if an invasion is carried out with more benevolent intentions, it is unlikely to succeed. If it is an attempt to overthrow a tyrant, it will probably create a power vacuum which the invading forces will have to fill, since in the nature of the case no internal political forces have been strong enough to do so. In the end, therefore, such an attempt is more likely to obstruct than to promote the authentic political life of the community. Whereas wars of intervention, then, are extremely difficult to justify in any terms, wars of resistance to aggression may be, on pragmatic grounds, more plausible candidates for justification.

Similarly, the theory of *jus in bello* points to the fact that some ways of waging war are worse than others. Some forms of warfare are indiscriminate and totally dehumanising. Others may at least pay some minimal respect to the humanity of the enemy, if only by directing the war against those on the other side who are themselves doing the fighting. The principle of non-combatant immunity does, albeit imperfectly, reflect relevant moral distinctions, even if it cannot furnish the conception of moral responsibility which 'just war' theory needs.

The theory, then, is not without its uses. It does not, however, succeed in its primary aim. It does not provide a way of rebutting the initial moral presumption against war in any form.

CHAPTER 6

Having no choice

THE CASE AGAINST WAR

My conclusions so far have mainly been negative ones. I have argued that the idea of 'respect for life', properly understood, sets up a very strong moral presumption against war. Since the waging of war almost invariably involves the deliberate taking of life on a massive scale, it will be immensely difficult to justify. I have argued that utilitarian justifications are not good enough. We cannot justify the taking of life simply by saying that the refusal to take life is likely to lead to worse consequences. An adequate notion of moral responsibility implies that other people's responsibility for evil does not necessarily justify us in doing evil ourselves in order to prevent them. We cannot sacrifice some people for others and claim that we are justified by a utilitarian calculus of lives.

I have also argued, in the previous two chapters, that the 'just war' tradition does not furnish adequate grounds for justifying war. The failure both of utilitarian arguments and of 'just war' arguments seems to be pushing us in the direction of a pacifist conclusion, that participation in war can never be justified, but I do not think that we are yet in a position to endorse such a conclusion. Though we start from a strong moral presumption against the taking of life, in war or in any other context, that presumption is not an absolute prohibition against the taking of life in any conceivable circumstances. I have said that killing cannot be justified by a simple calculus of lives, which would sacrifice some lives to preserve more overall, but I do not see how one could rule out the possibility that one might, in

extreme circumstances, have to kill in order to prevent some
enormous disaster involving huge loss of life. The only logical
basis for a strict absolutist position seems to me to be some kind
of religious belief. I have said that how one sees one's own moral
responsibilities will depend on what one takes other people's
responsibilities to be. I am not necessarily responsible for all the
consequences of my actions if other agents are responsible for
some of them. Clearly then it must make a difference if one
believes that those other agents include a divine being who in
some sense bears the ultimate responsibility for everything
which happens in the universe. One might then be in a position
to say 'It is wrong for me ever to kill, whatever the consequences,
and if the consequences of my refusal to do so appear to be
appalling, how things turn out in the end is in God's hands, not
mine.' I do not say that a religious believer has to take that
position, but it is a possible position, and one which is not
available to the non-believer. I am not certain that it can be
made coherent even if the religious context is supplied; I find it
difficult to see how one could decide where to draw the line
between those consequences for which we must assume responsibility and those which can be left to God. (This is, I
suppose, part of the general problem of giving a coherent
account of divine omnipotence.) I am not capable of judging
what conclusion one should come to here. Such a judgement
would require a greater familiarity than I have with the
intricacies of religious belief. Setting aside the religious option,
then, if we cannot be absolutists about the prohibition on
killing, I do not think we can as yet rule out the possibility that
even the large-scale killing involved in war might be morally
necessary in extreme circumstances. Without being simple
consequentialists, we still have to look at the possible consequences of waging war or refusing to do so.

Even from this point of view, however, the case for war does
not look good. What do wars achieve? To answer the question
fully we should have to look in detail at the historical record, but
one general fact stands out. The conclusion of any war typically
tends to sow the seeds of a future war. As pacifists have always
emphasised, violence breeds violence, and this is true not only at

the level of relations between individuals but also at the level of relations between nations. The settlement reached at the end of a war is, almost by definition, a coercive settlement, imposed by the victors on the vanquished. As such it creates resentments and fosters grievances which will in due course provide the pretext for another war, waged by the defeated to right the wrongs done to them. The classic example is the First World War, a war supposedly fought to end all war. The war concluded with the Treaty of Versailles which deprived Germany of territory and colonies, set strict limits to the future size of the German armed forces and imposed heavy economic reparations. The grievances thus created were nurtured by the Nazis and led directly to the even more destructive Second World War.

The Second World War itself may at first look like a more convincing example of a successful war. Recall A. J. P. Taylor's judgement, which I quoted previously (p. 73), that it was 'fought to liberate peoples from Nazi, and to a lesser extent Japanese, tyranny', and that it was 'a war justified in its aims and successful in accomplishing them'. It is true that the war did bring about the overthrow of Nazism, albeit at an immense cost, involving millions of deaths and appalling suffering. We should remember, however, that the purpose for which Britain declared war on Germany was not the defeat of Nazism as a political system, and that most of those who fought against Germany did so in complete ignorance of the concentration camps and the other distinctive features of Nazism. The reason for Britain's declaration of war was the German invasion of Poland and Britain's treaty obligation to come to Poland's defence. Although the war aim soon came to be formulated as German unconditional surrender rather than the restoration of Poland's independence, this had more to do with the inexorable logic of warfare than with any longstanding commitment to oppose Nazism. Insofar as the original aim was to free Poland, it is debatable whether this aim was really achieved. The war left Poland with formal independence and with a Polish government, but one which was firmly under the control of the Soviet Union. The direct result of the war was in fact forty-five years of Soviet repression in Eastern Europe, and the division of Europe into two military power blocs, posing the danger of an even more destructive war, a nuclear war which would have destroyed European civilisation and perhaps even eliminated the human race altogether. As far as I am aware, no one in 1939 foresaw such an outcome from the war. It is not surprising that wars often lead to results very different from those which they were intended to produce; a major war involves social upheaval on a huge scale, eluding effective human control, and its outcome is almost bound to be unpredictable.

The other general point to bear in mind, in assessing what wars achieve, is that we have to take seriously the alternatives. Consider again Taylor's statement. Whatever its other consequences, the Second World War did liberate peoples from Nazi tyranny, and his judgement therefore has some plausibility if we assume that the only alternative to waging war was doing nothing. We should consider, however, whether Nazi tyranny could have been opposed in other ways, and whether the same results, or better, might have been achieved by means more morally acceptable than this immensely destructive war. The judgement may then turn out differently.

What are the possible alternatives to war? There are the various possibilities which come under the general heading of 'non-violent resistance'. In chapter 2, I suggested that the concept of 'violence' was too ill-defined to play a central role in moral arguments about the rights and wrongs of war. However, though 'violence' is unhelpful as a moral category, the phrase 'non-violent resistance' has acquired a fairly specific use to refer to the various kinds of non-cooperation with an occupying force or an oppressive regime.[1] These include strikes, boycotts, sit-ins, demonstrations, non-violent sabotage (such as dismantling machines and equipment, or removing signposts to confuse an

---

[1] The most thorough discussion of the theory of non-violent resistance, with a full documentation of its varieties and with historical examples, can be found in Gene Sharp, *The Politics of Nonviolent Action* (Boston, 1973). For a succinct survey, see ch. 7 of *Defence Without the Bomb*, the Report of the Alternative Defence Commission (London and New York, 1983); the footnotes to that chapter give extensive further references.

invading army), and disobedience to unjust laws (such as using facilities reserved for the dominant racial group in a racist society). Though we may still have problems in determining what counts as 'non-violent' (is there a significant difference between blowing up an installation and dismantling it?), it is clear that we are talking about forms of non-military action, which do not involve deliberate killing or the deliberate infliction of physical injury. Some degree of success has been achieved by these methods both in internal campaigns for political changes (for example the civil rights movement in the United States), and in resistance to occupying powers. In some of the countries occupied by Germany in the Second World War, in particular Norway, Denmark and Holland, much of the resistance was of this non-violent kind, and was able to frustrate some of the aims of the occupying power. In Denmark, 95 per cent of the Jewish population was enabled to escape; in Norway, the most notable success was the defeat of the attempt to change the educational system along Nazi lines. Another notable example of non-violent resistance to invasion was the Czechoslovak response to the invasion by Soviet and other Warsaw Pact armies in 1968. This is a good example of what can and what cannot be achieved by non-violent resistance. There are obvious limits. People may sit down in front of tanks, as they did in Czechoslovakia, but a military advance cannot be halted non-violently if its commanders are sufficiently ruthless – if they are prepared to massacre those who obstruct them, for instance, as the Chinese authorities did in Tienanmen Square in 1989. More generally, a military occupation cannot as such be prevented non-violently. What we have to bear in mind, however, is that a military occupation is not an end in itself. It is always a means to political objectives, the exercise of continuing control over the civilian population, the imposition of a certain kind of political regime, the acquisition of resources or whatever. These are the objectives which can sometimes, in the long term, be undermined by non-violent resistance. Opposition to the invasion of Czechoslovakia achieved an initial success, in the period of intensive resistance. The Soviets, who would have liked simply to remove the Czechoslovak government, were forced to do a deal with it. The deal was massively disadvantageous to the government (who accepted it partly because they themselves were unaware of the extent and success of popular resistance), and over subsequent months the Soviets gradually imposed their control, removed the reformers from office and installed a puppet regime. The initial resistance had, however, been of crucial importance in establishing the illegitimacy of the new regime. Having once been defied, the Soviet occupation and its servants could never be genuinely accepted. Over the years, in immensely difficult circumstances, the hopes of the reform movement were kept alive, by organisations like Charter 77, leading to the re-emergence of active resistance again in 1989 and the victory of the democratic revolution. The continuity of the resistance is symbolised by the fact that Alexander Dubček, the leader removed by the Soviets, was in 1989 elected President of the new National Assembly. Of course the eventual success of democratic reform in Czechoslovakia would have been impossible without the coming to power of Gorbachev and the immense changes in the Soviet Union itself. However, the success of military resistance to occupation may likewise depend on political developments within the occupying country. What I want to stress is that though non-violent resistance cannot in the short term prevent a military invasion, it can in the long term, to some degree or other, deny it the fruits of political success. We cannot know what might eventually have been achieved by purely non-violent resistance to the Nazi occupation of Europe, but when considering the supposed success of the military overthrow of Nazism we have to bear in mind both the immense human costs of that military victory and the possibility of non-violent alternatives.

The other thing to remember, when comparing the efficacy of military resistance and non-violent resistance, is that historical examples of the latter have mostly been *ad hoc* and unplanned. Huge resources are devoted to preparations for military action, and those who execute it can draw on intensive training, detailed planning and lavishly provided equipment. As Robert Holmes puts it, to compare the supposed successes of war with 'non-violence in its present embryonic form' would be as though one had compared air travel with rail travel at the time of the Wright brothers and said, 'Look, we have only two pilots, no airports, and one plane that can fly a few hundred yards but we have thousands of miles of railroads and a nation accustomed to rail travel', and then argued on that basis against the development of the airplane.[2]

We have to ask what non-violent resistance might achieve if it too were thoroughly prepared and resourced, if the population were trained in its techniques and the preparations for it were an established part of the life of a society.

The various forms of non-violent resistance, then, are the alternative means by which people can combat the invasion or oppression of their society. And insofar as wars are also waged by third parties, seeking to protect societies other than their own from an aggressor or an oppressor, the alternative to war is likewise the various forms of economic and cultural sanctions which can be brought to bear. After the Iraqi invasion of Kuwait in 1990, for instance, sanctions were imposed in the form of a trade embargo, under the authority of the United Nations, in order to put pressure on the Iraqis to withdraw from Kuwait. The economic blockade put a stop to 90 per cent of Iraq's exports and imports. The country's economy was vitally dependent on oil exports, and sanctions were costing it about £41 million a day in lost oil revenues. Many people argued that this economic pressure offered a realistic chance of securing an Iraqi withdrawal without the need for military conflict. The United States and other governments claimed, however, that sanctions were not working quickly enough. Iraqi forces were imposing a reign of terror in Kuwait, and this, they said, could not be allowed to continue any longer. After five months of economic sanctions, therefore, the Allies turned to military means to eject the Iraqis from Kuwait. It is impossible to know whether continuing economic sanctions might have been successful. The Allies' argument was that the suffering of Kuwait had to be ended quickly. Their critics' argument was

---

[2] Robert L. Holmes, *On War and Morality* (Princeton, 1989), p. 278. Holmes' book is the most persuasive philosophical defence of pacifism which I know.

that sanctions were working but needed more time, and that the resort to war actually accelerated the killing and destruction in Kuwait, culminating in the ransacking of Kuwait City and the firing of the oil wells by retreating Iraqi troops. In view of the high death toll in the war, it is at least possible that a continued reliance on economic sanctions might have achieved success at a lesser cost in death and destruction.[3] Here, then, was a clear example of the choice between the military solution and non-military sanctions, with the typical costs and uncertainties of both options.

Like non-violent resistance, sanctions are limited in what they can achieve. In assessing them as an alternative to war, however, we again have to bear in mind, first, that war also is limited in its ability to achieve the political ends which are its real purpose, and, secondly, that the proper comparison is between the efficacy of war and the efficacy which sanctions could have if they too were implemented wholeheartedly, prepared and coordinated and resourced in the way that war is waged.

We should also be clear about the moral status of sanctions. They are not nice. Like war, they are a coercive threat. They involve the deliberate infliction of suffering in order to pressure people into compliance. Like war, they inflict suffering on people who are 'innocent' in the sense that they are not individually responsible for the actions which sanctions are intended to oppose. Typically, for instance, economic sanctions will deliberately create hardship and even starvation for ordinary people as a way of forcing their government to back down. For all that, there can be no denying that sanctions, if they work, are morally preferable to war. On any reckoning, they cause vastly less suffering and loss of life than war does. And though they are coercive, they leave the door open for

---

[3] It is a matter for debate whether the United States government was ever genuinely committed to making a success of sanctions. Jeff McMahan and Robert McKim, in 'The Just War and the Gulf War', *Canadian Journal of Philosophy*, vol. 23, no. 4 (1993), argue that economic sanctions could have worked, that the availability of this alternative undermines the claim that the Gulf War was a just war, and that the Bush administration opted for war rather than sanctions because it had other (illegitimate and partly unacknowledged) aims.

negotiation and compromise at every stage, whereas war is much more likely to close off such possibilities.

With these points in mind, it is instructive to return to the example of the overthrow of Nazism as a result of the Second World War, and to compare it with a recent example of the use of sanctions, against the apartheid regime in South Africa. I do not want to equate apartheid with Nazism – the advocates of apartheid did not actually propose anything equivalent to the extermination of the Jews – but both are examples of social systems based on a racist ideology and supported by the apparatus of a police state. We can therefore usefully compare the methods of war and of sanctions as ways in which other countries have tried to combat such a system.

We should first reiterate the point that Britain and its allies did not in fact declare war on Germany in order to eliminate Nazism. When it is said, then, that the Second World War was successful in doing so, this looks suspiciously like an *ex-post-facto* justification. Since the war ended with the demise of Nazism, that is held to have been its objective, and the fact that the original objective was not fully achieved is conveniently forgotten.

The point is strengthened if we go on to note that, despite the opprobrium which apartheid almost universally incurred, nobody seriously proposed declaring war on South Africa in order to put an end to it. If a war to end Nazism is supposed to be a classic example of a just war, one would also suppose that a war to end apartheid would have some claim to be a just war. On the contrary, however, many people, and especially politicians, who purported to be strongly critical of apartheid, opposed even economic sanctions against South Africa. This again suggests that objectives such as 'ending Nazism' would not normally be thought of as good reasons for going to war – except after the event.

Suppose, however, that we do compare the efficacy of the war in ending Nazism and the efficacy of sanctions against apartheid. It has to be agreed that, at least for the time being, Nazism was decisively defeated, but at a huge cost. Millions of people were killed, more than half of them civilians, whole cities were destroyed as well as thousands of smaller towns and villages, national economies were devastated. The struggle against apartheid has of course not been without its costs. Many black South Africans have been killed or maimed by the police or the military, the African National Congress itself turned to armed struggle (a decision which I shall discuss shortly), and there has been tragic and destructive violence between different sections of the population, both black and white. At the time of writing, the struggle is not yet over and could still culminate in a bloody civil war. Clearly, however, the deaths and suffering caused specifically by sanctions were as nothing compared to the costs of the Second World War, yet sanctions were also undeniably effective. They were slow to work. Many governments including the British were reluctant to participate, and the initiative came largely from popular campaigns rather than from governments. Nevertheless, sanctions played a decisive part in bringing about a dramatic change in South African policy, and the beginning of the end of apartheid. A particularly good example is the severing of sporting links with South Africa. It can hardly be said to have created great suffering, but it was an effective form of pressure. If compared with the methods of war, in respect both of its moral acceptability and of its efficacy, it has a great deal to be said for it.

I want to emphasise again the limits to what I am claiming for non-military sanctions. They are never completely effective, and sometimes they simply fail (as they did when deployed against the Italian invasion of Ethiopia in 1935). Even if they succeed, they are not morally unproblematic. What I am suggesting is that the possibility of economic and cultural sanctions, and of non-violent resistance, should affect our assessment of the efficacy of war. If we compare war with doing nothing, we may feel that despite the heavy moral price which it exacts, it is at least effective. If we compare it with other, morally more acceptable ways of pursuing the same aims, the case for war looks considerably weaker.

I want to re-emphasise also that the moral assessment of war should not be primarily a matter of utilitarian calculation. The primary case against war is that it is an overwhelming violation of respect for human life. Only when this has been acknowledged is it relevant to put the counter-claim that war is nevertheless effective. The counter-claim has to do a great deal of work. What has to be shown is not just that war is effective, but that it is an instrument so indispensable as to outweigh the strong moral presumption against it. What I have now been suggesting is that when we consider the availability of other more acceptable instruments of social action, the claim for war becomes unconvincing.

That, then, is the case against war. Though it cannot be simply deduced from the wrongness of killing, that is in the end the primary moral consideration. And the appeal here is not to some abstract principle, but to our deepest human responses, and to the shared understanding which those responses make possible. The moral rejection of war is often thought of as an abstruse stand taken by the morally fastidious. At the beginning of the first chapter I drew attention to the disparity between conventional moral views of war and the general recognition of the wrongness of taking life. I have now tried to show that the standard attempts to justify that disparity, with ideas of 'just war' and 'self-defence' and with appeals to consequences, are unsuccessful.

'WE HAVE NO CHOICE'

Many people would acknowledge the weight of these arguments, yet would still balk at a pacifist conclusion. Attitudes to war often seem to be positively schizoid. 'We know that wars are morally appalling', a common view appears to be, 'but we have to have them.' Sometimes this is merely an expression of moral inertia, a failure of moral imagination, a refusal to think through the implications of our moral beliefs and to act on those implications. Such remarks may also, however, have a deeper significance. They may express a genuine sense of the irreconcilability of two sides of our moral thinking. I want now to explore what may be meant by those who, having acknowledged the moral case against war, go on to say 'We have no choice but to fight.'

One of the attractions of the self-defence analogy is that it might seem to account for this idea of having no choice. In the case of literal individual self-defence, that phrase appears to be appropriate. If my life is threatened, and I can defend myself only by killing my attacker, then I have no choice but to kill him. Of course in a sense there is a choice: I can choose to kill the attacker or be killed by him. As philosophers such as Sartre have emphasised, in some sense there is always a choice, whenever we act. What can be said, however, is that it is not a real choice, because it is a *forced* choice. There are two aspects to this. First, it is a forced choice because the attacker is responsible for putting me in the situation where I can defend myself only by killing him. Secondly, I can avoid killing him only by sacrificing something of equal importance, my own life. It is the combination of these two features that, as I have argued, overrides the normally compelling moral presumption against taking another life.

I have also argued, however, that the purported analogy between war and individual self-defence does not work. When people fight for their country, they are not forced to kill in order to protect human lives – at least that is not the primary object – and it therefore cannot be in this sense that they have no choice. The possibility nevertheless remains that, at a more general level, some broadly comparable notion of 'having no choice' may apply to wars fought for social and political objectives. That is the possibility I want to consider.

I have referred already, for various purposes, to the example of the struggle against apartheid in South Africa, and I want to use that example again now. In 1961, the year after the massacre at Sharpeville, the African National Congress decided that it could no longer adhere to its longstanding policy of non-violence. It set up a new group, Umkhonto we Sizwe, to wage a campaign of armed struggle. After its first actions the group issued a statement which contained these words:

The time comes in the life of any nation when there remain only two choices: submit or fight. That time has now come to South Africa. We shall not submit and we have no choice but to hit back by all means within our power in defence of our people, our future and our freedom.

The government has interpreted the peacefulness of the movement as weakness; the people's non-violent policies have been taken as a green light for government violence ... We are striking out along a new road for the liberation of the people of this country.[4]

As in the case of individual self-defence, the form of words used here acknowledges that in one sense there *is* a choice. There are two alternatives: submit or fight. What the statement goes on to imply, however, is that submission is not a real choice. Why not? It is of course perfectly possible, indeed it might in some ways be the easier and more comfortable option. To say that it is nevertheless not a real option is an inescapably *moral* assertion. Submission is morally impossible. It is not just morally worse than the alternative; it is morally unthinkable. To submit, it might be said, is something which one could not live with. To do so would be to abandon one's deepest moral convictions, those convictions which are a precondition for making any meaningful moral choices at all.[5]

This may explain why submission can be described as not a real choice, but the further question remains: why should the Umkhonto manifesto assert that the only alternatives were to submit or to fight? I have been arguing in this chapter that there *are* alternatives to military struggle. Non-violent resistance is a real possibility. The African National Congress was perfectly well aware of this. Prior to 1961 its campaigns had been self-consciously of this kind, modelled on the example of Gandhi's earlier campaigns with the Indian population in South Africa, and on the Indian independence movement. Why then should it now see that form of action as no longer an alternative, and assert that there was no choice but to fight, and why should other people who are the victims of invasion or oppression make similar assertions?

At this point it is important to remember that the availability of different forms of resistance is a matter not just of abstract

[4] Mary Benson, *Nelson Mandela* (Harmondsworth, 1986), pp. 110–11.
[5] On the idea that some supposed alternatives might be morally 'unthinkable', see Bernard Williams, 'A Critique of Utilitarianism', in J. J. C. Smart and Bernard Williams, *Utilitarianism: For and Against* (Cambridge, 1973), pp. 92–3. And for the related idea of what one can or cannot 'live with', see pp. 103–4.

theoretical possibilities, but of *socially* available options. Political oppression is by definition a social phenomenon, and resistance to it likewise cannot exist except as a social phenomenon. A private individual may decide to disobey, to defy orders and perhaps to die for it, but this counts as resistance, as a challenge to oppression, only if it is publicly recognised as such and gets its meaning from a wider social movement, however informal. This means, however, that the availability of identifiable resistance depends on the existence of a tradition of struggle of the appropriate kind. Of course such a tradition has to start somewhere, and I am not denying that resistance can sometimes be improvised with no prior institutional structure to work from. The Norwegian campaign of non-violent resistance to the German occupation, for instance, developed spontaneously and there had been no pre-invasion plans for such a campaign. Nevertheless there may be situations where the only recognised form of resistance is military resistance, where alternative forms of struggle simply do not gain acceptance, and where it can therefore be said that 'we have no choice but to fight'.

This was not the case in South Africa in 1961. As I have mentioned, the freedom movement had a vigorous history of non-violent resistance, involving strikes and various kinds of civil disobedience. The problem was the total suppression of all these activities. Now if the judgement to be made was one of effectiveness, that in the circumstances non-violence appeared not to be achieving anything, and that armed struggle offered a better chance of success, this would not, I think, be properly expressed by saying that 'we have no choice'. Judgements of social effectiveness are always provisional; a movement which seems to be getting nowhere may triumph in the long run, and the temptation to look for a short cut may be delusive. What might be meant, however, is something along the following lines. Resistance has to be recognised as such not only by the resisters but also, at some level, by their opponents. Civil disobedience and other kinds of non-violent resistance are a statement, an assertion of the wrongness of existing institutions and practices. As such, they presuppose at least a minimal level of dialogue. The statement must be heard, it must be acknowledged as a statement even if it is rejected. If the authorities say 'You are wrong, your protest is misguided and inadmissible and we have to arrest you', that is at least a recognition of the protest, and those who take part in the non-violent resistance, though they may feel frustrated at the lack of success, can at any rate see themselves as genuinely resisting. But if they are simply crushed, ruthlessly and totally, if the authorities are prepared simply to massacre them without seeing any need to offer any self-justification, and if there is imposed a total censorship so that the would-be resisters cannot even communicate to their potential supporters what it is that they are doing, they may rightly feel that their actions cannot even serve as a statement of their opposition. There has ceased to exist a civil society within which rival political claims can be made, and in which disobedience can be civil disobedience. It may then be true that there is no alternative but to fight. It may be that only in that way can one force from one's opponents a recognition of one's existence as a political resistance. It will of course always be a difficult judgement whether that point has been reached. Out of frustration at the slowness of progress it will sometimes be tempting to say that non-violent resistance has become impossible when in fact that is not so. It could be argued that it was not really so in South Africa in 1961, for non-violent resistance has continued since then and arguably has been more impressive than the armed struggle. Nevertheless I am suggesting that we can, along these lines, make sense of the idea that in a particular social context the only available alternatives may be to submit or to fight, and that, submission being morally unthinkable, people can then intelligibly say that they have no choice but to fight.

Having said that, however, we have to add that by the same token the pacifist can also say 'I have no choice.' That assertion, I have been suggesting, is essentially a moral assertion. In a sense one always has a choice, but the point of the assertion is that the only alternative course of action may be morally unthinkable. So, just as someone who turns to military resistance may say 'I have no choice' because the only alternative is submission to an intolerable evil, the pacifist can likewise say 'I

have no choice' and mean that, however limited the alternatives, the resort to war and the deliberate wholesale destruction
of human lives is morally unthinkable. In saying this the pacifist
cannot be accused of incoherence. Even if the result of the
refusal to resort to war would be that others would, unresisted,
engage in widespread slaughter or some other terrible evil, still
one's view of one's competing responsibilities in this situation
will, as I have argued in chapter 3, be itself a judgement about
competing values. Killing and letting die cannot simply be
equated, and someone who refuses to endorse killing as a means
of saving life is not necessarily inconsistent. 'I have no choice',
then, can as well express the overriding moral commitment of
the pacifist as it can the moral commitment of someone who
finds war inescapable.

MORAL TRAGEDY

We appear to have reached moral deadlock. Confronted with
the dilemma where war seems to be the only way of resisting an
intolerable evil, we can apparently go either way, depending on
which moral commitment we take to be of overriding importance. There seems to be no further scope for rational
argument to determine which decision is right. This takes us
back to the concerns of my first chapter. Does it not confirm that
reason can play only a subordinate role in moral discourse, that
all moral views are in the end inescapably subjective, and that,
as Russell suggested, our judgements about war are ultimately
'the outcome of feeling rather than of thought'?

I do not think that this follows. Admittedly in the present case
we appear to have reached a position of deadlock, but it is
important to see why this is so. We have arrived at an impasse
because of the strength of the moral case on either side, and that
strength is an *objective* strength. To resort to war is a terrible
thing, and that assertion is not just an expression of subjective
feeling but a judgement rooted in our understanding of our
shared human life. There appear to be situations where war is
the only available means of resisting an intolerable evil, and
that too is an objective judgement, not a mere expression of

feeling. It is when these objective judgements clash that we appear to be faced with an irresolvable dilemma. In other situations, where they do not clash, assertions of the wrongness of war may be rationally and objectively grounded. Political leaders who, in search of popularity at home, cook up an excuse to attack a neighbouring community, and are prepared to squander the lives of their own citizens and of those on whom they make war, are wrong – objectively wrong. Political leaders who declare war on the basis of purely national interests are objectively wrong. Hitler and his supporters were wrong, all other similar warmongers and ruthless oppressors are wrong, and it is because of the objective strength of that judgement that the question of how to resist them is so problematic.

The dilemma, then, is of a special sort. It is an example of what we might call 'moral tragedy': a situation where whatever one does, though one may feel morally compelled to do it, is also wrong. As Thomas Nagel puts it, 'the world can present us with situations in which there is no honorable or moral course for a man to take, no course free of guilt and responsibility for evil'.[6] So here, there will be cases where the only way to resist aggression or oppression will be to engage in the wholesale destruction of human lives, but the refusal to fight and to kill will be a failure to resist intolerable evil. Hegel saw such irresolvable moral clashes as the very essence of tragedy, and as providing the theme for some of the great tragic dramas, especially those of the Greek tragedians: Aeschylus' *Oresteia*, for instance, where Orestes must avenge his father's murder but, to do so, must kill his own mother, so that, as he says, 'right conflicts with right'; or Sophocles' *Antigone*, where Antigone's loyalty to her brother and her duty to give him a proper burial requires her to defy her uncle Creon's edict and her loyalty to the city.[7]

---

[6] Thomas Nagel, 'War and Massacre', in *International Ethics*, ed. C. R. Beitz, M. Cohen, T. Scanlon and A. J. Simmons (Princeton, 1985), p. 73. The idea of tragic moral conflict has also been discussed by Bernard Williams; see his 'Ethical Consistency' in *Problems of the Self* (Cambridge, 1973), and 'Conflicts of Values' in *Moral Luck* (Cambridge, 1981).

[7] Hegel's theory of tragedy is most fully set out in his Lectures on Aesthetics. See G. W. F. Hegel, *Aesthetics*, trans. T. M. Knox (Oxford, 1975), Part III, Section III,

I have said that a subjectivist account cannot explain what makes such conflicts tragic. For the subjectivist they are, in the end, like all dilemmas, a matter of choice. Though the conflict may be acute it can always be resolved by an act of choice, and in choosing one is *ipso facto* committing oneself to regarding the chosen course as right and the alternative as wrong. Thus Sartre's famous example of the young man who has to choose between staying to care for his mother or leaving to join the Resistance looks like an example of a tragic conflict, but when Sartre, in the spirit of his subjectivist ethics, advises the young man, 'You are free, therefore choose', he implies that once the choice is made there is no need for further agonising.[8] Sartre does indeed recognise that choice is burdensome. In choosing, I have to assume full responsibility for all the implications of my choice, and it is 'bad faith' to try to make my choice easier by denying responsibility for its unwelcome consequences. For Sartre, however, responsibility does not imply guilt. By freely embracing my responsibilities I liberate myself from a sense of guilt, and it is then incoherent for me to retain a belief that I have nevertheless done a terrible wrong. It is interesting that Sartre's version of the Orestes legend, his play *The Flies*, is a deliberate repudiation of the Aeschylean version; his Orestes, unlike the citizens of Argos, refuses to be weighed down by a sense of guilt.[9]

If a subjectivist ethics cannot account for moral tragedy, neither can a utilitarian ethics. Utilitarians can recognise that we may encounter dilemmas where the alternatives are equally balanced. From a utilitarian point of view, however, what this must mean is that the overall utility, on balance, of one course of action is the same as the overall utility of the alternative. When we weigh up the likely happiness and suffering which will result, there is no advantage to be gained either way. In a sense, then, this is a situation where you cannot win, but also one

Chapter III.c.3. The phrase 'right conflicts with right' occurs in Aeschylus' *Coephoroi*, line 461.

[8] Jean-Paul Sartre, *Existentialism and Humanism* (Methuen, 1948), pp. 35–6.

[9] Jean-Paul Sartre, 'The Flies', in *Altona, Men Without Shadows, The Flies* (Harmondsworth, 1962).

where you cannot lose. The utilitarian has no need to see it as a situation of moral tragedy, but only of moral indifference. This is because for utilitarianism there are no incommensurable moral demands. Everything can be weighed on the same scale of happiness and suffering, and there is no room for the idea that in doing what I have to do I may violate another, distinct value. The fact is, however, that in endorsing war to resist oppression I am endorsing the destruction of human lives which cannot be cancelled by any positive achievement, and which is therefore inexpiable.

A further relevant feature of utilitarianism, as well as its failure to recognise the diversity of values, is its failure to recognise the diversity of our responsibilities. As I suggested in chapter 3, utilitarianism works with an undifferentiated notion of moral responsibility, as simply a general obligation to benefit everyone who might be affected by one's actions. In fact, however, our moral responsibilities arise out of our various relations to others, and these include not only the relations which we have to human beings in general and indeed to all living things, but also relations to specific groups and individuals. If, then, out of loyalty to our community or in pursuit of the liberation of our fellows, we kill or endorse killing in war, we are inescapably sacrificing some people for others. The relevant upshot is not just a net gain or net loss for the universe or for humanity in the abstract, but an irreconcilable clash between two different sets of moral responsibilities. Again, those who are sacrificed cannot be compensated by the gain to others, and our guilt in relation to them is in this sense inexpiable. As Hegel saw, tragic conflicts arise because we are each located within a number of different social groups and institutions which sometimes make incompatible moral demands on us.

Are we then helpless in the face of moral tragedy? The conflicts may be irresolvable but, as Sartre says, we have to choose. This is the difference between theoretical and practical conflicts. We can live with irreconcilable conflicts between, say, competing scientific theories. Though the position may be an uncomfortable one, we can say, for instance, that the wave theory of light and the particle theory both capture certain

aspects of the properties of light. If, however, we recognise the
force of saying that war is the only option but is also morally
unthinkable, we cannot leave the matter there. We have to
decide whether or not to support the waging of war, and to do
nothing is itself a choice. How we choose will therefore depend
ultimately on our sense of the relative importance of different
moral values and responsibilities. We have to decide *what matters
most*. This, as I have said, cannot be done by measuring the
alternatives on a single scale of value. It can be done only by
trying to put together a coherent overall picture of human life
and experience, within which we can understand the dependence of some items on others and within which some things
come into focus and others recede into the background. So we
may say, 'In the end what matters is the existence of individual
human lives, each one different and each one irreplaceable.' Or
we may, perhaps, say, 'In the end what matters is our loyalty to
the wider community which links us to the past and the future;
we die, but the community continues, and without it our finite
individual lives would lack any purpose or meaning.'

Almost inevitably, different people will come to different
conclusions. Nevertheless our conclusions can be the outcome of
thought and deliberation. This will not, for the most part, take
the form of logical inference; there is no set of premises from
which one can logically deduce conclusions about the relative
importance of different values. Rather, argument and deliberation here will consist in reminding ourselves and one
another of this or that feature of our experience, drawing
attention to the persistence of certain facts, noticing or pointing
out how things fit into a certain pattern, and so on. This may
sound like an incredibly vague and sloppy way of proceeding,
but in fact a great deal of our thinking takes this form and very
little of it actually consists in linear inferences. Take the case of
our characterisations of people. 'Is he a good friend?' 'Well,
he's rather dull, but he's always reliable, he never lets you down,
and in an undemonstrative way he is very sensitive to people's
moods and feelings and he knows just how to respond to them.
Did you notice how, the other day ...' Or 'Should we appoint
her to the job?' 'She's likely to be erratic, and she will put

people's backs up, but she will bring plenty of energy to the job, and that's what we need.' 'Is she really all that dynamic? I suspect that it's mostly talk, and that she doesn't really get things done. Look at her record...' Or take the case of comparing works of art or literature. 'Dickens' novels are wonderfully entertaining, but in the end they lack the moral seriousness of, say, Conrad.' 'But what does Conrad's moral seriousness really amount to? It is a superficial impression created by authorial intrusions which sound metaphysically profound but are not adequately brought to life by the substance of the novels. Whereas, in *Dombey and Son*, for example, a moral critique of a whole society is conveyed not by explicit pronouncements but through the characters and their interrelationships. Look at the way in which...' There are no logical arguments by which it can be demonstrated that he is a good friend, that she is dynamic, that Dickens' novels have greater moral seriousness than Conrad's. Nevertheless we can fruitfully argue and deliberate about such matters by drawing attention to features of our experience of them and by proposing ways in which they can be fitted into an overall pattern. If no final agreement is reached, this is not because the judgements are inherently subjective, but because the issues are extremely complex, because they involve the application of multiple criteria, and because the application of those criteria cannot be exact. Hence no conclusions can be definitive. There is always more to be said, there will always be new emphases to be proposed and new ways of looking at the facts. So also arguments about the permissibility of war will, in the end, appeal to conflicting conceptions of the relative centrality, within human experience, of respect for other lives, of loyalties to communities or of commitment to a self-respect which may have to be fought for. There is always room for further argument, always more to be said about the role of these things in our lives, and if the argument is interminable this does not make it pointless.

There is a sense in which the conclusion which anyone comes to will always be a *personal* judgement. It is significant that pacifists often speak of their position as a personal commitment, though it is not always clear in what sense this is meant. Any such judgement will necessarily be made in the light of one's own experience. Consider again the incident in *All Quiet on the Western Front*.[10] Paul's experience in the shell-hole with the dying Frenchman, whom he has killed, brings home to him the uniqueness and irreplaceability of each human life, and his own responsibility for the life he has taken. When he says to the dying Frenchman, 'Now, for the first time, I see you are a man like me', he is acknowledging that his experience has put things into perspective for him, and has made him aware of the importance of something which, at one level, he knew already. Others, looking at the world from the standpoint of a different personal history and set of experiences, might see things differently.

Though in this sense such a judgement is personal, this does not make it subjective. What Paul is rightly made to say in the novel is not 'Now I feel differently about it' or 'Now I want something different', but 'Now I *see.*' What he sees, anyone could see, for though his way of seeing things is the product of his experience, that experience is communicable. The example which I am discussing is, of course, not the experience of an actual individual, but an example from a novel, and it is precisely the function of imaginative literature to make available a shared experience. What imaginative literature does is not just to convey experiences in an anecdotal way, but to *shape* experience. Through the process of selecting and describing, giving prominence to this and pointing up that, it provides a pattern by which we can make sense of our own experience. Literary form is always also at the same time a possible form of life. And this shaping of experience is what I have said moral thought consists in, when we are concerned to judge the importance of our different values. Without having had direct experience of war, we can read and respond to the literature of war, we can relate it to things which we ourselves have experienced, such as our attachments to others and our grief at their deaths, and in that way we can come to recognise and perhaps to share the perspective of the writer.

A shared literary culture is, then, an essential precondition of

---

[10] See above, p. 180.

moral thought, providing shared ways of making sense of our experience. Another precondition is a shared history. Past wars are reference points against which we can compare new cases, looking for similarities and differences. Thus, confronted with the Iraqi invasion of Kuwait, many people compared Saddam Hussein to Hitler, with the implication that it was necessary to stand up to a ruthless aggressor. Assimilating the new to the old in this way, we are better able to respond to it. The comparison could, however, be contested, and others said that the build-up of armed forces in the Gulf was more like the prelude to the First World War, a process with an inexorable momentum which made it impossible for either side to back down. Much the same happened with the argument about nuclear armament and disarmament. Some said that nuclear disarmament would be 'appeasement', others characterised the continuing acquisition of nuclear weapons as an 'arms race', with the implication that it was carrying us into ever greater peril. The role of the appeal to precedents in these moral arguments is rather like the role of precedents in case law. In both, the judgement of new cases is made by appealing to past particulars – 'Isn't this case like that one?' – rather than by appealing to general principles which can be applied to the particular case in order to yield a conclusion. The difference is that in case law the judgements of past cases are authoritative, and what is up for discussion is the degree of similarity and difference between the new case and the old, whereas the historical precedents which are appealed to in moral argument are themselves contentious. There will be conflicting versions of the shared history. The history of past wars, for instance, may be seen as anything from a tradition of glorious exploits to a record of imperialistic oppression or a story of futile and self-perpetuating waste. Nevertheless, despite the variety of interpretations, the common history provides a set of common reference points to which arguments can appeal. Like a shared literary culture, a shared history makes available a common stock of experience which can be shaped in different ways, furnishing patterns with which we can then try to make sense of new cases, and giving us an overall view of priorities among our values.

Let me try to sum up the role that reason can play in resolving our moral dilemmas about war. We can, as I have done in previous chapters, try to clarify our fundamental values, showing how they are rooted in our experience and in our natural human responses. I have attempted to do this particularly with the idea of respect for life, suggesting that it is central to a great part of our moral thinking and that it generates a strong moral presumption against war. We can examine the standard justifications for war which purport to rebut that presumption, and I have tried to show in chapters 4 and 5 and the first section of this chapter that the commonest of these are incoherent or unconvincing. There is then a strong, rationally grounded case against war, but I cannot show it to be conclusive. There remain situations where some will plausibly say that there is no choice but to fight, since the only alternative is to submit and that is morally unthinkable. Since the pacifist can equally say that the wholesale slaughter which war involves is morally unthinkable, we are faced with a tragic conflict of values. The conflict is irresolvable in the sense that neither side can be convicted of error, but I have tried to show that the resources of reason are not necessarily exhausted at this point. We have to seek some overall perspective which gives priority to some values over others, and which matches and makes sense of our experience. The position which each of us reaches will in a sense be a personal one, but it can also be objective in the sense that, drawing on the resources of a shared literary culture and a shared history, it invites endorsement from others as a judgement of the proper importance of particular features of our lives.

THE PRACTICAL AVOIDANCE OF TRAGIC CONFLICT

There remains another respect in which the fact of moral tragedy does not leave us helpless. The existence of recalcitrant moral disagreement is itself a moral problem with which we can try to grapple, and to which we can seek a rational response. The apparent impossibility of resolving the conflict at one level can be the occasion for shifting the argument to a new level, at which we can try to find ways of living with our moral differences. This means especially looking for some kind of political accommodation. Pacifists and those who think that war is sometimes unavoidable have to live together in a society which will have to follow some policy or other with respect to the possibility of war. The society as a whole has to decide whether or not it wants to engage in military preparations and, if it does, what form they should take. Its decisions cannot be morally acceptable to everyone, but they can try to take some account of the strength of different moral positions.

The suggestion that we should look for some kind of accommodation between conflicting positions may look like a moral platitude, but in fact it runs counter to some influential philosophical views of the nature of moral conflict. I have referred to those moral philosophies (especially monistic theories such as utilitarianism) which fail to acknowledge the existence of tragic conflicts between different moral demands. At the other extreme, however, are moral philosophies which see tragic conflict as an almost endemic feature of moral argument and disagreement. I have in mind here those who say that standards of rational moral argument are *internal* to a 'practice' or 'tradition', and that there is a multiplicity of such 'practices'; therefore there can be rational argument *within* a practice, but when different practices make conflicting demands there can be no rational way of adjudicating between them. Moral practices are sometimes compared to games, insofar as the latter have internal standards determining what constitutes correct or incorrect behaviour. For anyone participating in the game, the rules of the game have a rationally binding force, since they serve to define the game as a practice. It is laid down by the rules of football, for instance, that one is not allowed to handle the ball, and one cannot play football without being bound by that rule. Unlike games, however, moral practices can come into conflict with one another and there is then no independent rational standard, outside the conflicting practices, to which one can appeal in order to resolve the conflict.

D. Z. Phillips and H. O. Mounce offer the example of promise-keeping as a moral practice:

within the practice of promise keeping, one has a reason for saying that a man ought to perform an action if he has undertaken to do so; within that practice this is what constitutes a reason for such a judgement ... It is only from within such a practice that one can speak at all of making a moral judgement or decision.[11]

As an example of a 'practice', promising is a very specific form of activity, but Phillips and Mounce also talk in a similar way about much broader and more general ways of life. The moral disagreement between a pacifist and a militarist is said to be a relevant example, and another which is offered is that of a disagreement about birth control between a scientific rationalist and a Catholic housewife. These broader ways of life they tend to speak of as 'traditions' rather than 'practices', but the logical point seems to be the same, that standards of moral judgement are internal to practices or traditions and that there is no external standpoint from which to adjudicate the conflicts between them. In particular, discussing the 'birth control' example, Phillips and Mounce reject the idea that there are any independent facts of 'human good and harm' which could settle the disagreement between the conflicting moral positions:

what they differ over is precisely the question of what constitutes human good and harm. The same is true of all fundamental moral disagreements, for example, the disagreement between a pacifist and a militarist. The argument is unlikely to proceed very far before deadlock is reached ... Their arguments are rooted in different moral traditions within which there are rules for what can and what cannot be said. (p. 59)

It is this diversity of incompatible practices or traditions which is said by Phillips and Mounce to explain the occurrence of 'moral tragedies' (p. 94).

A more complex version of this philosophical position can be found in the work of Alasdair MacIntyre.[12] He gives it a historical dimension. He distinguishes between the diversity of

---

[11] D. Z. Phillips and H. O. Mounce, *Moral Practices* (London, 1970), p. 12.
[12] See in particular Alasdair MacIntyre, *After Virtue* (London, 1981), to which subsequent page numbers refer.

moral conceptions characteristic of the pre-modern era, and the complete fragmentation of moral discourse characteristic of the liberal individualism of 'modernity'. Along with this goes a distinction between 'practices' and 'traditions'. In the ancient world there was a diversity of 'practices' involving different conceptions of the moral virtues, but these were located within a shared moral tradition. There were conflicts, for instance, between the heroic ideal exemplified in the Homeric poems and the alternative conceptions of the virtues more appropriate to the civic life of the polis. But the Greek dramatists were able to present these moral conflicts as tragic because they saw them as located within an objective moral order. For Sophocles, in particular, the moral order is not harmonious, it contains incoherences and therefore presents us with rival and incompatible claims, 'but our situation is tragic in that we have to recognise the authority of both claims' (p. 134). By contrast, in the modern world the tradition has fragmented completely, so that we are faced not with tragic conflicts but with a mere multiplicity of incommensurable moral ideas between which we can make only arbitrary choices. MacIntyre explicitly mentions the debate about the justification of war as an example of a moral disagreement which is apparently interminable (p. 6). The pacifist, the advocate of military deterrence to prevent aggression, and the advocate of wars of liberation on the part of oppressed groups, all invoke conceptually incommensurable values, and 'the rival premises are such that we possess no rational way of weighing the claims of one as against another' (p. 8).

Common to the theories of Phillips and Mounce and of MacIntyre is the idea that the only criteria for rational moral argument are internal to particular moral traditions. Consequently, when these come into conflict with one another, not only are there no independent criteria for deciding between them; it is not even possible for the disputants to acknowledge the rational force of rival positions. This might in a sense be possible insofar as one individual is the inheritor of a number of different moral traditions, but even then, strictly speaking, all that can be said is that one may oscillate between applying different standards of rationality, according as one locates oneself first in one tradition and then in another. There is no overall point of view from which the rational force of rival positions can be acknowledged. It must follow that there are strict limits to the possibility of seeking an accommodation between conflicting moral positions, whether about war or about anything else. Admittedly there could be practical reasons for attempting to achieve a compromise which would enable the disputing parties to live and let live. But, according to the philosophical theory we are considering, any reasons for seeking a compromise will themselves be reasons internal to another moral tradition, presumably the liberal tradition with its emphasis on the value of tolerance. What cannot provide the basis for such an accommodation, according to this theory, is any recognition on the part of the disputants that their opponents have a rational case to make.

The strength of this philosophical theory is that it emphasises the diversity of moral concepts and values, and hence the recalcitrance of tragic conflicts. At the same time it does not, as Russell's subjectivism would do, treat these diverse moral positions as resting simply on non-rational personal feelings; it properly emphasises that there can be rational standards of moral argument, rooted in a shared moral vocabulary. Where it goes wrong is in supposing that different moral vocabularies or moral traditions are sharply demarcated, separated from one another by clear boundaries. It fails to recognise that these different vocabularies and traditions all derive from common human experience, and are therefore, in some sense, accessible to anyone.

In his thumbnail sketch of arguments about war, for instance, MacIntyre attributes to the pacifist the argument that 'in a modern war … no practically applicable distinction between combatants and noncombatants can be made. Therefore no modern war can be a just war …' (p. 6). Against this he sets the argument for strong defence: that 'the only way to achieve peace is to deter potential aggressors … Otherwise you will not avoid war *and* you will be defeated' (ibid.). The first argument, he says, starts from 'premises which invoke justice and innocence', and these are at odds with the premises of the second argument 'which invoke success and survival' (p. 8). This is true as far as it goes, but it is an over-simple picture of how the argument proceeds. The advocates of strong defence cannot (and do not) simply ignore the questions of justice and innocence. As we have seen, they will typically argue (unsuccessfully, I have suggested) that defence against aggression *is* just. As far as 'innocence' goes, either they will have to redefine the concept of 'innocence' in war (again unsuccessfully, I have argued), or they will have to acknowledge that war involves killing the innocent but assert that we sometimes have no choice but to do this. They will thereby be acknowledging the heavy moral burden which is carried in the waging of war. Likewise the concepts of 'success' and 'survival' which MacIntyre says are invoked by the second argument are not the prerogative of any particular moral tradition. How we are to understand them is itself a matter for rational discussion. As we have seen, arguments about war are likely to revolve around the importance of the survival of certain kinds of community. Again, pacifists cannot simply ignore the importance of this, and they may therefore have to acknowledge that a refusal to fight may mean accepting the sacrifice of something valuable. So the pacifist and the advocate of strong defence, while not denying their differences, can both recognise the desirability of searching for ways of protecting or creating a good society without resort to war. And those of us who are trying to assess the arguments can recognise the rational strengths of the conflicting positions and can properly look for practical policies which take account of them.

MacIntyre is probably right to maintain that pluralism is a dominant feature of our modern moral culture. It does not follow, however, that this represents a 'state of grave disorder' (p. 2), a destructive fragmentation of moral discourse which condemns moral disagreements to be pointlessly interminable and leaves us with no rational resources for dealing with moral conflict. It may be that the extent of moral disagreement is the sign of a more open and democratic moral culture. Though it may represent, in a sense, the breakdown of a received moral tradition, this may be because a dominant tradition can no longer be imposed by religious or secular authority. On the issue of war and peace, in particular, there may be more disagreement because people are freer to criticise their country's wars without fear of persecution or imprisonment. Such disputes may then appear interminable, but this may be a healthy development, indicating not that rational discussion has become impossible but that it is being engaged in more freely than before. It need not imply that the advocates of opposed positions can have nothing to say to one another and no means of arriving at some form of rational accommodation.

I suggest then that the search for practical ways of living with our moral differences is one which we can profitably pursue. Recognising the rational case to be made for opposed moral positions, we can try to formulate political policies which might be, at least to some degree, acceptable to the holders of those different positions.

The policies to be adopted may not only be a kind of moral compromise; they can also be aimed at making it less likely that the irresolvable dilemmas will present themselves. If our social circumstances are such as to present us with tragic moral conflicts, we can try to change the circumstances so that such conflicts do not arise. I have mentioned that the idea of conflict between right and right is to be found in the ancient Greek tragedians. They recognise that such conflicts are to some extent ineradicable features of the human condition, but they also recognise (as does Hegel) that tragic conflicts are sometimes the expression of social contradictions which can be transcended. Aeschylus' *Oresteia* ends with the establishment of a new legal court which will replace the tradition of vengeance and vendetta and prevent the kind of irresolvable conflict with which Orestes was faced. Likewise, if we live in a world in which people can sometimes see no alternative but to resort to war, we can try to build up the alternatives so that in the future people are less liable to be confronted with the stark choice to submit or to fight.

How is this to be done? For reasons which I hope are by now apparent, I cannot claim to offer any simple general answer to the question 'What are we to do about war?' I do, however, want to consider certain practical policies which could constitute a rational response to the moral conflict. These are, first and foremost, policies for governments, but they are possibilities which we can all consider insofar as we are in any position to try to influence the policies of our governments. We start from a situation where military defence is the recognised form of defence, where military institutions are firmly entrenched in a dominant position within our societies and where huge amounts of resources are devoted to preparations for war. There is no way in which these institutions can be simply wished away, but also no way in which they can be reconciled with the moral case against war. The question is, then: are there feasible policies which could offer a more morally acceptable alternative – which would recognise the strength of the pacifist case, would draw on the positive insights which I have tried to retain from 'just war' theory, would do justice to many people's sense that there are situations where we have no choice but to resort to war, and might also make it less likely that such situations would continue to arise?

PACIFICISM

The position which I want to consider is one which could be labelled 'pacificist' rather than 'pacifist'. I take the term, and the distinction, from Martin Ceadel's very helpful classification of theories of war and peace.[13] Ceadel identifies five broad positions, which he defines as follows.

(a) Militarism: 'the view that war is necessary to human development and therefore a positive good'.
(b) Crusading: 'a willingness under favourable circumstances to use aggressive war to promote either order or justice'.
(c) Defencism: 'this theory accepts that aggression is always wrong, but insists both that defence is always right and

---

[13] Martin Ceadel, *Thinking about Peace and War* (Oxford, 1987), pp. 4–5. Ceadel says that his use of the term 'pacific-ism' was 'originally suggested in 1957 in a casual footnote by A. J. P. Taylor' (p. 102). Note that I have chosen to drop the hyphen.

that the maintenance of strong defences offers the best
chance of preventing war'.

(d) Pacificism: 'war can be not only prevented but in time
also abolished by reforms which will bring justice in
domestic politics too ... Pacific-ism rules out all aggressive
wars and even some defensive ones (those which would
hinder the political reform for which it is working), but
accepts the need for military force to defend its political
achievements against aggression.'

(e) Pacifism: 'the absolutist theory that participation in and
support for war is always impermissible'.

Defencism is, as Ceadel says, the dominant war-and-peace
theory in the modern world. As a theoretical position it is open
to the criticisms which I have directed against the first part of
'just war' theory in chapter 4. My criticisms tended in the
direction of pacifism, but since I have stopped short of a simple
endorsement of pacifism, I have to address the question whether
there is a coherent intermediate position, between defencism
and pacifism. Ceadel's definitions reveal the difficulty. Defencism and pacifism are both concerned primarily with the
question whether wars can be justified, here and now. They
offer relatively straightforward criteria for deciding whether or
not to fight. Pacificism, by contrast, is future-oriented rather
than present-oriented. It asserts that war will eventually be
avoidable, but leaves it unclear how, in the meantime, we are to
decide whether or not to support particular wars. The aspirations for the future are supposed, in some way, to furnish criteria
for present decisions; 'Pacific-ists insist that even a defensive
cause is just only if it is not also "reactionary", in the sense of
making it harder to achieve those political reforms on which it
ultimately pins its hopes of lasting peace' (Ceadel p. 74).
Clearly this is pretty vague. No doubt it can be made more
precise in the light of the particular recipes for political change
which the different schools of pacificism have offered as routes
to the abolition of war. (So, for instance, it may be said that
defensive wars are not to be supported if they are in defence of
colonial territory, or of 'autocratic' or 'imperialist' or 'capi-

talist' regimes.) The fact is, however, that historically pacificism has too often failed to provide clear guidance in the face of particular dilemmas. An example is the débâcle of 1914, when the left-wing parties of Europe, which were all in theory 'anti-war' and claimed to be able to point the way to a future without war, mostly fell into line behind their belligerent governments. In this way, for lack of clear criteria, pacificism is in danger of collapsing into defencism or even crusading. Alternatively, pacificism may sometimes appear indistinguishable from a disingenuous pacifism which dare not speak its name. One might get the impression that the position of the peace movement (of which I count myself a member) is, 'Wars can sometimes be justified, but not this one', where 'this one' means whatever war one's own government happens to be waging at the moment.

A related problem for pacificism is that it runs the risk of appearing naively utopian. As Ceadel explains, the different varieties of pacificism have typically taken their cue from standard positions in domestic politics. (Ceadel lists these as liberalism, radicalism, socialism, feminism and ecologism.) The danger is then of positing an implausibly sharp contrast between a world where militarism is now rampant and a world 'after the revolution' when all will be sweetness and light. This problem is connected to the previous one because, to the extent that pacificism postpones its solution until 'after the revolution', it has nothing to say to the dilemmas which arise in the meantime.

I do not know whether the eventual abolition of war will ever be possible. It may be that, in centuries to come, people will look back on institutionalised warfare as an outmoded barbarity, in much the same light in which we now regard, say, the slave trade. However, a pacifism which is to have anything to say to our present condition cannot pin its hopes on a remote future. It will have to address the question of what can be done, in the world that we know, to deal with the violence of aggressors and oppressive regimes. Its proposals will have to be both morally acceptable in their own right and at the same time a route towards decreasing reliance on the methods of war. One thing which pacificists can obviously do is to advocate the use of non-violent pressures such as economic sanctions, and the methods of diplomacy and negotiations, even if these appear to be less effective than a military response to the immediate threat. I have mentioned previously the example of the Falklands War. By resorting to war when negotiations still offered some prospect of success, the British government reinforced the prevailing view that the only way to deal with aggressors is to fight them. Conversely a negotiated solution, even if it had not been ideal, would have served as a valuable precedent, as well as being in itself morally much more acceptable. Likewise, if sanctions had been persisted with and had successfully ended the Iraqi occupation of Kuwait, this would not only have saved countless lives but would also have encouraged the employment of similar methods in future situations of the same kind. There are, however, difficult judgements to be made here, for the argument cuts both ways. If sanctions or negotiations are only partially successful, and if a refusal to resort to war leaves no alternative but to make significant concessions to the aggressor, this may encourage future acts of aggression. As Ceadel points out, this is the criticism which defencists can make of pacificism: 'the pacificist who argues that in certain circumstances states should not defend themselves ... appears to be encouraging their adversaries to start a crusade ... A retort which defencism can thus use against its moralistic critics is that it is the theory which most consistently disapproves of aggression' (p. 75).

Pacificists, therefore, since they do not rule out the use of military force, have to think seriously about when military defence is acceptable, and what form it should take. The starting-point has to be the acknowledgement, in agreement with defencism, that the defence of the autonomy of a political community is the cause for which the use of military force is most likely to be justifiable. I argued in chapter 4 that there is nothing sacrosanct about the territorial borders of nation-states, and that there is no difference in principle between justifying military resistance to an oppressive internal regime and justifying military resistance to external aggression. However, I also recognised that in practice the invasion of a community will nearly always create a more oppressive rule, and it is therefore a reasonable presumption that invasions need somehow to be resisted. The other empirical fact which has to be acknowledged is that defence against aggression is the purpose for which the use of military force is most firmly entrenched. There are established forms of non-violent resistance to oppressive regimes, but there is only a limited experience of non-violent resistance to invasion, and the institutional provision for it is minimal, in contrast to the massive institutional presence of military defence. Therefore people are much more likely to find themselves with 'no alternative but to fight' when it is external aggression that has to be resisted. In discussing the idea of 'having no choice' I considered cases, like that of South Africa, where people might respond in this way to internal oppression, if they feel that military resistance is the only way in which their rejection of that oppression can be socially expressed and recognised. But if external aggression is likely to lead to internal oppression, then why, one might ask, wait until the oppressive regime is installed in power before resisting it? If the invaders are at the borders, intent on subjugating the country, imposing their power and crushing all opposition, is this not the clearest case where people may feel that they have no choice but to fight? If all this is acknowledged, how should the pacificist position then differ from defencism? What sort of defence policy should pacificists advocate? It has to be one which brings together, again, the answers to the two questions: what kinds of military defence are, in themselves, morally least objectionable? And what kind of defence policy might, for the future, lead to a decreasing reliance on military force?

DEFENSIVE DETERRENCE

The approach which I want to consider is that which has been advocated by the so-called 'alternative defence' movement.[14] The central idea is that of 'defensive deterrence'. This means that defence preparations are geared to repelling an invasion. The intention is that potential aggressors should be deterred by the awareness that, though they may perhaps possess the military capacity eventually to overcome such a defence, success would be so costly as to be not worth it. 'Defensive deterrence' is therefore *strictly* defensive, in contrast to other so-called defence policies which envisage more than just the ability to repel an invasion. In particular, it is to be contrasted with 'retaliatory deterrence', where the intention is that potential aggressors will be deterred by the threat of counter-attack. Though 'retaliatory deterrence' may be defensive in the sense that its aim is to prevent invasion rather than to launch an aggressive war, the reliance on the threat of counter-attack means that it must incorporate the capability for offensive military operations such as attacks on the enemy's forces, military installations and perhaps even cities and industrial sites. 'Defensive deterrence' will thus require an emphasis on different kinds of weapons from 'retaliatory deterrence': anti-tank missiles rather than tanks, surface-to-air missiles and fighter aircraft rather than bombers and strike aircraft, light coastal patrol vessels and minesweepers and submarines rather than aircraft carriers. As we shall see in a moment, there is not a sharp division between defence and offence, and likewise the distinction between defensive and offensive weaponry is not a division between watertight compartments. Anti-tank missiles, for instance, could be used in an assault on an enemy position. Nevertheless the overall mix of weaponry will signal a tendency towards a strictly defensive or a retaliatory strategy.

---

[14] In a British context the most detailed and coherent set of proposals is to be found in the work of the Alternative Defence Commission. This was set up by the Lansbury House Trust Fund, and its report was published under the title *Defence Without the Bomb* (London, 1983). A shortened version was published as *Without the Bomb* (London, 1985), and was followed by a second report, *The Politics of Alternative Defence* (London, 1987).

The idea of deterrence has come to be associated especially with *nuclear* deterrence. (People talk of nuclear weapons as 'the deterrent'.) In the light of my discussion of 'non-combatant immunity' and the wrongness of indiscriminate killing, nuclear deterrence seems to me to be unacceptable. However, there is not necessarily anything wrong with the idea of deterrence as such. Any particular form of deterrence will be acceptable if (a) what you threaten to do is something which it would be morally permissible actually to do, and (b) the system of deterrence does not itself help to create precisely the danger it is supposed to prevent. Nuclear deterrence fails on both counts. It depends on the threat indiscriminately to slaughter millions of people. If we could be certain that such a threat would never have to be carried out, the making of the threat could perhaps be morally justified. Since, however, there is no such certainty, and since the carrying out of the threat would be just about the most appalling action which it is possible to imagine, nuclear deterrence is morally unacceptable. As to the second point, it can be argued that a system of mutual deterrence actually contributes to creating the danger of nuclear war. It gives rise to a nuclear arms race. The various nuclear powers strive to keep up with one another in introducing new weapons, thereby promoting suspicion and mistrust in one another, and this self-perpetuating process may well increase the possibility that a nuclear war will actually be started either by miscalculation or accident.

How does defensive deterrence fare on these two counts? I shall take the second point first. I think it can convincingly be claimed that a policy of defensive deterrence would make war less likely. At one level this would be true also of defencism in the broader sense. If all states followed defencist policies, there would be no war. However, the term 'defencist' as it is used by Ceadel refers to orthodox military policies which, though they take defence against aggression to be the sole *occasion* for military action, envisage uses of military force much wider than simply warding off an attack. 'Defencist' policies allow for the capacity to launch a pre-emptive strike, or to launch a counter-attack against an aggressor, and to engage in a retaliatory war aimed at destroying the enemy's capacity to initiate future aggression. Of course it remains the case that if all states followed defencist policies, there would never be any occasion to engage in pre-emptive strikes or retaliatory counter-attacks. Nevertheless, because defencist policies incorporate this capacity for wider forms of military action, they are provocative. Whatever the assurances given by states following defencist policies, the fact remains that their military forces *could* be used for aggressive purposes, and other countries will plan accordingly. In times of tension each state may, as the saying goes, be tempted to 'get its retaliation in first'. By contrast, strict 'defensive deterrence' focuses on non-provocative forms of defence. Defensive deterrence aims to deter by means of a military capacity which is not only defensive in intent, but cannot be interpreted by other states as potentially aggressive. It does not tempt them in turn to build up an offensive capacity, and thus does not fuel the fears and tensions which give rise to wars. Defensive deterrence is thus genuinely pacificist. It is a policy which not only says when and how war should be resorted to in present circumstances, but also offers the prospect of reducing the need to resort to war at all.

It would of course be simplistic to suggest that the fears and tensions provoked by arms races are the only causes of war. In the end, states and governments go to war because they perceive it to be to their political or economic advantage. Pacificists will therefore see defensive deterrence as part of a wider strategy aimed at creating the kind of world in which it is less and less in anyone's interest to go to war. This means in particular encouraging the tendency towards greater economic inter-dependence between states. The more one state is economically dependent on cooperation with another state, the more contrary to its interests it will be to go to war against that state. Similarly, pacificists will want to encourage the creation of diplomatic procedures and institutions which offer less costly ways for states to pursue their political interests.

What now of the other criterion by which any system of deterrence is to be judged? This was that the carrying out of the deterrent threat must itself be morally acceptable. Defensive deterrence, like any other system of deterrence, aims to avoid the need to carry out the threat. But, again like any other system of deterrence, it may fail. If it did fail, the ensuing military action would be a purely defensive war in the strict sense. Military force would be directed solely against those who were doing the attacking. In contrast to a retaliatory counter-attack, it would be much more likely to respect non-combatant immunity. Therefore, by the standards of 'just war' theory and the principle of not killing the innocent, such military action is morally acceptable.

I have, in chapter 5, cast doubt on those moral criteria. I do not think that the distinction between non-combatants and combatants corresponds to a morally relevant distinction between those who are and those who are not 'innocent'. All killing in war is to some degree, I argued, depersonalised and indiscriminate killing. I accepted however that there are differences of degree. The bombing of cities, whether by nuclear or non-nuclear weapons, is even more indiscriminate, even more incompatible with respect for human lives, than is the killing of enemy combatants who are attacking one's country. This does not mean that the latter are justly killed. Many or perhaps most of them are not in any strong sense responsible for the attack in which they participate. The most that can be said is that such killing is morally less appalling. We are, however, now arguing within a perspective where war may have to be accepted as inevitable, where military defence is the institutionalised form of resistance to aggression, and where people may find themselves with no choice but to fight. Within that perspective I think it can be agreed that a purely defensive military response to aggression is more acceptable than a policy of retaliatory counter-attack.

Directing one's defence solely against the invading forces is also a military response of which one can say most plausibly that one has no choice. If one is to resist aggression at all by military means, one has to resist those military forces which are doing the aggressing. If invading troops are crossing the border or coming ashore on the beaches, and one is to offer military resistance at all, then one has no choice but to fight them. If enemy aircraft are bombing one's country, the defending forces have no choice but to try to shoot them down. One cannot, however, retaliate against the invaders' homeland, bomb their factories and power stations and cities, and claim that morally one has no choice. To be sure, military and political leaders do say this. The idea of 'military necessity' is regularly invoked to justify any number of atrocities. What they mean by 'necessity' here is simply that they have to do these things if they are to maximise their chances of winning. This is very different from the sense which I want to give to the idea that one may have no choice.

Orthodox defencist critics of 'alternative defence' will say that this is just the trouble with defensive deterrence; it is a half-hearted acceptance of the idea of defence, which stops short of doing what is necessary in order to win. It is suicidal, they argue, to confine oneself in this way to a purely defensive response.[15] If you wait until you are actually attacked, it may be too late, and you may have lost your chance of successful resistance. It may therefore be necessary to launch a pre-emptive strike against the enemy's forces in order successfully to defend oneself. If, once a defensive war has begun, you limit yourself to repelling attacks, without ever launching a counter-attack against the enemy's military installations, you allow him to go on attacking you indefinitely, until eventually you must succumb. If territory has once been lost in a defensive war, the only alternative to surrendering it will be a counter-attack to recapture it. Moreover, there are modern forms of weapon against which there is no defence other than the threat of retaliation. As Ceadel puts it in his summary of the critics' case, 'Infallible defence has been rendered utopian by the development of the bomber plane and missile, which are harder to intercept and parry even than land armies ... All the alternative-defence movement can really hope to achieve is to reduce, rather than abolish, the retaliatory component of modern defence strategies' (p. 82). Finally, it may be doubted whether it is even possible to maintain a clear distinction between defence and offence. Is the bombing of an enemy tank

---

[15] The orthodox defencist criticisms of alternative defence are summarised by Ceadel, *Thinking about Peace and War*, pp. 78–86.

emplacement, or the sinking of enemy ships, defence or counter-attack? The difficulty extends to distinguishing between the different kinds of weapons, as the 'defensive deterrence' policy purports to do. 'The disagreement during the World Dis-armament Conference of 1932–4 over whether a submarine was aggressive or defensive is indicative of the conceptual problems involved' (Ceadel, p. 86).

The conceptual point is perhaps the easiest to deal with. It is true that a particular class of weapons may not, in the abstract, be simply classifiable as offensive or defensive. What has to be looked at, however, is the overall mix of weaponry deployed by a particular state. Anti-tank missiles, for instance, can be used in an attacking role, but if they are not part of an arsenal that includes, say, large numbers of tanks and landing craft and strike aircraft, then their use will necessarily be confined to a primarily defensive role. Though there are no sharp lines to be drawn, it is possible to distinguish between states whose range of weaponry puts the emphasis on a defensive capacity and those which possess an offensive capacity. What is true of the weapons is true also of particular military operations. A country fighting a defensive war may have to counter-attack against invading troops which have penetrated into its territory. It will never-theless be possible to identify the overall strategy as one of defending the country's territory rather than invading other countries either with aggressive intent or as punitive retaliation against an aggressor.

This still leaves tough practical dilemmas. It remains true that a country which limits itself to a defensive military capacity may, from a purely military point of view, be in some respects more vulnerable. At the extreme, there is indeed no military defence against nuclear missiles, other than the threat of retaliation. Anti-missile missiles are not sufficiently effective to offer full protection against an all-out attack, and a nuclear-armed power which was intent on destroying another country could not be prevented from doing so.

To some extent these criticisms can be answered at the level of arguments about military effectiveness. The claim to be made for a country committed to defensive deterrence is not that it could always prevail in any military conflict, but that it could usually make the costs of invasion unacceptably high for the invader. The aim would be to make the invader's loss of troops and equipment and resources so great as to outweigh the possible gains of persisting with an invasion at all costs. The fact remains that a militarily powerful country intent on defeating a country committed to defensive deterrence could probably do so. We then have to ask what political objectives it might hope to gain from its victory. If it can win only by wreaking massive destruction, this will limit the use it can subsequently make of the country it has defeated and destroyed. To take the extreme case, if a nuclear-armed state wished to obliterate a non-nuclear state by means of a nuclear attack, no doubt it could do so, but this would destroy the defeated country's industrial and economic resources and leave its land contaminated and useless for at least decades, and it is not clear what the fruits of such a 'victory' would be. Perhaps the greatest danger for a country committed to defensive deterrence is the possibility that the *threat* of, say, a missile attack, nuclear or conventional, might be used to force concessions such as surrender to an invasion. The threatened country might simply call the bluff of the threatener, and might successfully do so, but a sufficiently ruthless aggressor, possessing overwhelming forces, could demonstrate the seriousness of its intent by beginning on the process of destruction, city by city, leaving no choice but capitulation. Even so, the advantages to be gained by nuclear blackmail, or by equivalent non-nuclear threats, are not necessarily as great as one might imagine. They are limited by other political constraints. A state which employs such threats may find that its relations with other states with whom it wants to be on good terms, and its position in the international community generally, are damaged as a result. The historical record is significant. No nuclear-armed state has ever found it expedient to employ explicit nuclear blackmail against a non-nuclear state, presumably because the political disadvantages would outweigh any possible political gains.[16]

---

[16] The United States, for instance, though militarily it could certainly have done so, did not use the threat of a nuclear attack against North Vietnam, the conventional

These responses to criticisms of defensive deterrence are, however, only partial answers. In particular, they assume that states act rationally, and do not embark on military actions unless they stand to gain from them. Unfortunately this is not always the case. If it were, the problems of war would be greatly diminished, and war would indeed be a less prominent feature of human affairs. The historical record just mentioned is only a limited one, and the wider canvas of human history contains many examples of military activity guided by nothing more than wanton destructiveness. Against such an opponent, a country committed to defensive deterrence may simply find itself without recourse. It is at this point that such a policy is likely to appear naively idealistic, in contrast to the hard-headed realism of a state which sets a premium on military invincibility and provides itself with the necessary means to secure it. Is defensive deterrence thereby invalidated?

If so, it is not alone. Traditional 'just war' theory, as we have seen, likewise insists that not all means are permissible; certain kinds of military action have to be excluded, even if the price of foregoing them is defeat. Indeed, as far as invincibility is concerned, it is unattainable. Even nuclear deterrence will work only against a rationally self-interested opponent. A country which is prepared to go down in flames along with its enemy cannot be deterred.

More fundamentally, I want to question the implied division between 'naive idealism' and 'hard-headed realism'. Why

bombing campaign from 1964 to 1972 failed to achieve its objective of ending North Vietnamese support for the guerrilla movement in the South and political pressures forced an eventual American withdrawal from Vietnam.

The political constraints which tend to prevent nuclear-armed nations threatening to use nuclear weapons against non-nuclear nations are considered in Robert Neild, *How to Make up your Mind About the Bomb* (London, 1981), pp. 115–20. The problem of nuclear blackmail is also usefully discussed in Jeff McMahan, *British Nuclear Weapons: For and Against* (London, 1981), pp. 40–7.

The Alternative Defence Commission recognises that a country committed to defensive deterrence might have to yield to the threat of massive conventional bombing or a nuclear missile attack. It therefore proposes a fall-back strategy of non-violent civil resistance if military defence fails and the country is overrun. I have mentioned previously the possibilities and limits of non-violent resistance. The main problem with the policy proposal is that it is difficult to imagine many existing states providing their citizens with formal training in the techniques of strikes, boycotts, sit-ins, civil disobedience and non-cooperation.

should we attach so much importance to military victory? Why call it 'realism'? The vocabulary used to urge people to victory in war is quintessentially that of idealism. It is full of appeals to the virtue of heroism and the nobility of self-sacrifice. A willingness to sacrifice one's life for one's country is, in the context of a different sort of argument, regularly held up as the epitome of devotion to an ideal. If there is such a thing as 'hard-headed realism', a better example of it would be not an overwhelming commitment to military victory, but the attitude of the old Italian in Joseph Heller's novel *Catch-22*:

'You put so much stock in *winning* wars', the grubby iniquitous old man scoffed. 'The real trick lies in *losing* wars, in knowing which wars can be *lost*. Italy has been losing wars for centuries, and just see how splendidly we've done nonetheless. France wins wars and is in a continual state of crisis. Germany loses and prospers. Look at our own recent history. Italy won a war in Ethiopia and promptly stumbled into serious trouble. Victory gave us such insane delusions of grandeur that we helped start a world war we hadn't a chance of winning. But now that we are losing again, everything has taken a turn for the better, and we will certainly come out on top again if we succeed in being defeated.'[17]

He readily professes that he was a fascist when Mussolini was in power, and is now an anti-fascist; was fanatically pro-German when the Germans were in charge, and is now fanatically pro-American. The young American airman is suitably shocked:

'It's better to die on one's feet than live on one's knees', Nately retorted with triumphant and lofty conviction. 'I guess you've heard that saying before.'

'Yes, I certainly have', mused the treacherous old man, smiling again. 'But I'm afraid you have it backward. It is better to *live* on one's feet than die on one's knees. *That* is the way the saying goes.'[18]

But in truth not even this attitude has any special claim to the label 'realism'. Each of these stances, the moral rejection of certain kinds of military action, devotion to the victory of one's country, and a preoccupation with individual survival, is a particular choice of values, a particular judgement about the nature of one's relations with other human beings and about the importance of different aspects of human life.

---

[17] Joseph Heller, *Catch-22* (London, 1985 edition), p. 312.   [18] Ibid., p. 315.

So we are back with the question: what kind of choice is this? Is it just a subjective preference? A mere expression of feeling? Or can there be objective rational judgements of value about right and wrong ways of living?

CONCLUSION

I have tried to demonstrate, in this book, the scope of rational moral argument. I have argued that the idea of the wrongness of taking a human life is not something which we can just take or leave. It is a deep feature of our structure of moral understanding, grounded in our most basic human responses. As such it has an objective validity, and this remains true however much people may go against it in practice, and whatever further claims they may make about possible reasons for overriding it. I have argued that the standard theories used to justify war, and to override the importance of respect for human life, are objectively untenable. Utilitarianism grossly oversimplifies the range of our moral concerns. 'Just war' theory rests on untenable analogies, between individual and collective self-defence, and between individual and collective innocence and responsibility. And particular claims about the desirable results which can be achieved by war are often factually unconvincing.

I suggested that this amounts to a strong rational case against any resort to war. It is, moreover, not just an abstract theoretical argument; it identifies an objective anomaly within our moral thinking. The widespread moral acceptance of war is at odds with the importance we elsewhere attach to respect for human life. I also acknowledged, however, that the case against war is not definitive. There remain situations where people can intelligibly say that, though the resort to war is morally appalling, they have no choice, since not to fight would be to acquiesce in an intolerable evil.

This seems to leave us with an irresolvable moral deadlock. In a sense it *is* irresolvable. There is no 'solution'. This does not, however, confirm the view of philosophers such as Russell that disagreements about war, and other recalcitrant moral conflicts, in the end come down to a clash of subjective preferences. There is a tragic moral conflict here precisely because there are objective claims of right on both sides.

I also argued that the tragic conflict does not leave us helpless. There is always room for further rational reflection on the differing views of what is of overriding importance in human life. This reflection will not take the form of linear argument, from premises to a conclusion. It will be more the sort of thing which is done by imaginative literature, offering a way of looking at the world which claims to make sense of our shared experience, and which we can assess accordingly.

Finally, I have suggested that there is another form which further reflection might take. We can, as I put it, shift the argument to a new level, where the existence of recalcitrant disagreement is itself seen as a practical problem which we can try to deal with. We can aim to work out practical policies which might acknowledge the strengths of opposed moral positions, and which might also help to change things in such a way that the tragic conflict is less likely to arise.

I have been looking at the idea of 'defensive deterrence' as a practical policy which might commend itself in those terms. It builds on the pragmatic case which, I have suggested, can be retained from 'just war' theory, that resistance to aggression may be the most plausible justification for war. It builds on the recognition, again imperfectly registered in 'just war' theory, that indiscriminate killing is morally unacceptable. It builds on the sense which people have that there are situations where one has no choice but to fight. Though incompatible with pacifism, it is a policy which might contribute to the creation of a world where war is a less prominent feature. As such it could be labelled, if not 'pacifist', at any rate 'pacificist'.

The case for defensive deterrence would have to be made in much more detail, with fuller attention to the complex empirical questions about the consequences of following such a policy in a world of powerfully armed nation-states. I do not intend to continue the argument here. What I am more concerned to do is to emphasise that rational argument about the moral acceptability of such a policy is possible, and that it can be carried on between people with radically different moral perspectives. Despite the depth of our moral disagreements, we are not locked within separate and self-contained moral worlds. Those disagreements are themselves articulated within a common moral vocabulary. We can appreciate the force of one another's moral positions, and we can try to find ways of doing justice to them. In that sense, the resources of rational moral argument are never exhausted.

Index

254

Learning Resources
Centre